THE ILLUSTRATED PRACTICAL ENCYCLOPEDIA OF
FITNESS TRAINING

BODY-SHAPE • STAMINA • POWER

EVERYTHING YOU NEED TO KNOW ABOUT STRENGTH AND FITNESS TRAINING IN THE GYM AND AT HOME, FROM PLANNING WORKOUTS TO IMPROVING TECHNIQUE

AN EXPERT AND EASY-TO-FOLLOW GUIDE WITH STEP-BY-STEP INSTRUCTION SHOWN IN MORE THAN 700 FANTASTIC PHOTOGRAPHS

ANDY WADSWORTH

HERMES
HOUSE

This edition is published by Hermes House, an imprint of Anness Publishing Ltd
Hermes House, 88–89 Blackfriars Road, London SE1 8HA
tel. 020 7401 2077
fax 020 7633 9499
www.hermeshouse.com
www.annesspublishing.com

If you like the images in this book and would like to investigate using them for publishing, promotions or advertising, please visit our website www.practicalpictures.com for more information.

Publisher: Joanna Lorenz
Project Editors: Brian Burns and Anne Hildyard
Photographer: Phil O'Connor
Illustrator: Peter Bull
Designer: Nigel Partridge
Copy Editor: Charlotte Judet
Indexer: Diana Lecore
Production Controller: Pirong Wang

ETHICAL TRADING POLICY
At Anness Publishing we believe that business should be conducted in an ethical and ecologically sustainable way, with respect for the environment and a proper regard to the replacement of the natural resources we employ.
As a publisher, we use a lot of wood pulp to make high-quality paper for printing, and that wood commonly comes from spruce trees. We are therefore currently growing more than 750,000 trees in three Scottish forest plantations: Berrymoss (130 hectares/320 acres), West Touxhill (125 hectares/305 acres) and Deveron Forest (75 hectares/185 acres). The forests we manage contain more than 3.5 times the number of trees employed each year in making paper for the books we manufacture.
Because of our ongoing ecological investment programme, you, as our customer, can have the pleasure and reassurance of knowing that a tree is being cultivated on your behalf to naturally replace the materials used to make the book you are holding. Our forestry programme is run in accordance with the UK Woodland Assurance Scheme (UKWAS) and will be certified by the internationally recognized Forest Stewardship Council (FSC). The FSC is a non-government organization dedicated to promoting responsible management of the world's forests. Certification ensures forests are managed in an environmentally sustainable and socially responsible way. For further information about this scheme, go to www.annesspublishing.com/trees

CONTENTS

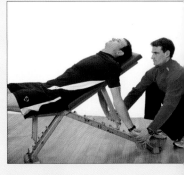

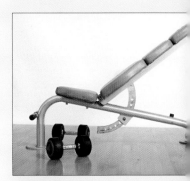

Introduction to Exercise

Going to the gym and jumping on the treadmill will not necessarily give you the results you want from your exercise regime. There are so many different exercises that you can do, some of them far more beneficial than others.

This book will give you an understanding of which exercises will help you to achieve your goals, with detailed descriptions of how and when to do them so that you can be confident that you are exercising correctly. To achieve fast, effective, long-lasting results you will need variation in your training. Each exercise lists the muscles used so you can determine which part of your body is being exercised, giving you the chance to change your exercises and challenge your body to promote better results.

This is a chance to create the new you – a healthy mind and a fit body. You will grow in confidence as you learn more about yourself, how to test your fitness, and which exercises work for you.

Before you begin exercising, decide what you want from your exercise routine. Do you want a six-pack for a summer beach holiday? Is building muscle or losing weight important for you? Whether it is looking great for your wedding day or staying fit through pregnancy, de-stressing or keeping fit while travelling, beating the opposition on the sports field or trying to stay young that interests you, there is a plan for achieving your goal in this book.

It's not just exercise that will make you fit and healthy; nutrition is just as important. Everything you eat has some effect on you – your food can turn to fat or energize you; it can help you to improve your fitness level, recover from exercise, change your body shape and alter your self-image. This book will provide you with an understanding of the effect that different foods have, the optimum nutrition combination and the best time to eat and drink.

There is always some exercise you can do. Even if you are injured, there are exercises that will help you to recover. This book provides you with basic knowledge to help with diagnosing injury, understanding the recovery process and preventing the injury from recurring.

Exercise is not just about sweating buckets in the gym. Core stability and flexibility training are just as important to prevent injury and give you the strength to train harder, push big weights, run marathons or cope with the demands of everyday life.

Regular exercising will not only help you to gain physical fitness, providing a big boost to your self-esteem; you will also have increased energy, and benefit from a more active and positive outlook.

Right: There are no short cuts to getting fit, but it is much easier if you have the right information about appropriate training.

GETTING STARTED

Before you begin your journey to a fitter lifestyle, this chapter outlines a realistic approach to a successful fitness training programme, including accurately assessing your starting point, setting achievable goals, taking and analysing body measurements, performing fitness tests to measure your progress, keeping a training diary, and determining which exercises are best for you. Armed with this new knowledge, you will come to appreciate why you are not intended to live a sedentary lifestyle, and commit to making health and exercise priorities in your life.

Above: Whatever your fitness goals may be, you will certainly enjoy achieving them.
Left: Fitness training will help you discover more about yourself.

Three Steps to Fitness

We are bombarded today, on one hand, by news items stressing the importance of a healthy lifestyle, and on the other by pictures of glamorous celebrities. Can you ever look that good? Yes, but not by wishing for it – it takes determination, motivation and knowledge.

As everyone knows – or should – there is no such thing as overnight success in any walk of life, and certainly not in the area of health and fitness. Unfortunately, we live in a culture of conflicting messages that do nothing to nourish our wellbeing. On the one hand, it is impossible to escape media images of thin, toned, buffed and sculpted role models of quite out-of-reach physical perfection. On the other, advertising and the food industry pump fat-filled, sugar-coated, carbohydrate-rich food at us from every direction. Consequently, we

Below: Hours of training steps up all the systems in your body and helps you to run faster.

Above: You don't need to be in the gym for this type of floor exercise; you can easily do it at home.

Above: The buzz you get from being supremely fit will help you continue your fitness regime.

have become an unfit society in thrall to endless aspiration, and sold on the promise of nips, tucks, jabs, instant gratification and quick fixes. Quite simply, becoming fit and healthy – safely, effectively and in the long term – does not and will not happen quickly. You will, however, get real results if you follow this three-step plan:

Determination Look at other areas of your life in which determination has been a force for change, such as passing exams, bringing up your children in the best way possible, getting a better job or making more money. Transfer some of this determination to the job of making yourself fit and healthy.

Motivation Have a goal in mind, such as running a half-marathon, fitting into a wedding dress or simply getting up the stairs without being out of breath.

Fitness can't be bought
Simply paying a monthly subscription to a gym is not enough to help you get fitter. You can buy many things in life, but fitness involves regular, hard work.

Correct training

Watching people exercising in the gym and copying them is not the way to get the best results, because many people cheat to make the exercise easier.

Use this chapter to determine your goals by analysing all aspects of your life and making a note of your strengths and weaknesses. Once you have set your goals, keep visualizing how great you will feel once you have achieved them. This is something you are doing for yourself and no one else. Family and friends can try to motivate you but until you actually want to do it for yourself, it won't work. After all, no one is asking them to make sacrifices – you are the one who has to change your lifestyle and do the physical training.

Knowledge Gather as much knowledge as possible to plan your new personal training plan. It is not possible to get results without understanding how your

Below: If you want to succeed in your aims quickly, get help and advice from professionals in the field.

Above: Just a little extra fitness can mean the difference between winning and losing.

body works and what type of training will be best for you. Be aware, though, that a little knowledge can be a bad thing. For example, the suggestion that resistance training will make you gain weight is a myth. The truth is that resistance training will make you gain lean muscle mass, which will have a positive effect on your metabolism and therefore make you lose fat.

Knowing what to eat, and when to eat it, is also essential. Without good nutrition, you won't have the energy to train, recover from training or see the benefits of your training. There are no short cuts or quick fixes – your nutrition plan will require preparation to make it practical for you to stick with it every day.

Know yourself

Once you have the basic knowledge, you can apply the correct training to achieve your goals. In some ways you have far more knowledge of yourself than a gym instructor because they have only known you for a matter of hours, whereas you have known yourself since the day you were born. You know how determined you can be and what your motivation is. You know what you enjoy and what you dislike. You can be honest with yourself about how you look and

how you want to look. You know how much energy you have and how much more energy you would like to have. Your exercise plan has to suit you and no one else.

Plan ahead

Be practical and think ahead. For example, if you are travelling for business or on holiday, plan your training to be harder in the week before and after you are away. Don't use the time away as an excuse – there is always some kind of training you can do, whether it's going for a run or doing exercises in your hotel room. Keep your goal in sight and remember that consistency is the key to achieving it.

No excuses

There are two types of people who want to get fit: those who think about results and those who think of excuses. If you look for excuses, you are setting yourself up to fail. If you focus on achieving results, you will win. From the moment you pick up this book, the excuses stop and you set yourself on the path to success – to fitness and health.

A Lifestyle that Works for Your Body

One of the main reasons for a general lack of fitness in developed societies is that so many people lead sedentary lifestyles, and abuse their bodies daily through poor diet and other bad habits. The simple fact is – we are not designed for the way we live.

Compare your lifestyle with that of someone who lived approximately 10,000 years ago. When people lived as hunter-gatherers, constantly on the move looking for food, they led very active lives.

From hunter-gatherers to channel-flickers

Today, many people lead an unhealthy desk-bound, sofa-lounging, channel-flicking lifestyle, their longest walk being to the car and back. It's time to take stock of the fact that although we live in post-industrial, urban environments, our bodies have not evolved to keep pace with the demands of life in this developed world. We are still built to live as our ancestors did, many thousands of years ago. Unfortunately, that's causing us a lot of problems. Take control of your lifestyle before it's too late.

Below: If children are encouraged to try a sport when they are young, it will stand them in good stead later on.

Life expectancy and lifestyle

There is a direct correlation between life expectancy and lifestyle. A person who drinks excessive amounts of alcohol, smokes, eats unhealthily and lives a sedentary lifestyle will have a shorter life expectancy than someone who looks after their body and takes regular exercise. However, it is not just about the length of your life. Quality of life is just as important, and if you don't take care of yourself, your life will not only be shorter, it may well be unpleasant too.

Most disturbing of all, there is ample evidence that these bad habits are starting earlier and earlier in life. Little to no exercise or outdoor games, endless hours sat in front of computer games and a diet high in sugar and saturated fat have triggered escalating and alarming rates of obesity and related illnesses among children. The net result will be, if left unchecked, a generation of children likely to live shorter lives than their parents.

Above: Children thrive on fresh air and exercise; limit the time spent playing computer games indoors.

Our healthy ancestors

We know people lived relatively healthily 10,000 years ago because there are people still living the same lifestyle in some areas of the world today – the last 84 tribes of hunter-gatherers in the world, who can be found in Australia, Africa and South America. Fit with lean muscular physiques, these people continue to live very active and healthy lives, and experience markedly lower levels of diseases such as cancer and heart disease.

This much we know

People in the developed world cannot go back in time, but they can get an understanding of what they should do to find a balance in their lifestyle, in order to stay healthy. We know that exercise makes you fitter, boosting your immune system and protecting you from

Above: Sea air and exercise is a great combination for a healthy and happy way of life.

disease. We know that some exercise each day will counteract the negative effects of sitting at a desk all day staring at a computer screen, and will give you the get-up-and-go to have fun with family and friends. We know that eating certain foods will give you energy and make you look good and feel good. Let's take this knowledge and put it to good use so that we can all live longer and happier lives.

Below: Your body is not designed to sit in a car all day. Try to change your mode of transport to include walking.

The perils of modern-day life

There are many aspects of modern life that are intrinsically bad for our physical and mental wellbeing. From the daily grind of office life to the stresses and strains of travel and the junk food that we consume, living in a developed country has a downside.

Desk-bound injuries Sitting still in front of a computer all day long, and doing no exercise, contributes to back and neck problems. Physiotherapists and osteopaths owe most of their income to this fact. Correct exercise would prevent all of these problems – problems that didn't exist generations ago. We didn't need core-stability exercises to avoid such aches and pains, because working the land made these muscles strong.

Mental exhaustion We are not designed to work long hours and feel stressed about hitting deadlines. The body is designed to hunt and gather, then rest and build strength for the next day. Having to retain huge amounts of information can be exhausting; it leaves you feeling too mentally tired to do any exercise. Of course, taking exercise will provide you with the energy to continue to hit targets and deadlines at work, and enable you to work long hours.

Travel woes We were not intended to travel in planes or for any great length of time by other means of transport.

Above: Fast food is fine occasionally, but it is good to be aware of your body's nutritional needs and eat healthily.

Travelling through time zones, especially at altitude in a short space of time, can be very tiring, and of course there are the additional negative effects of sitting still for hours.

Junk food and booze We are not designed to eat convenience foods, which are often full of sugar that will affect your energy levels and body weight. Alcohol is viewed as a natural accompaniment to food, but even modest amounts of alcohol can lead to a number of illnesses and damage to some of the major organs of the body. Even if food is 'natural', the nutritional content may only be a fraction of what it was many years ago. In many areas, the land has been over-farmed and saturated with chemicals, which leaves crops tainted with an unhealthy chemical residue.

Labour-saving, life-shortening We were not designed to use labour-saving devices. We were designed to use our hands and the materials from the land to build shelters and weapons to catch animals and provide food. Today, there is a gadget or machine for almost everything, which simply encourages us to become lazier still.

The Importance of Exercise

Regular exercise leaves you full of vitality and a get-up-and-go attitude. People who do physical training regularly already know that if they skip a few days they start to feel tired and lethargic, which is how many people feel who never exercise.

The right exercise and nutrition can dramatically reduce the risk of many common illnesses and diseases, including cardiovascular disease, various cancers and type II diabetes:

Heart disease Exercising three to four times a week and eating healthily have a positive effect on your heart. Exercise also lowers cholesterol levels and blood pressure, which considerably reduces the chances of suffering a heart attack.

Osteoporosis Regular weight-bearing exercise helps to build bone tissue and prevent age-related bone-density loss.

Cancer Exercise reduces the risk of some cancers. Two ovarian hormones that are linked to breast cancer, estradiol and progesterone, are reduced by exercise. Studies have shown that regular exercise can help prevent breast cancer by up to 60 per cent. Several studies also show that obese people who live sedentary lives are at increased risk of endometrial, colon, gall bladder, prostate and kidney cancers.

Below: If you attempt to practise a healthy lifestyle, you are less likely to worry about the doctor's findings.

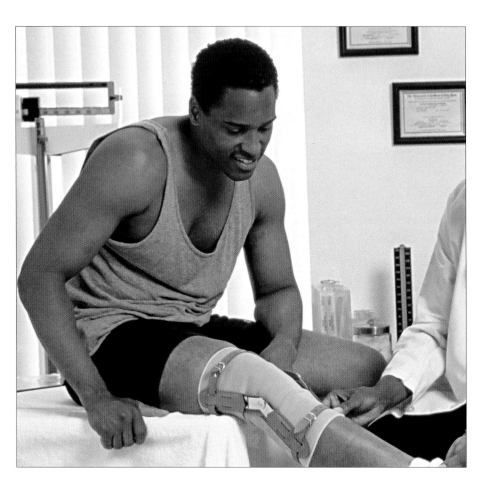

Above: Sporting injuries should always be assessed by a professional.

Type II diabetes Regular exercise will dramatically reduce the risk of developing type II diabetes. A weight increase of 5–10kg/11–22lb doubles the risk of developing type II diabetes. More than 80 per cent of people with type II diabetes are overweight or obese, which is why it is also referred to sometimes as 'diabesity'.

Joint and back pain These common ailments can be reduced with the correct physical training, which will build muscle and increase flexibility and core stability.

Obesity A combination of cardiovascular and strength training will increase the metabolism and improve the body's capacity to burn calories. This helps to

Right: Regular physical exercise can greatly reduce unpleasant neck pain and headaches.

reduce the risk of developing one of the many obesity-related diseases as well as increasing wellbeing.

Psychological health The symptoms of depression and anxiety can be reduced by regular exercise. Stress is part of everyday life but exercise can equip you to cope with it. Exercise will give you greater endurance to tackle daily tasks, improve your sleep, increase your energy and give you an improved body shape, which will improve your self-esteem.

Above: Lack of exercise can have the effect of making you feel lethargic and demotivated.

Below: Fruits are a healthy alternative to sugary or fatty snacks.

General health Regular exercise has many health benefits. It can boost some vital processes in the body, such as stimulating your digestion, liver function and your glycogen system (stored glucose, mainly in the muscles and the liver). Exercise will lead to an improved immune system, it can revitalize and enhance your sex life, and may well add some years to your life. Strength training has the ability to tone, build and improve the speed of muscle contraction and reaction time through the development of strong neuromuscular pathways. You will also become more agile and benefit in many ways from improved co-ordination and balance.

Don't put it off
Fear is one of the biggest factors in motivating exercise. If you were to stand in a line of 100 people waiting for a heart attack, where in the queue would you be? If you are near the front, then fear will probably be the motivating factor that drives you to a healthier lifestyle, but why should it be this way? Be healthy before you get to the fear stage. Most importantly, respect your body – it's the only one you've got – and aim to feel good on the inside and the outside by exercising regularly.

Below: Regular strength, flexibility and core-stability training can help to prevent back pain.

Setting Your Goals

Before you start to exercise, you must be clear about what it is you want to achieve. Do you want to run a marathon, lose weight or gain muscle? These are all big goals and in order to achieve them, you need to prepare both your body and your mind.

Begin by setting out smaller goals. For example, if you want to run a marathon in six months' time, set yourself deadlines, such as being able to run 10km/6.2 miles after the first two months of training, and 20km/12.4 miles after three months. A gradual improvement in stamina and ability will help you to focus on the big goal.

There are also other factors to take into consideration, such as what it will be like to run among so many other athletes. Research the marathon course and talk to people who have run it previously so that you are familiar with its organization and structure. Consider the equipment you intend to use, your fluid intake and tactics for the big event. Running a half-marathon is an excellent way to get first-hand marathon experience. Plan when to change your training shoes in order to get the best

out of them, but do not turn up on the start line with shoes that are worn out or brand new shoes that may give you injuries or blisters. Read around the subject of injury so that you can identify early signs of injury immediately.

If you want to lose weight, follow a six-week plan that incorporates a low GI diet and exercise. So that you can monitor your weight loss and progress, keep a training diary.

When you want to gain muscle, plan your training sessions carefully, enlisting the help of a personal trainer if necessary. They will be able to help with the appropriate type of exercises for specific muscles.

Make your own goal wheel
It is important to focus on other factors in your life that will have an effect on your goal. For example, if you want to

Above: Even if you don't succeed immediately, there is nothing wrong with setting long-term goals.

lose weight, you will struggle if you have low self-esteem, suffer from lack of sleep and work too hard to do any exercise. Use a goal wheel to help you change your lifestyle and keep achieving. The goal wheel is similar to the wheel of a bicycle. The wheel has an outer rim, a hub in the centre and spokes running between the rim and the hub. Each of these spokes represents a different factor in your life. Because people's lives are very different, you can make the spokes represent whatever you like.

An example would be spokes for physical exercise, social life, nutrition, sleep, family, work, injury and psychology. Each spoke has a score on it going from ten at the hub to zero at the rim. You personalize your wheel by putting a cross on each spoke. For example, if you take little or no physical exercise, you would put a cross close to the rim of the physical exercise spoke. If your exercise routine is going well and you really enjoy it, mark a cross close to the hub.

Once you have put a cross on each spoke, join the crosses up. It is highly likely that you will have a jagged pattern within the wheel. Some crosses will be close to the hub and others will be farther away. Every spoke that has a cross close to the rim of the wheel represents the lifestyle factor that you need to work on. It is important to

remember that all the factors are related. For example, your psychology score may be low if you never take any exercise and your nutrition is poor. If you spend all your time working and socializing and especially if this involves a lot of drinking alcohol, you won't be able to run a marathon successfully.

Above: Always keep in mind the goals you have set yourself; this should help you stick to the training.

There simply won't be enough time to train adequately, and if you try to take part, it could result in feelings of depression and even physical injury.

Below: Getting weighed weekly will help you assess the progress you are making in your training plan.

Goal wheel

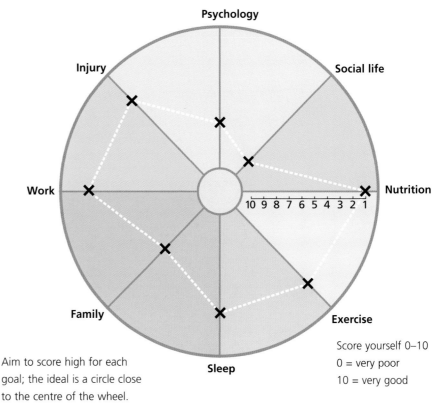

Aim to score high for each goal; the ideal is a circle close to the centre of the wheel.

Score yourself 0–10
0 = very poor
10 = very good

Training Diary

Keeping a training diary will help you to achieve your goals and stay motivated. Make the diary realistic and useful. Don't cram it with information that will become irrelevant later on in training – only note facts that motivate you and help you to track your progress.

A diary can help to re-motivate you as you look back through all the other fitness improvements you have made.

When losing weight you may find that over the first six weeks of training you lose 10kg/22lb but then you don't lose any in the seventh week, which can lessen your motivation. However, it's not just the weight loss that matters; for example, if you have been walking in an effort to accelerate your weight loss, and could only walk for 1.6km/1 mile in your first week, but can now manage 4.8km/3 miles, this progress will motivate you to keep going.

If you are training for a marathon, keep a diary of all your training, including details such as whether your training is road or off-road running, the time of day, your nutrition and hours of sleep. This way, if you do suffer from any problems, such as an overuse injury, a coach or physician will be able to use your diary to see when the problems may have started and may be able to determine what caused them. Noting what you eat will help you determine which foods work best for your performance and recovery.

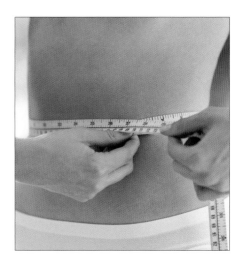

Above: By taking your measurements, you can work out that you have lost fat and are more toned than before.

Above: If you step up your walking, note the details in your diary, to allow you to assess your progress better.

How to keep your training diary
You should record details of your training, the goals you want to achieve and an assessment of your training to date. Include test results, nutrition information and body measurements.
Daily records Record the following information in your diary every day:
• The physical training you intend to do against the actual physical training that took place, marked out of ten.
• Hours of sleep the previous night.
• Resting heart rate, taken first thing in the morning.
• Any injury or signs of fatigue.
• All food and fluid intake, including what time you ate or drank.

Also note what you did on rest days, as your activity on these days will have a significant effect on your performance. For example, if you stayed up late on a rest day, or drank alcohol on two rest days before a big competition, your performance will suffer and when you check the diary you will know why.

Above: Your training needs to work the way you want it to. You can discuss your progress with an instructor at the gym.

Big goals and small goals At the front of your diary list the goals you want to achieve, and when you want to achieve them by. For example, if you weigh 70kg/154lb on 1 January and you want to lose 10.8kg/24lb over six months, or 1.8kg/4lb per month, mark your desired weight – your small goal – on the appropriate page for each month; so on the page for 1 February, you would note that you want to weigh 68kg/150lb, and on the page for 1 March, you would note that you want to weigh 66kg/146lb, and so on.
Weekly assessment At the end of each week assess how your training has gone. Note the average score you have given to your training and how you felt each day. Look back over your nutrition for the week and mark down any changes you want to make. Assess your fluid intake for the week and check that you are drinking enough. Add up the total number of hours you have been

Below left: Note any injury; what you were doing and for how long. It may help you alter your training plan.

Below middle: An accurately filled-in training diary can prove to be an invaluable asset at a later date.

Below right: Keep a record of the hours that you sleep to get an insight into your sleeping patterns.

training and compare it with the week before. Make a note of measurements such as body fat, weight and Body Mass Index (BMI).

Weekly review If the overview of your week is not positive, consider where you may have gone wrong and note the changes that you intend to make in order to get more from your training. These changes might involve a different combination of exercises, taking more

Above: Even if your goal seems daunting at times, try to meet the challenge and stay on track.

rest days or working harder to achieve intensity levels in certain sessions. Look back at the goals you have set yourself, written at the front of the diary, and make changes to the small goals – adding new ones and ticking off the ones that you have achieved.

Body Type

We are all born with a body type, some naturally physically stronger than others. However, with the right exercise and nutrition, we can become stronger and fitter, change our type and fine-tune our strengths for specific sports and physical activities.

Your body type will have a direct influence on your sporting performance. For example, if you are a gymnast or Tour de France cyclist, being lightweight is a priority. However, if you take part in contact sports or weightlifting, you need to be heavy enough to hold your ground in the scrum or have the muscle power and strength to lift weights.

American psychologist W.H. Sheldon (1898–1977) developed a system in the 1940s that recognized three body types: endomorph, mesomorph and ectomorph. Most people share many, but not all, of the features of one of these body types.

Endomorphs

People with this body shape carry the most body mass of all three types. They are pear-shaped and often overweight. Endomorphs are likely to have the most sedentary lifestyles of all of the body types. They are not good at endurance activities, but if they have strong enough muscles, they can lift weights and use their own weight to provide power. Consequently, disciplines such as javelin and hammer throwing naturally suit them. People of this body type have a high Body Mass Index (BMI) and are at a greater risk of poor health than any other body type.

Mesomorphs

The most athletic and muscular-looking of the three body types, mesomorphs find it easy to compete in most sports and are able to build lean muscle, lose and gain weight fast, and maintain low body fat. They are stronger and fitter than other body types and will be good at adapting their body to cardiovascular and strength-training exercises. Mesomorphs are at less risk of health problems than any other body type. Mesomorphs can train harder than any other body type but need to watch their diet to make sure they are getting the correct fuel for their activity; they can get away with eating unhealthy food much of the time, but it won't provide them with the fuel for activity or aid their recovery after exercise.

Ectomorphs

These are the most fragile of the body types. They are thin in appearance and struggle to gain weight. Their low level of body fat makes them more susceptible to health problems. However, they are the best body type for endurance activities such as running marathons or cycling long distances. With the correct training, ectomorphs can have very high power-to-weight ratios, making them fast over long distances and good at climbing hills, for example.

Left: Some people are more flexible than others, but this degree of flexibility requires more than just genetics.

Above: Try a regime to change your body shape and, as a result, you will be happier with the way you look.

Making the changes

You may be an endomorph now but this doesn't mean you have to stay that way. The right exercise and food will change your body shape and decrease the risk of health problems. If you want to have a more athletic figure, you will need to follow a plan that involves burning as many calories as possible, while eating healthily, using the glycaemic index as a guideline in order to balance your blood sugar levels and prevent you from depositing fat. You will need to exercise three to four times a week,

---

A combined approach

To change your body type, you will need to adjust your training and your nutrition. One without the other will never get you the desired result. Once you have changed the way you look, you will need to continue working hard to maintain your new body shape.

Above: Ectomorphs are naturally thin and have a low level of body fat. They often find it hard to gain weight.

Above: Mesomorphs are the fittest, with more lean muscle and low body fat. They easily lose and gain weight.

Above: Endomorphs have the largest body mass and may be overweight. They often have a sedentary lifestyle.

incorporating: cardiovascular training to burn calories and build a better and more efficient aerobic system (which in turn will allow you to burn yet more calories); and resistance training to build muscle and increase your metabolism.

Endomorph to mesomorph If you are an endomorph, the chances are that you constantly struggle to motivate yourself to eat healthily and exercise. To make the necessary changes, you will need to alter your habits. Focus on reducing your calorie intake and increasing cardiovascular fitness and resistance training to increase your metabolism and lose weight. As you feel the benefits and increase your energy levels, you should see results more quickly, which will, in turn, reinforce your motivation.

Ectomorph to mesomorph You will need to consume more calories to feed your muscles and help them grow. At the same time you need to reduce your cardiovascular training time and focus more on resistance training, which will help you to build muscle.

Mesomorph to endomorph This is the easiest transformation and one that, unfortunately, usually happens quite by

Left: If you eat a healthy diet and exercise appropriately, you will be able to alter your body image.

accident. People who were athletic in their youth but have less time for exercise as they grow older, and perhaps have a sedentary job, are likely to change body type in this way. The bottom line is that if you consume more calories than you expend, then an endomorph you will become.

Mesomorph to ectomorph If you have bulky muscles, you may want to change shape, but this is hard to do. It requires you to lose muscle, not just fat. You can try to lose muscle by reducing your calorie intake so that you have to burn up muscle and use it as an energy source. Add long-distance endurance running or cycling, but avoid resistance training, as this will build muscle.

Altering your body type

Expect changes to your body shape to take time. Don't be discouraged by this. Keep the end goal in sight and stay motivated. If your body type changes too quickly, you will not be able to sustain the transformation.

Body Measurements

There are many different ways of measuring your body on a regular basis and assessing your progress. As you see your body shape gradually but definitely changing, it will help to give you the motivation you need to keep training.

The weighing scales are one of the oldest but most effective ways of recording your weight. Always use the same scales to weigh yourself at the same time of the day, on the same day of the week. Place the scales in the same place on a hard floor each time to get a true measure. If your goal is to lose weight, only weigh yourself once a week to give yourself a chance to see the weight decrease. Weighing yourself first thing in the morning will reduce the chance of the measure being affected by what you have eaten, as you probably won't have eaten anything for at least 8 hours. However, dehydration after a heavy night of drinking alcohol can make you seem lighter on the scales, so don't be fooled by this.

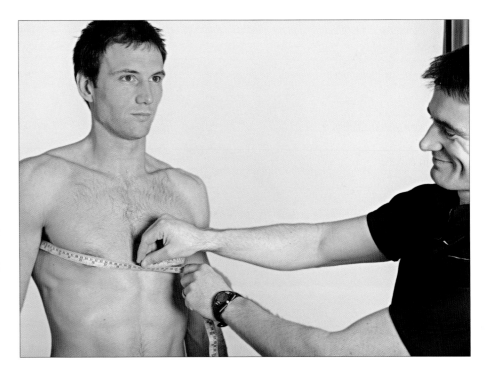

Above: Using a tape measure is an accurate indicator that your fitness regime is working well.

Measuring tape

A measuring tape is another useful way of monitoring your progress. Take measurements once a week at the same time as weighing yourself. Measure several different areas of the body each week. Breathe normally and don't suck your belly in when you measure.

Below: Scales don't always tell the whole story. You may have changed shape, but muscle is heavier than fat.

If the scales don't show a change in weight, the measuring tape might be your saviour. If your measurements are reducing, you know you are going in the right direction, even if you haven't lost weight. This change in shape and weight may be a result of more training, as muscle weighs more than fat – in fact, the same volume of muscle weighs nearly twice as much as the same volume of fat.

Use your body measurements to create your long- and short-term goals, but remember to be realistic. If you are trying to lose weight and your waist measures 102cm/40in, set a goal to lose 1cm/½in every two weeks until you reach your end goal of a 81cm/32in waist. If you are trying to gain muscle and change body shape, and your chest is 97cm/38in, set targets of a 2.5cm/1in increase in size until you reach your goal.

How to measure yourself

Chest: measure around the body, in line with the nipples.

Waist: measure around the body, in line with the belly button.

Hips: measure around the widest part of the hips.

Thighs: measure around the leg 15cm/6in up from the top of the knee.

Calves: measure around the mid-point of the lower leg.

Biceps: measure around the mid-point of the upper arm (decide whether you want to do this with the muscle tensed or with a straight arm, and use the same method of measurement each time so that you will be able to record any differences accurately).

Shoulders: measure from the middle of the side of one shoulder across the back to the middle of the side of the other shoulder.

Neck: measure around the mid-point of the neck.

Photographs and mirrors

One of the best ways to measure your progress is to look in the mirror and assess what you see. Obviously, you will not be able to remember what you see from one week to the next, so take photographs to compare the difference. This is especially important if you are trying to lose weight, change body shape or put on muscle mass. You can also use the mirror to assess your muscle definition if you are trying to put on muscle and look leaner. If you use a tape measure to measure your biceps, and the measurements don't change from week six to eight but the mirror and photograps show a distinct change in appearance, you will be instantly motivated to continue training. If you have been working on your running technique for your next 10km/6.2-mile race or marathon, run in front of the mirror or use photographs or a camcorder to see the difference in your technique.

Using a mirror for most weight-training exercises, especially with free weights, is essential. You need constantly to check whether you are using the right technique. Many people use weights that are too heavy for them and so fail to work the correct muscles, because the

Below: By regularly examining your body in a mirror, you will notice any areas that look different.

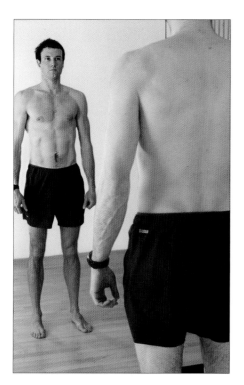

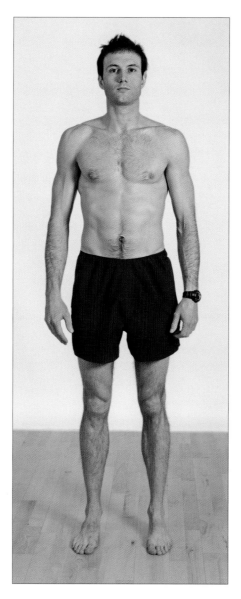

Above: If you have photographs taken at intervals, you will easily be able to see any bodily changes.

weight forces them to use other parts of their body instead of isolating the muscles they really want to work.

Clothes that fit

How your clothes fit is one of the best measures of your progress. The scales and the tape measure may at times suggest that your body has not changed at all, but if you go down a dress, trouser or shirt size, you will be inspired to continue training – it clearly is working. Clothes can tell you more than any measuring tape; for example, it is hard to use a measuring tape to measure the size of the buttocks but if your trousers feel looser, then obviously you have become thinner – in that area

Above: How your clothes fit is a good indicator of losing body fat. After weight loss, they feel much looser.

at least. Buy clothes that you want to fit into in the future, and use this as a small goal on the path to achieving your goal.

Above: If you are prepared to put in the required effort, you will achieve the results you want.

Measuring Body Fat

If you are trying to gain weight in the form of muscle, and you are eating more and taking supplements, measuring body fat regularly will help you to see whether you are gaining muscle or fat, and keep you on track to reach your goals.

As already stated at the beginning of this book, fad diets simply don't work. Many of them, in fact, can result in a higher percentage of body fat because a diet that leads to fast results often causes you to lose just as much muscle as fat. This reduction in muscle means that your metabolism will be lower, and as a result you will put on more fat, especially after the diet has come to an end – which, invariably, it will.

If your weight on the scales is the same as before you started the diet, but your body fat has dropped from 15 to 10 per cent, you will know that you have gained a considerable amount of muscle.

Below: Don't be discouraged if you are not losing weight quickly; slow and steady ensures it stays off.

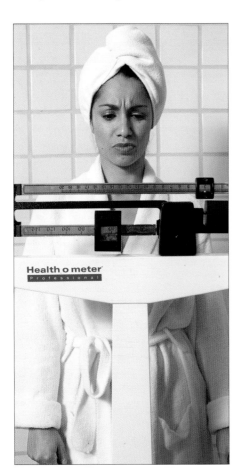

Body fat table			
Once you have calculated your body fat, compare your percentage with the figures on this table. You should try to stay within these boundaries – having some fat is essential for regulating the body's temperature and protecting vital organs.			
Age	**up to 30 years old**	**30–50 years old**	**50+ years old**
Female	14–21 per cent	15–21 per cent	16–25 per cent
Male	9–15 per cent	11–17 per cent	12–19 per cent

How to measure body fat

There are several different ways to measure body fat. The most accurate is hydrostatic weighing, which works by submerging the subject in a tank and measuring the water that is displaced. It is one of the most reliable tests, as factors such as how much fluid has been drunk in the last hour will not affect the results. However, you are unlikely to have a suitable tank at home and you won't find one at many sports clubs either. Instead, you are more likely to encounter body-fat scales and callipers.

A set of body-fat measuring scales will give you a rough estimate of your body fat. A low level electrical current is passed through the body and the impedance (opposition to the flow of current) is measured. The result is used with your weight and other factors to give you a body fat percentage. However, your body's impedance level can be affected by the amount of water in your body, any recent exercise and your skin temperature. If you are going to use body-fat scales to measure body fat don't eat or drink for at least 3 hours before measuring and avoid exercise for 12 hours before measuring.

Using body-fat callipers is more accurate if the same person does the measuring each time; the same amount of skin is pinched; the same side of the body is measured (usually the right-hand side); and the same equation is used to calculate body fat. If you repeat the same test in a month's time, and your fat

percentage has gone down, you know your training plan is working. There are a few rules you should stick to:
• The same person should measure you every time.
• Measure at the same time of day.

Below: This woman is having her fat measured in a hydrostatic weighing pool, which is a very accurate method.

Body fat by sport

Average body-fat percentage for athletes.

Sport	male	female
Baseball	12–15	12–18
Basketball	6–12	20–27
Football	9–19	15–30
Cross-country running	5–12	12–18
Tennis	12–16	16–24
Triathlon	5–12	10–15

• Avoid drinking and eating for at least 3 hours before measurement.
• Avoid exercise for at least 12 hours before measuring.
• Hold the skin fold between the thumb and the index finger.
• Apply the callipers at a depth equal to the thickness of the fold.
• Repeat the measurement three times and take an average, so that you get an accurate reading.
• Add the readings for the different areas of the body together and use the equations that follow.

Instead of converting your skin-fold measurements into an actual body-fat reading, you could just add up your skin-fold measurements and use this to determine whether you are losing or gaining fat. If you want to focus on one area, such as losing weight from your stomach, then simply take one skin-fold measure from your abdomen using the following method. With a thumb and finger, pick up a skin fold with two thicknesses of skin and subcutaneous fat. Grip the skin with the callipers 1cm/½in from the fingers, at a depth the same thickness as the skin fold.

Measurements

Remember that muscle weighs more than fat so if the reading on the scales doesn't change don't feel defeatist. To check if you are losing fat, take body measurements using a tape measure, measure your skin folds with callipers and use your mirror to see the changes. Use your scales only twice a week unless you are an athlete in training.

How to calculate body-fat percentage

Specially calibrated callipers that grip the skin and fat are used for the measurement; three readings are taken at each site and an average is used for the calculation of body fat.

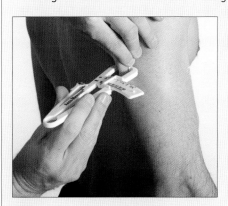

Triceps: *the back of the arm located halfway between the shoulder and the elbow. Measure vertically.*

Sub scapular: *situated just below the shoulder blade. Measure at a 45-degree angle.*

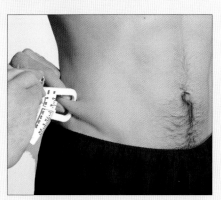

Supraspinale: *on the side of the abdomen just below the line of the belly button. Measure horizontally.*

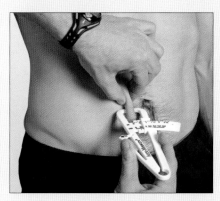

Abdominal area: *this is just beside the belly button. Measure the fat vertically.*

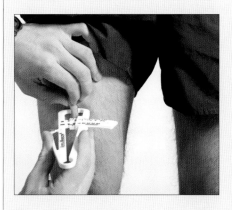

Thigh: *at the midpoint of the front of the thigh. Measure vertically.*

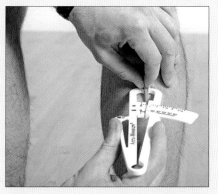

Calf: *taken at the back of the largest part of the calf. Measure vertically.*

Calculate your body-fat percentage using an equation such as this:
Equation for males: percentage body fat = (0.1051 x sum of triceps, sub scapular, supraspinale, abdominal, thigh and calf) + 2.585
Equation for females: percentage body fat = (0.1545 x sum of triceps, sub scapular, supraspinale, abdominal, thigh and calf) + 3.580
Yuhasz, M.S., *Physical Fitness Manual*, University of Western Ontario, 1974

Body Mass Index and Health Measurements

While the Body Mass Index is generally a useful way to assess whether your body mass is obese, overweight, normal or underweight, it is not always a straightforward measure, depending on who you are. It pays, therefore, to understand it in some detail.

Body Mass Index (BMI) is a measure of a person's weight scaled according to their height (see box 'Measuring your BMI'). This parameter is a useful tool for monitoring your progress in health and fitness. However, it is not accurate in all cases. For example, power athletes may have the same BMI score as an overweight person, even though they are carrying no fat. The reason for this is that the BMI does not account for the amount of lean muscle the athlete is carrying. Likewise, many endurance athletes have a BMI score indicating that they are underweight, even though they are actually a healthy weight. In older people, BMI

Above: Muscular people may have a higher BMI. This does not, however, mean that they are unhealthy.

Right: Long-distance runners who are lightweight will generally have a low BMI.

readings may be of little use, as they will not take into account loss of muscle mass. Neither can the BMI be an accurate measure for children or breastfeeding mothers. However, those exceptions aside, the BMI provides a good basic guideline to follow for the general population.

Measuring your BMI

Use the following methods to find your BMI:

Metric
BMI = body mass in kilograms/divided by height x height in meters

Example:
A 1.78m tall person, weighing 79.83kg would have a BMI of 25:
79.83kg/(1.78 x 1.78)
= 79.83/3.16
= 25

Imperial
BMI = body mass in pounds/divided by height x height in inches multiplied by 703

Example:
A 5ft 10in (70in) tall person, weighing 176lb would have a BMI of 25:
176lb/(70 x 70) x 703
= 176/4,900 x 703
= 25

How to measure your waist-to-hip ratio

Take your waist measurement by measuring round your body at the midpoint between the bottom of your waist and hips. Measure your hips by measuring around your body where your buttocks stick out the most. Divide your waist measurement by your hip measurement. For example, a 81cm/32in waist and 102cm/40in hip would be calculated as a waist-to-hip ratio of 0.8. This ratio is reasonable for a man but is the upper limit for a woman.

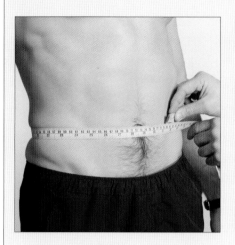

Above: To measure your waist, hold the tape measure between the lower part of the waist and the hips.

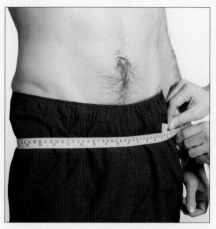

Above: The hips are measured by holding the tape measure at the widest place.

Blood pressure

If your blood pressure is higher than 140/100, you should consult a doctor before you start any exercise routine. It is easy to measure blood pressure yourself with a blood pressure monitor that you can buy from larger pharmacies. It is best to take the test before you have done any exercise that day, as that may affect the result. However, if you have already exercised, then make sure that you rest for at least 30 minutes before you take a reading.

Cholesterol

Your doctor can check your cholesterol level by a simple blood test. The result is reported in millimoles per litre (mmol/l) or milligrams per decilitre (mg/dl). A cholesterol level of 5 mmol/l/200mg/dl or less is desirable, 5 to 6 is borderline, and above 6 puts you at a high risk of a heart attack. In the UK, 75 per cent of adults aged over 40 have a level higher than 5, and 54 per cent of heart attacks are linked with levels of over 5.

Waist-to-hip ratio

Other body measurements are also useful for monitoring health. Simply measuring your waist and hips, then calculating your waist-to-hip ratio, can be just as effective as the BMI measurement for highlighting health risk factors, especially for heart disease

Below: There is no need to visit the doctor to take your blood pressure; you can easily measure it yourself.

and type II diabetes, as it has been proven that people who carry excess fat around their middle are more at risk of these illnesses.

The risk of health problems has been found to increase if a man has a waist measurement of over 102cm/40in, or a woman has a waist measurement of more than 89cm/35in. A waist-to-hip ratio of more than 1 for men and 0.8 for women is highly detrimental to your health. At this point, the risk of heart disease, hypertension and type II diabetes is dramatically increased.

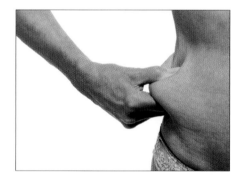

Above: The amount you can firmly pinch indicates extra weight and also the state of your wellbeing.

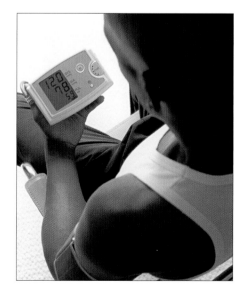

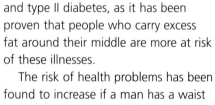

BMI and health risks

Studies show that the BMI score is linked to health risk factors. Compare your score with those on the chart below. If your health risk is high or very high, you should consult a doctor and start taking exercise and eating sensibly immediately.

BMI score	Classification	Health risk
Less than 18.5	underweight	moderate
18.5–24.9	normal	very low
25–29.9	overweight	low
30–34.9	obese class 1	moderate
35–39.9	obese class 2	high
Above 40	extreme obesity	very high

Cardiovascular Fitness Tests

It is essential when following a training programme that you test your cardiovascular fitness, and there are a number of ways you can do this. It is equally important that the test you choose is appropriate to the sport you will be doing.

Tests vary depending on the sport and the first step when testing your cardiovascular fitness is selecting the right test for you and your sport. If you are a sprinter, you need to set yourself tests on the track covering the distances, or similar distances, that you will be running in competition. Testing yourself over 5km/3 miles will be of little use to you.

If you are a cyclist, test your fitness with a 8km/5-mile or 16km/10-mile time trial over a familiar route – one that you can use in the future for comparison.

For invasion sports such as basketball or netball, test yourself by running different lengths of the court and timing

Measuring up

When testing your fitness, use a treadmill or run on an athletics track so that you can easily measure your distance.

The VO2 max table fitness assessment

Female

Age	Very poor	Poor	Fair	Good	Excellent	Superior
13–19	<25	25–30.9	31–34.9	35–38.9	39–41.9	>41.9
20–29	<23.6	23.6–28.9	29–32.9	33–36.9	37–41	>41
30–39	<22.8	22.8–26.9	27–31.4	31.5–35.6	35.7–40	>40
40–49	<21	21–24.4	24.5–28.9	29–32.8	32.9–36.9	>36.9
50–59	<20.2	20.2–22.7	22.8–26.9	27–31.4	31.5–35.7	>35.7
60+	<17.5	17.7–20.1	20.2–24.4	24.5–30.2	30.3–31.4	>31.4

Male

Age	Very poor	Poor	Fair	Good	Excellent	Superior
13–19	<35–36	36–38	38.4–45.1	45.2–50.9	51.0–55.9	>55.9
20–29	<33.0	33.0–36.4	36.5–42.4	42.5–46.4	46.5–52.4	>52.4
30–39	<31.5	31.5–35.4	35.5–40.9	41.0–44.0	45.0–49.4	>49.4
40–49	<30.2	30.2–33.5	33.6–38.9	39.0–43.7	43.8–48.0	>48.0
50–59	<26.1	26.1–30.9	31.0–35.7	35.8–40.9	41.0–45.3	>45.3
60+	<20.5	20.5–26.0	26.1–32.2	32.3–36.4	36.5–44.2	>44.2

Cooper, K.H., *The Physical Fitness Specialist Certification Manual*, The Cooper Institute for Aerobics Research, Dallas, Texas, 1968

Below: Sprinting demands a fast delivery of oxygen to your muscles. This is known as 'aerobic exercise'.

Below: If you enter a triathlon, you need to ensure that you do regular cardiovascular training.

Below: Games require a fast, efficient cardiovascular system to enable rapid recovery between points.

Above: If you have a high level of fitness attempt the Cooper 12-minute run test, in which you run or walk for 12 minutes.

yourself. Try starting at the back of the court and running to the halfway mark and back five times, and then running to the far end of the court and back five times and getting an overall time.

For rowing, set a distance such as 2,000m/2,187yd and time yourself. Then test yourself again in the future to check for fitness improvements.

There are three useful measurements that test either aerobic fitness or the cardiovascular system: the VO2 max, the Cooper 12-minute run and the Harvard step test.

VO2 max The VO2 max test measures the maximum volume of oxygen (O_2) that an athlete can use during intense exercise. The test is suitable for elite athletes who are able to push

---

Repeatable test

Only use a fitness test that will be easy for you to repeat. You should note your fitness test results in your training diary and repeat the tests every four to six weeks to monitor your improvement and help determine if your training is working for you. If you are training correctly you will see a change.

---

themselves hard without risk of injury or other health problems. It is also one of the best measures of cardiovascular fitness because it shows you how efficient your body is at utilizing oxygen and represents your maximum aerobic capacity. It is expressed as ml/kg/min (millilitres of oxygen per kilogram of body weight per minute).

The most accurate way to test VO2 max is to exercise to failure (when you reach the point that you simply cannot push your body any further) and use laboratory techniques to work out the exact amount of oxygen you are able to utilize by measuring the air that you exhale. However, there is a simple test you can do to predict your VO2 max without using specialist equipment, and which does not involve exercising to complete failure:

The Cooper 12-minute run Like the VO2 max, this test is also suitable for elite athletes used to pushing themselves hard. It measures the body's ability to use oxygen while running. Run or walk as far as possible in 12 minutes, then measure the distance in metres/yards to predict your VO2 max. Use the following formula to calculate your estimated VO2 max in ml/kg/min (milligrams of oxygen/ kilogram body weight/minute):

Miles: VO2 max=35.97 x miles - 11.29
Kilometers: VO2 max=22.4 x km - 11.3

An endurance athlete, such as a marathon runner would generally have a high VO2 of around 70ml/kg/min, an average level would be 35 and a poor level is 25 or below.

The Harvard step test Anyone who wants to get fit can use the Harvard step test, which monitors the cardiovascular system. This is a basic test that involves stepping up on to a 40–50cm/16–20in high gym bench once every 2 seconds for 5 minutes and recording your heart rate. Note your heart rate 1 minute after finishing the test (HR1), again after 2 minutes (HR2) and, finally, again after 3 minutes (HR3). Use the following calculation to assess the state of your fitness:

The Harvard step test results

>90	excellent
80–89	good
65–79	above average
55–64	below average
<55	poor

McArdle, W.D. et al, *Physiology: Energy, Nutrition and Human Performance,* 1991.

Fitness level = 30,000/2 x (HR1 + HR2 + HR3). For example, 30,000/2 x (120 + 100 + 80) = 50.

A high level of 80 or 90 is good, indicating a healthy cardiovascular system, while 50 or below is poor. Before you attempt any form of cardiovascular test for the first time, you should consult your doctor. Always have somebody with you during the test.

Below: The Harvard step test is a way of noting your heart rate to assess your state of fitness.

Strength Tests

When devising a training plan – and before you actually embark on it – it is important to find out how strong you are. Otherwise, you could quickly overreach yourself and do yourself an injury. When measuring your strength, use a test that best suits you and your specific goals.

The test that you choose should be determined by the goal you have in mind. If you want bigger arms, then use bicep and tricep exercises to generate a test that will assess your performance on the way to achieving your goals.

To recover from a knee operation using exercise to build strength in your quadriceps, use a leg extension test to assess the strength in your quadriceps and monitor your rehabilitation programme.

If you want stronger, wider shoulders, do shoulder presses in order to assess shoulder strength.

Below: Test your body for strength on the areas that you most want to work out.

Above: The bench press test is a method for assessing the strength of the pectorals and shoulders.

Above: You can easily find out how strong your legs are by using the leg press.

To assess hamstring strength (muscles at the back of the thigh), use a hamstring curl machine.

For upper-back strength, do chin-ups and add weights, wearing a weights belt to test your strength.

Take precautions

Before you do any strength test for the first time, consult your doctor. If you are testing to find your one repetition maximum (ORM), make sure to have a training partner to help you when your muscles tire. Use supports and foot rests on exercise machines when you start to fail on a weight. Struggling to lift a weight that is too heavy for you is one of the most common causes of injuries.

One Repetition Maximum test

This is the gold standard of strength tests. Most ORM tests involve the bench press and leg press, as these two exercises involve the majority of the large muscles in the upper and lower body. Follow this procedure to find your ORM:

1 Warm up for three sets using a weight you can lift for at least ten repetitions.
2 Add 5–10 per cent to the weight and complete three repetitions.
3 Add a further 5–10 per cent to the weight and try to complete three repetitions.
4 Continue to add 5–10 per cent to the weight until you can only do one repetition (ORM).

Strength assessment					
Bench press	**Poor**	**Fair**	**Good**	**Very good**	**Excellent**
Male	0.6	0.8	1.0	1.2	1.4
Female	0.3	0.4	0.5	0.6	0.7
Leg press					
Male	1.4	1.8	2.0	2.4	2.8
Female	1.2	1.4	1.8	2.0	2.2

*Left: The sit-up test lifts the head and
shoulders up. It measures the strength
of the abdominal muscles and hip flexor
muscles. The more sit-ups you can do in
1 minute, the stronger your muscles.*

Once you have found your ORM for
the bench press and leg press, divide
the weight you have achieved by your
body weight to get a score. This is the
calculation if your ORM for the bench
press is 100kg/220lb:

100kg/220lb (ORM bench press)/
80kg/176lb (body weight) = 1.25

A good result for a male would be more
than 1.4; a poor result is less than 0.6.

Strength endurance assessment					
Sit-ups	**Poor**	**Fair**	**Good**	**Very good**	**Excellent**
Male	20	30	40	50	60
Female	10	20	30	40	50
Press-ups					
Male	10	20	30	40	50
Female	10	20	30	40	50

Strength endurance test
You can easily do this test at home.
It involves doing as many sit-ups and
press-ups as possible in 1 minute.
Because women do not have the same
upper-body strength as men, women
can do the press-ups with their knees on
the floor. Use the scores in the table to
assess your strength endurance.

Using the strength tests
Anyone can adapt the strength tests to
their chosen sport. For example, if you are
a cyclist, use the leg press to find your
ORM. For the strength endurance test, see
how many step-ups or squats you can do
in 1 minute. If you want to build a bigger,
stronger chest, do an ORM test using the
bench press, and for strength endurance,
do as many press-ups as you can
manage in 1 minute. Repeat every four
to six weeks to monitor your progress.

*Right: For the female press-up test, the
knees balance on the floor.*

*Above right: The male technique for a
press-up test lifts the body off the floor.*

Equipment for Cardiovascular Training

Before you use cardiovascular equipment, in the gym or at home, you need to take into account a number of important factors. These include, location, space, value, safety, hygiene, familiarity with the controls and, most of all, using machinery that 'fits' you.

Whether you decide to train at home or in a public gym, the location and its surroundings are very important. The place you choose for your training must be somewhere that you really want to go. It must be somewhere to look forward to, especially if you are going to train after a long day's work. If you are going to join a public gym, there are a number of factors to consider.

Gym conditions

Always check the level of instruction on offer at the gym. Find out whether the instructors are qualified, and to what level. Find out how much help is on offer. If you have not used a gym before, you will need all the help you can get to set up machinery and feel safe with what you are doing. There also needs to

Below: Understanding the equipment will make your workout more enjoyable and useful.

be plenty of natural light or, failing that, good-quality artificial lighting and ventilation to keep you supplied with plentiful fresh air. Air-conditioning will help to cool you down, but it may lead to greater dehydration, especially during cardiovascular exercise, so take care to carry a drinks bottle with you at all times.

Spend some time at the gym before you join and study closely what it is like at different times of the day. It may be very quiet on your first visit at 10 a.m., but it may be packed with people waiting to use the machines at 6 p.m. – the very time you are most likely to want to train, if you have a regular job. Make sure, too, that the machines are kept in good order and are hygienic.

The machines that you will be using for cardiovascular training include treadmills, exercise bikes, cross-trainers, rowing machines, steppers, trampolines and vibration plates.

Measuring up and splashing out

You may not feel like using the gym close to you; a gym environment is not ideal for everyone, in which case, you should consider training at home, but check carefully the amount of space you have, and the access, before ordering any unnecessary gym equipment. For cross-trainers and treadmills, you will need considerable ceiling height. Buying cardiovascular equipment can be very expensive. It doesn't have be the most state-of-the-art to be useful to you but, generally, the more costly it is, the more functional and robust it will be. If you want to work out using smooth machinery with lots of built-in cardiovascular programmes, then spend more money. Many manufacturers describe

their cardiovascular equipment as being for 'domestic use' or 'commercial use'. The commercial use equipment will be more expensive, but it will last longer because it is designed for continual heavy use in a public gym.

Below: The heart-rate monitor is worn around the chest, over the heart. A reading can be seen on the wrist device.

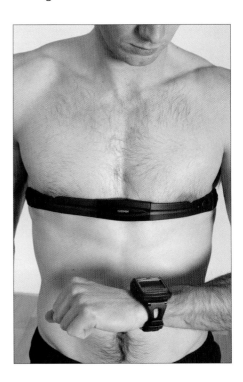

Above: It is essential to wear a supportive sports bra when doing vigorous training.

Above: Always check your equipment for safety. For hygiene, wear only your own boxing gloves.

Above: Swimming aids such as floats and pull buoys will help to improve your technique.

From treadmills to rowing machines, the choice of cardiovascular equipment is endless. If you can afford it and have the space, have at least two pieces of cardiovascular equipment so that you can vary your exercise routine. There should be a number of programmes to stop you getting bored. Also, keep in mind that treadmills have different maximum speeds and levels of incline. Rowers use different pulley mechanisms, while cross-trainers vary in size and motion. Some stationary bikes are more adjustable than others. Try out the equipment before you buy and make sure the machine is right for you.

Heart-rate monitor

Constantly use a heart-rate monitor to analyse your training efforts. Most good heart-rate monitors allow you to set zones for your desired level of intensity. You can buy more expensive versions that allow you to download the data to your PC and copy the workout data into a diary, if you wish. However, being able to view your heart rate easily during your training session is the most important factor. Make sure that your

Divert and motivate

Distractions when you are doing cardiovascular exercise are good. Use an MP3 player or watch television to turn your routine into a pleasant experience and make the time go faster. Knowing that you can watch a favourite TV programme may motivate you to get to the gym.

heart-rate monitor is coded so that it only picks up a signal from you and not your training partner's signal.

Clothing

For running, rowing or other similar cardiovascular exercise, wear loose-fitting, lightweight, breathable clothing. Always wear good footwear with plenty of support and cushioning. Females should wear good-quality supportive tops to prevent them feeling uncomfortable or self-conscious in front of others.

For boxing, it is essential to always have the correct protective pads and gloves. For hygiene reasons, always try to use your own gloves in a public gym. If you do have to use other

people's gloves, remember to wash your hands thoroughly afterward. Remove all your jewellery and watches to prevent injuries.

For swimming, wear a well-fitted swimming costume that is supportive but will allow you to move with maximum efficiency through the water. Use pull buoys and floats to help you improve your swimming technique. Choose goggles that attach firmly to your face with suction before you've even put the strap around your head. This is the sign of a good fit; wearing loose goggles when swimming are next to useless; they will allow water to get into your eyes, and will only interfere with the smooth timing, enjoyment and effectiveness of your session.

Suitable equipment

If you are training outdoors, always take a pack with the necessary clothing, including waterproof outerwear, and sun cream, when appropriate. Also, remember to take with you a water bottle, other drinks and snacks.

Equipment for Strength Training

With both free weights and machines, expensive equipment, though preferable, is by no means necessary. It is much more important that you combine different pieces of equipment for maximum effect – and know how to use them correctly and safely.

You don't need to spend lots of money on strength-training equipment, but if money is no obstacle, then having expensive, well-built equipment may well help to motivate you to exercise. This equipment is normally the easiest to adjust to suit your personal needs; it will offer a greater range of movements and require less maintenance.

You can choose between using free weights, body weight or machine weights, such as weight-training benches, squat stands, single stations and multi-gyms. Or, you can use a combination of all three for the best workouts. No single piece of equipment is better than any other piece. The most important factor is how you use the equipment. If used correctly, you will benefit from it; if used incorrectly, you may do yourself more harm than good.

Below: In a gym, dumbbells are stored on a convenient rack according to their size.

Use of free weights

Free weights such as dumbbells or barbells require you to recruit more muscle mass to provide balance and stability, unlike machines, which simply require you to push a weight in one direction. Free weights demand that you control the weight in all directions.

Free weights

Free weights involve barbells or dumbbells.
Barbells These are long, straight bars with weight plates attached at each end. Some gyms have a variety of barbells, with the plates permanently fixed to the bar. Sometimes, the plates can be removed so that you can adjust the barbell size and weight. If you intend using adjustable barbells, make sure that you use the safety collars on each end to retain the weights.
Dumbbells These are short bars with weighted plates on each end. The plates

may be fixed or removable, depending on the size of the weights area. Most gyms have a variety of dumbbells with permanently fixed plates.

If you want to use equipment at home, free weights are a good option compared with machines. Machines take up a lot of room and may give you the option of working only one or two different exercises – unless you've bought a multi-gym (a unit with lots of exercise stations coming off it). By contrast, free weights take up very little room and can be used for a variety of exercises.

Weight machines

Machines with multiple weight stacks give you an easily adjustable weight. You simply adjust the weights stack with a connecting pin that runs through the middle of the weight you want to select.

Below: This weights bench is adjustable to most sizes but it is best to check first that it is suitable for you.

Above: Before exercising, adjust the machine to fit you correctly. If it does not feel comfortable, do not use it.

Machines are often seen as safer because you cannot drop the weights on the floor or lose your balance, or even control of the weight, and injure yourself. Be warned: machines can sometimes be designed in such a way that they do not 'fit' you very well. Setting up machines in the correct position for you takes experience and, possibly, some assistance from a qualified instructor. You could unknowingly put yourself in a position that will cause muscle or joint pain. For example, sitting on a chest-press machine with the handles set too high will force your shoulders to do all of the work, not your chest. Some machines are designed as 'one size fits all', but they do not always live up to their billing. If you are particularly short or tall, you need to ask yourself whether a

particular machine is going to be best for you. How can you tell? Quite simply, if it feels wrong or awkward when you try to use it, use free weights instead.

Make sure that you are completely familiar with the safety aspects of each machine that you will be using before you start training on it. For example, if you are going to use a leg-press machine, before you release the weight and start bending your legs back toward your body, be clear about what you need to do in case you fatigue and you cannot straighten your legs again. Always check to see whether there is any kind of safety mechanism to stop your legs being crushed.

Body weight
If you are in a restricted space, or have a limited budget, then simply use your body weight – it's highly effective. Even top bodybuilders use exercises such a press-ups and lunges. To make these exercises effective, make sure that you are using the correct technique to isolate the muscles you want to work and avoid injury. Using just your body weight in warm-up exercises is also a great way to stimulate the muscles you intend to work using free weights or machines, giving you a better workout all round.

Getting started
If you do join a gym, you are most likely to be shown how to use the machines for your strength training. But if you find

you are mainly using machines in your workouts, take time to vary your exercise and introduce exercises that involve just your body weight and free weights. That way, you always have a familiar exercise programme when you are staying away from home and have limited or no access to a gym.

For weight-training, wear comfortable clothing that allows you the full range of movement. Clothing that fits close to your skin will enable you to see if the correct muscles are working. Always wear a number of layers to make it easy to adjust to changes in the temperature you are working in, and to keep your muscles warm.

Below: You can easily assess your position and ensure good technique by looking in a full-length mirror.

Use a mirror

Where possible, when exercising, you will need to use a full-length mirror, especially when doing free weights and body-weight exercises. Looking into the mirror will enable you to check your technique, and confirm that you are working the correct muscles. Use a mirror to adjust your training procedures.

Start right

Make sure the machines you use are set up correctly, with the back, seat and any handles or levers involved in the correct position. Once you are actually pushing or pulling the weight, there should be no strain on any part of your body; it should feel comfortable and natural.

CARDIOVASCULAR TRAINING

Any form of exercise that raises your heartbeat is cardiovascular, whether it is walking to the shops or swimming a long distance. What matters is finding the exercise that suits you best and slowly building up your level of intensity in order to achieve your goals. At the outset, you do not need to suffer to feel the benefits. However, to challenge your body, make it fun and get the best results, include variety in your training, and keep a record of your exercise to monitor your progress and stay motivated.

Above: Training in groups can make fitness fun.
Left: Running can be enjoyable, as well as helping you to achieve fitness.

The Benefits of Cardiovascular Exercise

Whether you are planning to run a marathon, take part in a triathlon or simply improve your general health and fitness to deal better with everyday demands, cardiovascular training has the added advantage of promoting your wellbeing.

Cardiovascular exercise has a beneficial effect on the body. It will promote weight loss and enable your heart and lungs to work more efficiently and become stronger. It will help to increase bone density, reduce stress and decrease the risk of heart disease and some cancers, particularly colon, prostrate and breast cancer. Regular cardiovascular exercise relieves depression, increases your level of confidence, improves your sleep patterns and gives you more energy to combat challenges at home and at work. It can help to lower cholesterol, triglyceride (fat in the bloodstream and fat tissue) and blood pressure levels. Glucose tolerance (how your body breaks down blood sugar) and insulin sensitivity (how well the insulin in the body controls blood sugar levels) will also improve. For athletic performance, the more cardiovascular exercise you do, the faster your heart rate will recover, and metabolize glucose to give your muscles the energy they need.

Below: The cardiovascular system consists of the heart and a closed system of arteries, veins and capillaries. Because the heart and lungs are made from muscular tissue, they need to be trained, just like other muscles.

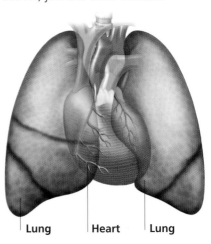

| Lung | Heart | Lung |

Appropriate exercises
Different exercises will benefit different people, depending on their fitness level and injuries. For example, a big muscular person will benefit more from rowing, in which there is no impact and they can use a large amount of muscle mass. Running, however, involves constant impact and is more likely to cause injury. It relies on the legs to carry the weight and doesn't use the upper-body muscles.

Losing weight
• To achieve weight loss and maintain your new lower weight, you must combine cardiovascular training with resistance training, because resistance training will increase your muscle metabolism and help you to burn more calories.
• To lose weight, do exercises that use greater muscle mass. The rowing machine and the cross-trainer work both your upper and lower body and will burn more calories compared to other cardiovascular exercises.

Above: Boxing provides a complete workout for your cardiovascular and endurance systems.

Enjoy yourself Choose a cardiovascular activity that you enjoy, so that you'll want to do more of it. If you dread going to the gym, try training with a partner, perhaps competing side by side on a bike or doing some boxercise. Use music to distract yourself from the exercise, especially if you are exercising at low intensity to burn fat. To motivate yourself before a training session, think about how great you will feel after you have completed a good cardiovascular session – energized, fresh and stress free.
Challenge yourself If you run for 5km/ 3 miles on the treadmill every other day, your body will soon get used to this exercise, and the lack of challenge will result in fewer calories being burnt and only a small improvement to your fitness level. Rather than doing the same exercise at the same level of intensity, combine different exercises and levels of intensity all the time to give your body new

Above: Eat a healthy, nutritious diet to prepare for and recover from cardiovascular workouts.

Above: Rowing trains your cardiovascular system without the impact of running.

Above: Make running a more challenging experience by trying out different surfaces and terrains.

challenges. For example, run for about 3 minutes at a steady pace, then accelerate and hold a fast pace for the fourth minute, before returning to a steady pace. When out walking, adjust

Below: Weights alone will not benefit your cardiovascular system – you need a mixture of different types of exercise.

your training route to include more hills to challenge your body and increase your heart rate, thereby making you work harder to achieve fitness.

When to train
Everybody has a preferred time of day to train. If you train first thing in the morning before eating, you will burn

straight into your fat stores as your glycogen stores (stored glucose, mainly in the muscles and liver), which you usually use in the first 20 minutes of exercise, will have depleted overnight. If you follow resistance training with cardiovascular training, you will also burn straight into fat stores. This may seem like a more efficient way of burning fat but be careful – you may start to feel dizzy and you may even pass out if your glycogen levels are low. Training will increase your energy level, so you may want to train during your lunch break so that you have greater energy for the afternoon's work.

Training tips
• To start burning fat, your exercise regime should last for at least 20 minutes.
• To feel the maximum benefits of cardiovascular exercise, you should train at least three times a week at between 60 and 90 per cent of your maximum heart rate.
• Elite athletes need to train at between 75 and 95 per cent of their maximum heart rate if they want to make significant fitness improvements.

Cardiovascular Energy Expenditure

When estimating the number of calories you will burn in an exercise session, you need to take into account duration, speed and intensity of exercise, along with your body type and the muscle requirement of each exercise.

The longer you exercise, the more calories you will burn. If you are unfit, you should exercise at a lower intensity so that you can exercise for longer before fatigue sets in. For example, if you are trying to run for the first time, begin by alternating 1 minute of jogging with 3 minutes of walking, then repeating for as long as possible. If you attempt to jog continuously, the chances are that you will last less than 10 minutes. By alternating walking and jogging, you may be able to last for up to 1 hour.

Below: Boxing is extremely demanding, and around just 3 minutes of hard boxing can seem a very long time.

Speed of exercise
The faster the exercise, the more calories you burn. Going faster will force your body to work harder, and muscle cells to contract faster. You have to burn more calories to maintain a fast work rate.

Intensity level
The greater the intensity of the exercise, the higher the number of calories you will burn. Intense exercise will not only

Above: If you constantly paddle out, catch a wave and surf in again, you will burn more calories.

burn calories during exercise, it will also make you burn more calories after the exercise has stopped. Interval training and sprinting will have this afterburn effect because your muscles need energy to recover, which in turn burns more calories.

Body type
Mesomorphs are naturally leaner and possess more metabolically active muscle cells. This means that they will have a higher metabolic rate, even at rest, and will, therefore, burn a greater number of calories, further helping them to stay lean.

Appropriate nutrition

If you are quite lean already, make sure that your food intake is sufficient to keep up with your exercise demands. If it is not, you may be forced to break down muscle to provide energy. In the long term, this means less muscle mass and, therefore, a reduced potential for burning calories.

Above: Cycling at speed uses up a lot of calories and they continue to burn even after the exercise has stopped.

The heavier a person is, the more calories he or she is likely to burn during exercise because they have got more weight to move around. For example, the energy required for a runner who weighs 63kg/140lb is far less than the energy needed for a runner who weighs 90kg/200lb, or almost twice as much. The lighter runner burns off fewer calories.

Below: For someone of average weight, baseball burns up around 350 calories in 1 hour.

Muscle use

There is a simple equation to keep in mind when it comes to exercise and calorie burn. Exercises that involve using greater amounts of muscle will burn more calories. For example, a training session on the rowing machine will burn more calories than a similar session on a static bike because rowing uses both your upper and lower body. However, cycling, when riding at speed, may burn up a lot of calories, even though it uses only your leg muscles. Competitive sports require high-speed running or sprinting and can burn off hundreds of calories in an hour.

Calorie burn by exercise

The following list shows an estimate of how many calories you can expect to burn in 1 hour of constant exercise, depending on your body weight, and the speed you are going at, for a variety of popular sports and activities.

Exercise	59kg/130lb	70kg/155lb	86kg/190lb
Aerobics, general	354	422	518
Aerobics, high impact	413	493	604
American football	593	783	866
Baseball	295	352	431
Basketball	472	563	690
Cycling <16kph/10mph	236	281	345
Cycling >32kph/20mph	944	1,126	1380
Cycling, mountain bike	502	598	733
Boxercise	531	633	776
Rowing, racing	708	844	1035
Rowing, leisure	17	211	259
Dancing, fast	325	387	474
Dancing, slow	177	211	259
Football	531	633	776
Golf	236	281	345
Handball	472	563	690
Hockey	472	563	690
Horse riding	236	281	345
Ice hockey	340	485	592
Rugby	590	704	863
Running 16kph/10mph	944	1,126	1,380
Running 13kph/8mph	796	950	1,165
Running 10kph/6mph	590	704	863
Ice-skating	413	493	604
Skateboarding	340	495	604
Skiing, cross-country	826	985	1,208
Skiing, downhill	354	422	518
Skiing, water	354	422	518
Squash	708	844	1,035
Surfing	177	211	259
Swimming, fast	590	704	863
Swimming, leisure	354	422	518
Tennis, singles	472	563	690
Tennis, doubles	354	422	518
Volleyball	472	563	690
Walking 6kph/4mph	236	281	345
Walking 5kph/3mph	207	246	302
Walking 3kph/2mph	148	176	216
Weightlifting	354	422	518

Heart Rate

The heart circulates oxygenated blood from your lungs to the working muscles. Using a heart-rate monitor will help to monitor the stresses you are putting on your heart and will reduce the risk of injury and overtraining.

Your heart rate is measured in beats per minute (bpm). You can measure your heart rate by using the pulse on your wrist or neck and counting the number of pulses in 6 seconds and then multiplying it by ten. However, the best way to monitor your heart rate is to use a heart-rate monitor. It's easy to use: simply place the strap around your torso just underneath the top of your chest or bra line. The best time to measure resting heart rate (RHR) is first thing in the morning when you wake up – before the stresses of the day, eating and exercise can affect the reading. For an average reading, take your RHR every day for three days.

Heart rate can be used as a measure of how fit you are. The sooner your heart rate returns to its resting value after exercise – 55bpm for example – the fitter you are. It is worth monitoring your average heart rate (AHR) throughout similar exercise sessions to compare your fitness levels and keep you motivated. For example, if you regularly do a 4.8km/3-mile cycle ride in 15 minutes and your AHR reading is 155bpm, and you do the same bike ride a month later, in the same time, and your heart rate averages 145bpm, you know you are getting fitter.

Maximum heart rate

The maximum number of times your heart can contract in a minute is called the maximum heart rate (MHR). This is the best indicator to use to work out the intensity levels of your training. There are two methods to determine your MHR: the first involves increasing the intensity of exercises, step by step, over the space of 10–20 minutes until you reach total exhaustion. For example, ride the exercise bike at 16kph/10mph and increase the speed by 1.6kph/1mph every minute until you can't go any farther. You should not try this test unless you have a doctor with you, in case you have cardiac problems. The second method uses the following formula: MHR = 220 - your age.

Heart rate and health

You can use your heart rate to monitor your health and prevent yourself overtraining. If your RHR is five to ten beats higher than normal, this

Above: The strap of a heart-rate monitor, worn around the chest, sends information to the wrist monitor.

indicates that you may be coming down with an illness. You should, therefore, consider adjusting your training or taking a rest before you do any more damage. If your heart rate will not increase to the values you normally see when you are doing high-intensity

Below: The heart rate can easily be calculated by feeling for, and taking, your pulse.

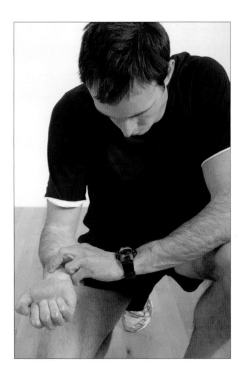

HRZ

To train safely and effectively, you need to establish your correct heart rate zone (HRZ) for the various training levels. To do this, you first need to calculate your heart resting rate (HRR), using this formula:

HRR = maximum heart rate (MHR) – resting heart rate (RHR)

Calculating HRR

220bpm (MHR) – 60bpm (RHR)
= 160bpm (HRR)

Your HRZ can be set using percentages of your HRR, using this formula:

HRZ = (HRR x percentage level of intensity) + RHR

Use the formula to work out your heart rate zone (HRZ) for all your training levels of intensity. Most heart-rate monitors will have a facility to set training zones. The watch will flash or make a noise if you go above or below the appropriate zone.

Calculating HRZ (Level 3 high intensity)

75–90 per cent (160 HRR x 75 per cent) + 60 RHR = 180bpm (bottom of L3) HRZ;

(160 HRR x 90 per cent) + 60 RHR = 204bpm HRZ (top of L3 HRZ).

Above: In the gym, many of the machines have heart-rate monitors built into the mechanism.

training, then you may be overtraining. Your body is telling you that it needs to rest – and you should listen to it.

Using your heart-rate monitor regularly in training sessions outdoors is a useful measure of how the weather conditions are affecting your performance. For example, if you are out on your normal cycle route and it is wet and windy, and you are cycling or running directly against the direction of the wind, you may find that you cover the ground slower. Your heart-rate monitor, however, tells you that you are working at the same intensity – if not higher – as you would if there were no wind. This shows that the wind is probably the limiting factor on your time. So, rather than overexerting yourself to beat your previous best time, and in the process increasing your risk of injury, use the heart-rate monitor to keep yourself in the correct zone. If you have not been exercising regularly or you are an athlete

returning from illness, consider using a heart-rate monitor to monitor your heart rate while exercising, that way you won't overdo your first few sessions on the way back to fitness. Avoid letting your heart rate go above 75 per cent of its maximum.

Above: Adverse weather conditions, such as rain or snow, can affect your heart rate.

Below: Cycling against a headwind slows you down and makes you work harder. This causes an increase in the heart rate.

Breathing Technique

There is an art to breathing correctly and getting the most out of each breath. Good breathing technique will help lower blood pressure, purify the blood, increase metabolism, improve digestion, promote rapid recovery after exercise and help you to relax.

Take a look at a gym full of people exercising and the chances are that you will notice most people resorting to shallow, fast breaths, because they are using only the top part of their chest to breathe. This type of breathing is inefficient and ineffective. Excessive panting is a waste of energy and does not deliver enough oxygen to your lungs. This rapid, shallow breathing may trigger what is known as a 'flight-or-flight' response: your heart rate increases as the heart pumps faster to use what little oxygen it has been given. This increases the stress on your body, which leads, in turn, to poor physical performance and increases the recovery time needed after your training session. Your brain is tricked into thinking you are exercising at high intensity when, in fact, if you were breathing correctly, you would be aware that it is not high intensity at all. Using only the top of the lungs with this type of short, shallow, chest breathing does not make use of the bottom half of your lungs, where

the most efficient exchange of oxygen takes place. It is important to exhale fully before you take in another breath or you simply won't have enough room for the new oxygen to come in.

Above: After strenuous exercise, you will feel less stressed and your recovery will be much quicker if you have been breathing correctly.

Shallow breathing

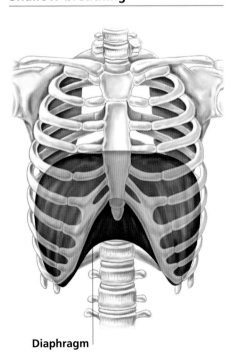

Diaphragm

Breathing exercises

During the week, try to regularly make time for some simple breathing exercises. Remember to keep your posture as upright as possible: relax your shoulders but keep your chest up and make sure your ears, shoulders and hips are all in line to maintain good posture.

If you add these two breathing exercises to your training plan twice a week, you will see the benefits within a few weeks.

Left: When breathing hard during exercise make sure you use the bottom half of the lungs to get maximum oxygen supply to your muscles. The most efficient exchange of oxygen takes place in the bottom half of the lungs. The diaphragm is shaped rather like a parachute.

Emptying your lungs

Breathing out correctly can be likened to emptying your garbage bin to make room for more. You need to empty the whole bin before you start filling it up again. Likewise, you need to empty your lungs completely before you take in another breath.

During any type of exercise, once you have completely breathed out, avoid holding your breath. If you do not breathe in again, you take the risk of depriving the body of oxygen and a dangerous rise in blood pressure. Also, if you are not breathing properly, your performance would be unsatisfactory and you may feel unwell.

After training, slow, deep breathing and slow exhalation can help to relax the body.

Abdominal or diaphragmatic breathing

Practise this technique when you are resting and relaxed, then start to incorporate the technique into your workout sessions. You will soon be able to increase the intensity level of your training session and sustain it at a higher level for longer.

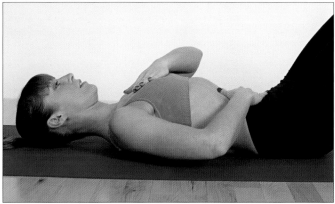

1 *Place one hand on your stomach and the other hand on your chest. As you breathe in, look at your hands. The hand on your stomach should be moving more than the hand on your chest. When this happens, you know you are making good use of the space at the bottom of your lungs.*

2 *Next, take a deep breath in through your nose and out slowly through your mouth. When you think you have breathed out fully, contract your stomach muscles to help empty your lungs completely. Breathing out should take twice as long as breathing in. Repeat this technique for 3 to 4 minutes at a time.*

Bellows breathing

Athletes often use this technique at the start of a competition because, by making the muscles involved in heavy breathing ready for action, it conditions the body to overcome the shock of a sudden demand for more oxygen. This method of breathing can help to combat fatigue, as it releases energizing chemicals to your brain.

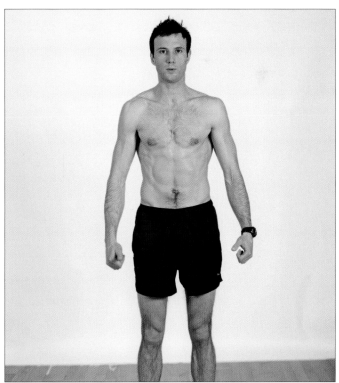

1 *Sit in a chair the first time you attempt bellows breathing because it can cause hyperventilation, and in some cases people may pass out. When you are confident that you can use the technique safely, do it standing up, with your arms out to your side.*

2 *Breathe in fast through your nose and mouth, then breathe out fast through your mouth, using your abdominal muscles to empty your lungs completely. Try bellows breathing for 10 seconds, then increase by 5 seconds each time you practise the exercise.*

Levels of Intensity

Doing the same 30 minutes of cardiovascular exercise every day will not continue to give you the results you need. To prevent your body from getting used to any one style of exercise – and so making it ineffective – you need to vary your intensity levels.

To achieve dramatic results through cardiovascular training, you need to learn more about your training and apply levels of intensity to your training routine. Heart rate is perhaps the best measure of intensity because it indicates how hard your body is working. To get the best results from your exercise routine, follow the four levels of intensity.

Level 1: Steady, long-duration training

This lasts for at least 1 hour. Your heart rate should be between 40 and 60 per cent of maximum and you should be able to hold a normal conversation without effort or panting. If you are new to exercise, this is the level at which you will spend most of your time for the first few weeks. It is the least demanding, but it will start to promote an efficient cardiovascular system. If you are unfit, there is no point in trying to go above

Below: Level 1 is simply walking steadily for about one hour, while still being able to drink and eat.

this level quickly, because you will tire too early to get a beneficial session. Walking fast for 40 minutes is far more beneficial than running for 5 minutes and being too tired to go any farther. Top athletes use this level of intensity to begin their warm-ups.

Level 2: Medium-intensity training

You should use this for 15 to 60 minutes of cardiovascular training. Your heart rate should be between 60 and 75 per cent of maximum – a rate at which you can only hold a conversation in short sentences. This level is great for weight loss and improving aerobic capacity without the risk of injury, but you have to make a conscious effort to stay at this level. (Aerobic capacity is the

Above: At Level 2, the pace is faster but still allows joggers to be able to speak comfortably.

highest amount of oxygen consumed during maximal exercise in activities that use the large muscle groups in the legs, or in the arms and legs combined.)

Fat burning myth

It is a myth that to burn fat you need to keep your heart rate low and keep going for a long period of time. In fact, the best way to lose fat is to adjust your intensity to challenge your body by making the exercise much harder, which in turn will burn more calories.

Pyramid of intensity

Imagine a pyramid where the base of the pyramid is Level 1. As you start to go up the pyramid, your level of intensity increases until you are training at Level 4, at the top. The base of the pyramid is wider indicating the amount of time you need to spend at this level of intensity to make your body efficient at coping with the demands of your exercise. If the pyramid has a narrow base, it will be more likely to topple over when you are at the top. This theory applies directly to your training. If you try to train at a high-intensity level without building a good base, you will be prone to injuries and overtraining.

Level 3: High-intensity training

This should last from 1 to 10 minutes, although trained athletes can continue at this level for longer due to their high aerobic capacity. Your heart rate should be between 75 and 90 per cent of maximum. You should only be able to give one-word answers during this type of training as you will be fully focused on breathing in as much oxygen as possible. Athletes often use this level of training in the form of intervals. For

Right: At Level 3, the going gets tougher, with the person running so hard that they start to get out of breath.

Below: The maximum level is Level 4, in which the runner pushes as hard as possible for a short sustained effort.

example, 10 minutes at Level 2, then 2 minutes at Level 3, then 2 minutes at Level 2, followed by 4 minutes at Level 3. This is often called Aerobic Interval Training. It is important to vary the duration of the intervals to achieve the best results. This is hard to begin with, but your body will adjust and be able to recover quickly between the intervals. This is the fastest way to develop muscle and increase your fat metabolism.

Level 4: Maximum-intensity training

This should last between 10 seconds and 2 minutes. This level is 90 per cent and above of maximum heart rate.

You will not be able to talk comfortably and you will feel out of breath from start to finish. As with Level 3, this level is used for interval training. For example, after 10 minutes' warm-up, walk for 1 minute, sprint as fast as possible for 30 seconds, then walk for 1 minute and, finally, sprint again for 30 seconds.

Sports people who play in positions that require the maximum amount of speed over short distances should adopt this type of intensity training. Do not, however, attempt to start this extreme type of training unless you have already been doing some reasonably intense training for some time.

Climate and Performance

Temperature, altitude, wind and humidity can all have significant effects on the body's ability to perform. It is absolutely essential that you understand these factors before attempting to train or compete in conditions that could have very serious adverse effects on your body.

One of the biggest factors that can affect your performance when training or competing in sports events is the prevailing temperature.

Your core body temperature is regulated at 37°C/98.6°F. If your body temperature changes by even just a few degrees above or below this level, you will become extremely unwell. Our natural reaction to combat overheating is to sweat. This creates a layer of water on the skin that helps to cool the body. Conversely, if we are too cold, we shiver, which increases muscle activity and in the process generates heat. We can, of course, also help to regulate our temperature by adding or removing layers of clothing.

Extreme heat

Exercising in the heat can be just as dangerous as exercising in low temperatures – and you should never attempt it without a full understanding of all the factors involved and being properly prepared. As soon as the air temperature rises above 32°C/89.6°F, you are entering the danger zone of heat cramps, heat exhaustion or even heatstroke. Heat cramps are similar to muscle cramps, and are caused by exertion and insufficient salts. Heat exhaustion is caused by a lack of the bodily fluids that would normally help cool you down. The signs of heat exhaustion are excessive sweating, pale skin, faster pulse and breathing rates, general weakness, nausea and vomiting. Heatstroke occurs when there is an increase in core body temperature due to a lack of fluids, or when the heat is so extreme that it overpowers your body's cooling mechanism. Too much water is lost via sweating and the volume of blood decreases so that there is less blood flow between the muscles and skin and less cooling, so that the body overheats. The

signs of heatstroke are the same as heat exhaustion, with possibly the additional symptom of dilated pupils. Heatstroke can be fatal. To avoid overheating, make sure you do not exercise in extreme temperatures, and avoid dangerous dehydration by drinking plenty of fluids before, during and after exercising. The amount you drink will depend on how hard you are exercising, your weight and the prevailing air temperature.

Wind

Weather conditions such as wind will either help or hinder your performance. For example, if you cycle with the wind

Above: Athletes at the Athens 2004 Olympics lie on the track suffering from heat exhaustion.

behind you, it will help you to go faster. If the wind is blowing toward you, it will slow you down. You should take this into consideration when you are trying to train at certain levels of intensity – there is no point in trying to beat a personal best time if you are cycling or running into a headwind.

Wind will take away the warm air close to your body and replace it with cooler air, lowering your body temperature in the process. The wind

Exercise and high temperatures	
Temperature – °C/°F	**Type of heat injury**
32–40/89.6–104	Heat cramps
40–54/104–129.2	Heat cramps, heat exhaustion, possibility of heatstroke
54/129.2+	Heatstroke very likely

chill factor is a scale that shows the equivalent temperature given to a particular wind speed. In hot conditions, wind will interfere with your body's natural cooling mechanism by drying the layer of sweat on your body that would normally cool you down.

Humidity

The ratio of water in the air at a particular temperature to the total quantity of moisture that could be carried in that air is defined as humidity. It is expressed as a percentage. If the level of humidity is high (30 per cent and above), you will sweat more, but the sweat cannot evaporate, hampering the body's ability to cool itself. This will lead to dehydration and the same problems associated with exercising in hot temperatures. To help overcome high humidity, drink fluids containing essential salts and minerals to keep your body functioning as normally as possible.

Below: When exercising in very cold weather, it is important to keep moving around and to wear adequate clothing.

Above: In hot or humid conditions, drink plenty of liquids before, during and after your exercise programme.

Altitude

As altitude increases, atmospheric pressure drops and there is a decrease in the amount of oxygen available. Your maximal aerobic ability is reduced by

Above: If you run in the mountains, where there is an increase in altitude, you will need a few days to adapt.

1 per cent for every 91m/300ft above 1,372m/4,500ft. To exercise at high altitude, your body will have to go through short- and long-term adaptive changes. At first, you will experience a more rapid breathing rate and increased blood flow when exercising, and you will find yourself tiring very quickly. You may get acute mountain sickness, feelings of nausea, headaches, insomnia, dizziness and muscle weakness.

However, in just one or two days, your body will have adapted. Your resting heart rate will increase, as will your cardiac output (blood flow), in order to compensate for the lack of oxygen. After three to four weeks, your blood haemoglobin level will increase – every drop of blood that supplies the muscle will deliver an increased amount of oxygen. (Haemoglobin is a protein in the blood that contains iron and transports oxygen from the lungs to the rest of the body.)

If you live at high altitude for some time, your body will naturally adapt to the atmospheric conditions by producing more of the myoglobin, mitochondria and metabolic enzymes used for aerobic energy transfer.

However, you can also expect to lose muscle mass and body fat, which may affect your performance.

Walking

It's tempting to think that there's nothing to walking beyond putting one foot in front of the other and setting off. True, it is a very accessible form of exercise. However, getting the best from it calls for the right technique, pace, clothing and footwear – and a schedule.

Walking has many benefits. It's free, it's an independent mode of transport and environmentally friendly. It is also a great way to get fit before progressing to harder forms of exercise, such as running or preparing yourself for a bigger goal such as a marathon. Walking at a brisk pace will burn between 300 and 400 calories per hour and because walking has only one-third as much impact as running, it is an ideal form of exercise for people who suffer from bone-degenerating diseases such as osteoporosis.

Technique

Try to focus on a different aspect of your technique each time you walk. It is important to keep your head still with your chin parallel to the ground to eliminate using unnecessary energy. Stand tall when you walk, keep your abdominals and buttocks tensed to keep your spine in a good neutral position, and bend your elbows at 90 degrees. To make your walking workout even more demanding, carry dumbbells or

Below: Listening to the radio or music through headphones will keep you company while you are walking.

Above: Carrying dumbbells while walking very briskly gives you a much more vigorous workout.

hand weights. The key to walking more efficiently is to increase your stride rate and maintain flexibility in the hips. Your foot should strike the ground with your heel first, before rolling forward on to your toes.

What to wear

It is essential to have the right clothes and footwear for walking exercise. Make sure that you are properly fitted

Walking speed

The following chart will give you a guide to your walking speed. The next time you are walking for an exercise session, try counting the number of strides you take in 1 minute.

Steps per minute	kph	mph
70	3.2	2
90	4	2.5
105	4.8	3
120	5.6	3.5
140	6.4	4

for your walking shoes. There should be a certain amount of comfort to begin with, but be aware that shoes will get more comfortable as the material softens and you wear them in. Therefore, you should buy shoes that are a half to a whole size too large so that you have room for your feet to expand when they get hot. If you are going to walk on the side of the road or on smooth walking tracks, you can wear normal running shoes. However, if you are going off-road, you will need a shoe with ankle support to protect your ankles from turning over on rough terrain. You should also wear several layers of clothing so that you can adjust them as necessary.

Below: Correct clothing and footwear suitable for the weather conditions and terrain are essential.

Walking exercises

Follow this six-week walking programme for four days a week, to improve your fitness. Although fast walking has less impact than running, equip yourself with comfortable walking shoes, and wear layers of clothing that you can peel off if you become overheated. The total walking time each week should increase week by week as you progressively get fitter and faster. If you are serious about stepping up your fitness, consider other aspects such as flexibility, core stability, strength and nutrition to get the desired results. After just six weeks of working through these exercises, you should be able to walk across hilly terrain for 60 minutes without stopping. Your recovery should be good enough for you to continue without taking any rests. To avoid dehydration, make sure you take fluids with you if you are out walking for more than 45 minutes.

Time	Intensity/environment
Week 1	
20 minutes	flat terrain
30 minutes	flat terrain, alternating 1 minute fast, 2 minutes slow
30 minutes	hilly terrain
20 minutes	flat or hilly terrain, with hand weights or a backpack

Weekly total: 1 hr 40 minutes

Time	Intensity/environment
Week 2	
25 minutes,	flat terrain
30 minutes	flat terrain, alternating 2 minutes fast, 2 minutes slow
35 minutes	hilly terrain
20 minutes	flat or hilly terrain, with hand weights or a backpack

Weekly total: 1 hr 50 minutes

Time	Intensity/environment
Week 3	
25 minutes	flat terrain
30 minutes	flat terrain, alternating 2 minutes fast, 2 minutes slow
40 minutes	hilly terrain
20 minutes	flat or hilly terrain, with hand weights or a backpack

Weekly total: 1 hr 55 minutes

Time	Intensity/environment
Week 4	
30 minutes	flat terrain
35 minutes	flat terrain, alternating 2 minutes fast, 1 minute slow
40 minutes	hilly terrain
20 minutes	flat or hilly terrain, with hand weights or a backpack

Weekly total: 2 hrs 5 minutes

Time	Intensity/environment
Week 5	
35 minutes	flat terrain
40 minutes	flat terrain, alternating 2 minutes fast, 1 minute slow
50 minutes	hilly terrain
25 minutes	flat or hilly terrain, with hand weights or a backpack

Weekly total: 2 hrs 30 minutes

Time	Intensity/environment
Week 6	
35 minutes	flat terrain
40 minutes	flat terrain, alternating 2 minutes fast, 1 minute slow
60 minutes	hilly terrain
25 minutes	flat or hilly terrain, with hand weights or a backpack

Weekly total: 2 hrs 40 minutes

Running

Like walking, running is a cheap form of exercise enjoyed by many people – though not everyone. Again, however, you don't just put your shoes on and go until you stop. Technique, stride, uphill and downhill terrain, and correct breathing are all important.

Running is one of the best forms of cardiovascular exercise as it doesn't require any expensive equipment and you can run just about anywhere.

Anyone can run, at any age. People have different motives for running: the initial reason may be to lose weight, then the person finds that they enjoy running and want to progress further in the sport, progressing until they can take part in races. For others, running is a simple form of exercise that can be done anytime, anywhere when convenient, and involves only the purchase of a good pair of running shoes and tracksuit.

Muscles used in running

The major muscles used in running are listed below. They are involved in driving you forward as well as taking the shock of the impact as your feet hit the ground. They also prevent injury and loss of energy caused by unnecessary movement.

The next step is technique. Good running technique is essential to enable you to run faster and avoid injury. As your foot strikes the ground, it should be in line with your hips and below your centre of gravity. Make sure that you have some flexion in your knee in the impact, and keep your hips stable to provide a strong base for driving forward.

Also, you need to be aware of lateral movement in the hips when you strike the ground, as this can lead to injuries. Do one-leg squats and superman exercises for the sides of the hips. To check for a weakness in the hip area,

stand on one leg and squat down, trying to keep your hips from pushing out to the sides. Your waist line should be level throughout the squat.

After your foot strikes the ground, let your leg stretch fully behind you and at the same time drive your other leg forward to make contact with the ground. Throughout the running movement, keep your arms bent, but relaxed, at 90 degrees at the elbow. Your opposite hand should drive forward as your knee drives forward and upward. Don't let your lower back do all the work. It is a common mistake to twist the upper body from the lower back, rather than pumping the arms forward and back.

The importance of stride

Stride length and stride speed are both important. Generally, stride length will make you run faster, but this is not always the best way to gain speed. Do not try to lengthen your stride until your stride pace is sufficient. Most people make the mistake of overstriding: they have a stride rate of 70–80 strides per minute, when, in fact, the most efficient

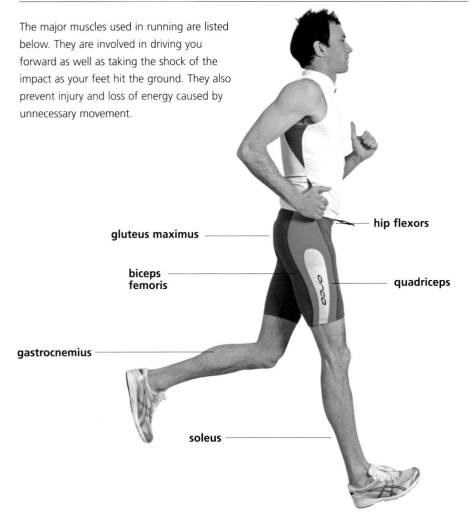

gluteus maximus

biceps femoris

gastrocnemius

soleus

hip flexors

quadriceps

Run away weight

Running can burn between 400 and 1,500 calories per hour, depending on the speed and the body mass of the individual runner. The faster you go and the heavier you are, the more calories you will burn.

Above: When running, the foot should strike the ground in line with your hips and below your centre of gravity.

Above: When running faster, the opposite leg to the arm drives forward. The momentum helps to increase speed.

Above: For smooth, injury-free running, try to avoid lateral movement in the hips, and keep the legs moving forward.

stride rate is approximately 90 strides per minute. Next time you run, keep a count of your strides – if you are running at less than 90 strides per minute, try shortening your stride slightly and increasing your stride rate. Don't be put off if you find you cannot manage to change your stride at once. It could take a month or two before you naturally run at the higher stride rate.

Uphill and downhill
When you run uphill, try to keep the stride rate high. Shorten your stride to avoid early fatigue and overstretching the muscles in the back of the legs. Use your arms more – a sprinter gets around one-third of propulsion from the arms. When you are running downhill, try to keep your stride length short and fast, in order to avoid injuring your legs – as a greater stride length creates more impact and increases the chances of injury.

Right: One-leg squats, which can be done in the gym, exercise the same muscles involved in running.

Breathing
To complete the correct technique, your breathing has to be right. There are a number of ways to try to breathe when you are running. Most runners use a 2:2

technique, that is, two strides on each leg (a total of four strides) to every time you breathe in, and two strides to every time you breathe out. You can use a 3:3 or even 4:4 technique, if you prefer.

Running: Warm-up to Workout

You might be eager to get on with your actual exercise routine but, before you do, it is vital that you have a warm-up that combines walking, jogging and stretching. In fact, from now on, get into the habit of thinking that warm-up is part of your 'real' routine.

Before you run, have a good warm-up, which should include at least 2 minutes walking, 5 minutes of light jogging or fast walking, and some stretches. The best stretches will be a hamstring, quadriceps and calf stretch. Perform each one twice for 10–20 seconds. Don't get chilled during the warm-up and always have a cool-down period after running. A slow 3- to 5-minute jog or walk, followed by some stretches, including the ones you did in the warm-up, constitute a good cool-down.

Jogging programme
If you are new to jogging, begin by jogging for 1 minute and walking for 2 minutes after your warm-up. Repeat this until you have been exercising for 30–45 minutes. When you have

completed three sessions of this combination in a week, build your jog time up to 2 minutes and walk for 1 minute for three sessions per week. Each week, add another 2 minutes to your jog time, so after six weeks of jogging/walking three times per week, you should be able to jog for 10 minutes and walk for 1 minute for a total of 30–60 minutes. At this stage, try to jog continuously for 15–20 minutes. Time yourself over distances of 2km/1.2 miles and 5km/3.1 miles. This will allow you to measure your improvement and set new targets. To maximize the benefits and avoid injury, aim for a steady rate of

Left: Treadmills provide a softer bed to run on so there is less impact than running on a hard surface.

Weekly sessions to improve running fitness

The following four running sessions are suitable for people at any level from beginner, through intermediate to expert. Just be realistic and make the appropriate choice for you, depending on whether your fitness level is below average, average or above average. Do not stick to your usual run, but instead, use these sessions to improve your training fitness and performance. Try to fit in at least three to four runs a week, using the appropriate session for you. *See* Levels of Intensity on pages 46–47.

	Fitness level	Distance/time	Intensity
Session 1: timed run –	Below average:	2km/1.2 miles	L3
do this every other week to	Average:	5km/3.1 miles	L3
compare your fitness level	Above average:	10km/6.2 miles	L3
Session 2: intervals to	Below average:	40 minutes	4 minutes easy run L1, then 1 minute fast L3: keep repeating
build aerobic capacity	Average:	40–60 minutes	3 minutes easy run L1, then 2 minutes fast L3: keep repeating
	Above average:	40–60 minutes	2 minutes easy L1, then 2 minutes L3 fast: keep repeating
Session 3: long endurance	Below average:	30–40 minutes	steady run L1–L2
run to aid aerobic efficiency	Average:	45–60 minutes	steady run L1–L2
and fat metabolism	Above average:	60–90 minutes	steady run L1–L2
Session 4: hill run to build	Below average:	20 minutes	2 minutes hills L3, then 8 minutes on the flat L1 x 2
power; attack the hills and	Average:	35–40 minutes	3 minutes hills L3, then 6 minutes on the flat L1 x 4
go easy on the flat	Above average:	45–50 minutes	4 minutes hills L3, then 4 minutes on the flat L1 x 6

progress – your body needs a chance to build the correct muscles and to establish stability to cope with the physical demands of running.

Treadmill versus outdoors

The treadmill is a good way to begin running, as the base of the treadmill provides some cushioning to help avoid injury. Running on a treadmill also allows you to assess your fitness as you can cover the exact distance and not be affected by terrain or weather conditions. When running outdoors, the fresh air can cool you down faster. Using off-road tracks will soften the impact of your foot striking the ground and will prevent injury

The right level
• Stay on one fitness level for six weeks before you consider moving up to the next level.
• Wearing a heart-rate monitor or occasionally using the sensors on the treadmill will help you to choose the appropriate level of intensity.

to joints. Try not to run on ground that is too soft, unless you are being coached to do a specific session. Soft ground will make the back of the calves – the Achilles – work too hard and may cause injury.

What to wear

Comfortable footwear that absorbs impact is vital; you will need running trainers that have been specifically designed to provide the proper support and cushioning. Visit a shop where the sales advisors are trained to watch you and suggest shoes that suit your style. If possible, test running shoes on a treadmill before you buy them.

Wear comfortable, breathable clothes. If it is cold, wear tights to trap body heat. This is especially important to protect joints with poor blood supply, such as your knees. On your top half, wear a few layers so that you can take them off and on as the temperature and the speed of your running session changes. Wear a cap to protect your eyes from bad weather, to keep the sun

Above: Wear layers and gradually take them off only once you have warmed up and your body feels at a comfortable temperature while you are running.

off your head and to prevent sweat getting into your eyes. Finally, carry water to maintain your hydration levels.

Running trainers

A good pair of running shoes is a very important purchase, so take your time before buying them. There are a number of factors you should consider before choosing the right shoes.

Get expert advice from a running shop if possible where they will be able to show you shoes which are correct for you. Try them on and run around the shop to see if they feel comfortable.

There should be sufficient room for you to fit a finger between your heel and the back of the shoe to allow enough room for your foot to swell when running.

The upper material of the shoe must provide good stability to prevent too much foot movement, especially on impact with the ground. If your foot moves forward in the shoe you will damage the front of toes and blister easily.

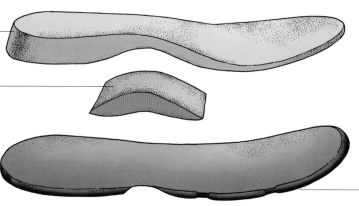

The mid-sole must provide cushioning and support to prevent injuries caused by impact. If your feet turn inward as you land you need more support on the inside of the shoe, if you turn outward as you land you need more support on the outside of your foot.

The lower-sole varies depending on the terrain. More grip is required if venturing off-road. It is important for the sole to have some flexibility to allow your foot to bend easily.

Cycling

Although not as cheap as walking or running, cycling is a relatively inexpensive and highly enjoyable way to keep fit, lose weight and enjoy the great outdoors. As ever, good technique, proper kit and an effective schedule will pay fitness dividends.

Cycling is an excellent form of low-impact aerobic exercise that burns up calories. Calorie burn ranges from 150 calories per hour for a small person travelling at 8kph/5mph to over 800 calories per hour for a bigger person travelling uphill or at over 32kph/20mph.

Technique

If the saddle on your bike is too low, you won't be able to make full use of the power in your legs. If the saddle is too high, you will feel your hips roll from side to side as your legs are stretched too far at the bottom of each pedal stroke. To get the saddle height correct, sit on the bike with one of the pedals at 6 o'clock. In this position, your leg should be almost straight.

To adjust the fore and aft position of the saddle, put one of the crank arms at 3 o'clock. The front of your knee should be in vertical line with the axle of the pedal. If the saddle is too far back or forward, you will put too much pressure on your knees and be at risk of injury.

If the handlebars are too low, you will get backache, so make sure the bars are not much lower than your hips. Put the

Above: When the saddle is the correct height, your leg should be almost straight in the 6 o'clock position.

bars higher than this for added comfort. The distance between the saddle and bars is also important. Make sure you can reach the bars with arms still slightly bent. If they are too close, your back will not be in the neutral position and will become rounded. If they are too far away, you will have to work your core muscles to stay in the right position, and this may result in lower back pain. Check constantly to make sure your neck and shoulders are relaxed to prevent unnecessary aches or pains.

To get the most efficient pedal stroke, pedal in circles rather than squares. In other words, use the whole of the pedal stroke to generate power rather than just pushing down from the top to the bottom. Pulling the pedal back up on the recovery part of the pedal stroke will give your hamstrings a good workout. As you reach the bottom of the pedal

Muscles used in cycling

The major muscles used in cycling are listed below. They are used to push the pedals down and pull them back up in a circular movement. Other muscles help to maintain stability and position on the bike.

hip flexors

gluteus maximus

quadriceps

biceps femoris

gastrocnemius

triceps

Cycling exercises

The following four cycling sessions are suitable for people at any level from beginner, through intermediate to expert. Just be realistic and make the appropriate choice for you, depending on whether your fitness level is below average, average or above average. Do not stick to your usual route. Instead, use these sessions to improve your training fitness and performance. Try to do cycling exercises three to four times a week using the sessions that match your fitness level. Always cool down at the end of your workout with about 5 minutes of easy pedalling as well as some stretches.

	Fitness level	Distance/time	Intensity
Session: time trials to monitor your progress	Below average:	5km/3.1 miles	fast as possible L3
	Average:	8km/5 miles	fast as possible L3
	Above average:	16km/10 miles	fast as possible L3–L4
Session 2: interval exercise to increase aerobic capacity and fitness time	Below average:	4 x 2 minutes	L3–L4 with 4 minutes easy L1 between efforts
	Average:	6 x 3 minutes	L3–L4 with 4 minutes easy L1 between efforts
	Above average:	6 x 4 minutes	L3–L4 with 3 minutes easy L1 between efforts
Session 3: sprints to improve anaerobic ability, recovery and leg speed. Revolutions per minute above 100 for the sprints	Below average:	20 minutes	L2 with 20-second sprints L4 every 4 minutes
	Average:	40 minutes	L2 with 30-second sprints L4 every 4 minutes
	Above average:	60 minutes	L2 with 30-second sprints L4 every 3 minutes
Session 4: hill exercises for leg strength and aerobic capacity. Use a harder gear and drop revs to 60–70 per minute.	Below average:	4 x 2 minute hills	L3 with 4 minutes on flat, L1 between hills
	Average:	6 x 3 minute hills	L3 with 3 minutes on flat, L1 between hills
	Above average:	6 x 4 minute hills	L3–L4 with 3 minutes on flat L1 between hills

stroke, push your heel down to get the full range of movement and make use of all the muscles at the front and back of your legs.

Below: For comfort, bend arms slightly at the elbow. To prevent soreness, keep your shoulders and neck relaxed.

The optimum pedal stroke rate is around 90–100rpm, which keeps you on top of the resistance and helps you to get the oxygen supply that is essential for your legs. Hard gears lower your pedal stroke rate and can cause you to build up lactic acid in your muscles, which may impair muscle contraction and cause a very unpleasant burning sensation.

Keep your upper body as relaxed as possible. Apart from pulling on the bars when you are going up a steep hill, try to conserve your energy and have a more comfortable ride by working your legs and consciously keeping your grip, neck and shoulders as relaxed as you can.

Getting started

If you want to use cycling for improved cardiovascular fitness, incorporate the sessions above into your training plan. Warm up with 5 to 10 minutes' easy pedalling that gradually becomes harder, followed by light stretches for your lower back, hamstrings, quadriceps and calves.

What to wear

A well-fitting helmet is essential – it could save your life if you are involved in an accident. Wear gloves to help you grip the handlebars and avoid sores and blisters. Your footwear will vary depending on your level of cycling. The most efficient shoes have stiff soles so that you can get maximum power through the pedals. Wear cycling shorts to give you protection and comfort.

Exercise bike versus outdoors

For anyone who prefers a more controlled environment, an exercise bike offers simulated hills and flats, and allows you to monitor your heart rate while you are exercising. Using an exercise bike requires little co-ordination and there is less strain on the ankle, knee and hip joints, especially for beginners, anyone elderly or people who are recovering from injuries.

However, if you like being outdoors, enjoy looking at the scenery and experiencing different terrains, riding a dynamic bicycle is a great way to get fit.

Cross-trainer

The cross-trainer is a highly effective, all-over body exercise that uses a large number of muscles. It offers a great alternative to running and is an excellent way to exercise for people who suffer from back and joint problems.

The cross-trainer is a low-impact alternative that works the same muscles that you use when running, but without the same physical impact of pounding the floor. The action of pushing and pulling with the arms simulates the action of cross-country skiing and hill-walking with poles. It also gives you great upper-body tone. If you are looking to do an all-over body weight-training session, the cross-trainer will provide you with a great warm-up.

Technique

Before you begin exercising on the cross-trainer, check to see if you are in the right position. If your feet are too far apart, your stride may force you to overstretch, which could cause an injury. Adjust the step length until you feel comfortable. Keep your posture upright

Below: Unlike running, the cross-trainer works all the major muscle groups in the body.

Target problem areas

Change the emphasis of your workout according to the body parts that you want to work hardest. For example, if you want to work your arms, then relax your legs and just let them follow as you drive the machine with your arms. Conversely, relax the arms so you can work the legs.

– your back should be straight, your shoulders back, chin up and your core muscles, especially abdominals, switched on to work hard. Try not to let your arms do too much of the work. Instead, really use your legs to drive the machine forward. When your leg drives the foot plate back, ensure that the back of your leg is fully extended to have maximum effect on the muscles at the back of your leg.

Avoid wearing training shoes that have too much grip. Your feet need to be able to move slightly in the shoes to find their natural position as you push down on the footplates.

To make the best use of your legs, resist bending forward when you start to feel fatigued. Bending forward will force your lower back to provide the power to drive the machine, and it will quickly tire. If this happens for long periods of time, you may be at risk of a lower-back overuse injury.

Warning

If you suffer from hip and lower back problems, do not at first spend too much time on the cross-trainer. Start with a maximum of around 10 minutes and gradually build it up, by around 3 to 5 minutes every session, until you are comfortable exercising for about 30 minutes.

Above: This position is too far back on the cross-trainer to have any significant effect on the muscles.

Above: The ideal position is a straight back, shoulders back and chin up. Let your legs do all the work.

Above: Leaning too far forward will cause strain on the arms and the back and neck will feel uncomfortable.

Getting started

Each cross-trainer will have different resistance or gradient settings. You should adjust these settings depending on your fitness level and weight. Your level should be adjusted depending on the type of training session that you want to do: long and steady to train your endurance; or fast, powerful intervals to increase your aerobic threshold. Rhythm is the key. You should feel as if you are keeping up with the machine or, ideally, you should stay slightly ahead of the machine, rather than losing rhythm and feeling as if you are struggling. To set your training levels, follow the principles relating to levels of intensity set out earlier in the book.

Post injury

If you are recovering from a running injury, use the cross-trainer to do similar training, but without the same physical impact on your joints and muscles, especially after Achilles tendon, feet, knee, pelvic and lower-back injuries.

Cross-trainer exercises

Include the following training sessions in your weekly programme to get the most out of this type of cardiovascular exercise. Check that you are in the correct position on the cross-trainer. Before you begin any of the sessions, make sure you do at least 5 minutes' warm-up at Level 1 intensity, including some stretches for the lower back, quadriceps, hamstrings and calves.

	Fitness level	Distance/time	Intensity
Session 1: aerobic endurance	Below average:	20 minutes	L2 continuous
	Average:	40 minutes	L2 continuous
	Above average:	60 minutes	L2 continuous
Session 2: improved fitness and aerobic capacity	Below average:	4 x 3 minutes	L3 with 3 minutes L1 easy between efforts
	Average:	5 x 4 minutes	L3 with 3 minutes L1 easy between efforts
	Above average:	6 x 4 minutes	L3–L4 with 3 minutes L1 easy between efforts
Session 3: a new level of fitness, and anaerobic workout	Below average:	20 minutes	L2 with 20-second sprints L4 every 4 minutes
	Average:	40 minutes	L2 with 30-second sprints L4 every 3 minutes
	Above average:	60 minutes	L2 with 30-second sprints L4 every 3 minutes

Rowing

Few cardiovascular exercises use the upper body to the same extent that rowing does. Rowing burns 600–1,000 calories per hour, making it one of the most effective exercises for burning calories and losing weight.

As well as giving you an excellent cardiovascular workout, rowing also exercises all the major muscles.

Technique

Hold the handle in front of you, arms straight and in line with the rowing chain. Your body should be curled up toward the front of the machine like a coiled spring. Initiate the pull by driving your legs as if you are doing a leg press. Take your arms with you as you straighten your legs. As your legs straighten, pull the handle in toward your lower chest and abdomen. Pause for 1 second – the recovery phase – then straighten your arms and bring your legs back to the coil position. Take your time in the recovery phase. Check your stroke rate, which will change depending on whether you are doing speed-work intervals or long-distance endurance. Aim for 25–35 strokes per minute. Your breathing needs to be correct, because the large number of muscles used in rowing demand a lot of oxygen. Breathe in as you recover into the coil, and out as you explode back in the pull.

Muscles exercised during rowing

Most of the muscles in your body are used for rowing; the picture below shows the major muscles working. Rowing regularly is a good cardiovascular exercise that is ideal for strengthening your shoulder, arm, abdomen and back muscles.

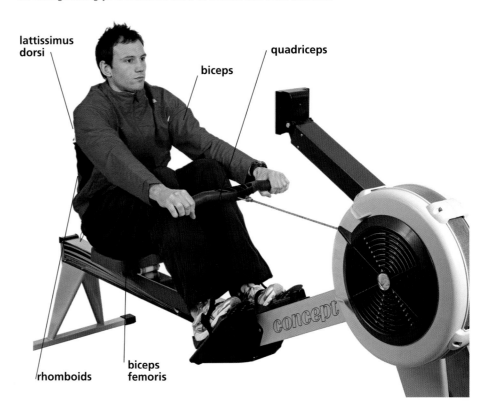

lattissimus dorsi

quadriceps

biceps

rhomboids

biceps femoris

Rowing exercises

Include the following training sessions in your weekly programme to get the most from this cardiovascular exercise. Before any of the sessions, make sure you do at least 5 minutes' warm-up at Level 1

intensity, and because rowing strengthens all the main muscles, it is best to warm them up first with some stretches for the lower back, quadriceps, hamstrings and calves.

	Fitness level	Distance/time	Intensity
Session 1: time trials to	Below average:	1km/0.6 miles	L2–L3
help monitor your fitness	Average:	2km/1.2 miles	L2–L3
	Above average:	2km/1.2 miles	L2–L3
Session 2: improving	Below average:	4 x 200m/219yd	intervals with 60 seconds' rest between each one L3
fitness level and aerobic	Average:	8 x 200m/219yd	intervals with 45 seconds' rest between each one L3
capacity	Above average:	16 x 200m/219yd	intervals with 30 seconds' rest between each one L3
Session 3: improving rowing	Below average:	2km/1.2 miles	long-distance, steady row L2
efficiency and burning calories	Average:	5km/3.1 miles	long-distance row L2
for weight loss and maintenance	Above average:	1km/0.6 miles	long-distance row L2

Above: Before starting your rowing exercises, the body is set in a coiled spring position.

Above: Drive the machine back with the legs, pulling the arms back with you as you begin to straighten your legs.

Above: As the legs are extended, pull your arms toward your lower chest and abdomen.

There are a number of technique faults that you should look out for and correct in order to prevent injury and make your rowing more energy-efficient.

Common faults
• Leaning forward as you go into the coil position: keep the back straight and bend your legs more in the coil position so that you don't have to lean forward to get a long stroke.
• Bent arms in the pull phase: correct bent arms by using your legs more. Your legs are approximately five times stronger than your arms, so keep your arms straight until your legs are almost straight, and your legs will do most of the work.
• Leaning back too much at the end of the stroke: leaning back will give you a

longer pull but can cause lower back injuries. Try to keep your back as upright as possible until you have the core strength to allow you to lean back slightly.
• Grip too tight: a tight grip is fine for short, fast-interval sessions because you get a chance to put the handle down and relax between efforts. However, for longer distances, such as those over 1km/1,094yd, you need to keep your grip relaxed in order to prevent your forearms from getting too tight and cramping. If you are rowing long distances, try changing the position of your thumb. Instead of wrapping it under the handle, rest it on top to use different hand muscles.

Getting started
If you are using the rowing machine for the first time, start with the below-average fitness sessions (*see* Rowing exercises). After six weeks, move up to the average fitness sessions. Wait at least another six weeks before you attempt the above-average fitness stage. Before you do any of these sessions, start with a 500m/547yd warm-up at Level 1, followed by back, arm and leg stretches.

> ### Set your target
> Professional rowers are able to row 2km/1.2 miles in less than 6 minutes. If you are starting out, 8 minutes is a good target to try to achieve for this distance.

Below: Leaning too far forward means that you have to expend far more energy to drive back.

Below: Wait for the legs to be fully extended before pulling the arms in toward your chest.

Below: Leaning back too much at the end of the stroke can cause injury to your lower back.

Swimming

For many people, swimming is simply an enjoyable bit of splashing about at the pool or the seaside. Beyond that, though, it can improve your cardiovascular fitness as well as muscular strength without any impact, because it is non-weight bearing.

There are a number of different swimming strokes you can use, which use different muscles. Try to use a combination of strokes to ensure that all your muscles are worked.

Freestyle

Front crawl is usually now referred to as freestyle. The arms are mainly used to get the forward motion, with the legs producing only 10 per cent of the forward energy. However, your legs do play a vital role in keeping your body balanced and in preventing excess drag. Keep your hand slightly cupped as it enters the water and reaches forward

Muscles used in swimming

These are the main muscles used in swimming. Each stroke will place different demands and movement patterns on the muscles. Using these muscles in conjunction with correct technique will improve your swimming.

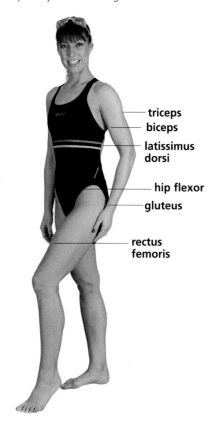

- triceps
- biceps
- latissimus dorsi
- hip flexor
- gluteus
- rectus femoris

Above: Take a breath as your arm and head come out of the water and before your hand re-enters the water.

and outward to catch the water. Sweep your hand outward and press the water laterally to your body, then sweep your hand in toward your hips. To finish the stroke, press the water down toward your hips, extending your arm as much as possible. On recovery to the next stroke, your elbow leaves the water first. You then reach forward, keeping your elbow high so that you don't slap the water as your hand re-enters it. Keep kicking with your legs at all times.

Tip At mid-stroke, slightly dropping the shoulder of your arm under the water will promote a better stroke and help the opposite arm to recover.

Butterfly

The butterfly is one of the hardest to perfect. The timing of the arm pull and leg kick is essential for a continuous efficient stroke. Your fingers should enter the water first, just as your legs finish their big kick. At this point, your arms should begin to bend as they press laterally, and the small leg kick begins. You then turn your hands and press them toward your body as the small leg kick finishes. You finish the stroke by pushing your hands toward your feet with straight arms, followed by the

Above: For the butterfly, as you reach forward for the next stroke, your upper body comes up out of the water.

quick exit of the hands from the water and the start of the big leg kick as your arms recover and reach forward to re-enter the water.

Tip Arch your lower back as you do the big kick so that you can help to get your upper body reaching forward for the next stroke.

Backstroke

Your legs are vital in the backstroke and should be kicking all the time below the surface of the water for maximum efficiency. Your little finger

Below: In the backstroke, the arms supply forward movement. One arm is in recovery while the other is in the water.

Swimming exercises

If you include the following three sessions as part of your main set of exercises, you will get fitter and faster in the water. Keep a diary of your times and comments to help monitor your improved performance. For the cool-down after you have done the main set of three sessions, choose any stroke you prefer and carry out at least 100m/109yd of easy swimming, focusing on breathing and trying to remain relaxed.

	Fitness level	Distance/time	Intensity
Session 1: time trials to help monitor your fitness	Below average:	10 minutes' continuous	go as far as you can L2–L3
	Average:	800m/875yd continuous	L2–L3 and note the time
	Above average:	1,500m/1,640yd continuous	L2–L3 and note the time
Session 2: improved fitness level and aerobic capacity	Below average:	8 x 25m/27yd intervals	with 60 seconds' rest between each one L3–L4
	Average:	10 x 50m/55yd intervals	with 30 seconds' recovery between each one L3–L4
	Above average:	10 x 100m/109yd intervals	with 30 seconds' recovery between each one L3–L4
Session 3: improved endurance	Below average:	20 minutes	L2
	Average:	40 minutes	L2
	Above average:	90 minutes	L2

should enter the water first, then your whole arm, with hand cupped to catch the water. Flex your elbow and press the water laterally, then downward, until your hand is just about level with your chest. To finish the stroke, press your hand down toward your feet, keeping it close to your body. When your arm is fully straightened, start the recovery by taking your thumb out of the water first and rotating your shoulder joint, allowing your little finger to enter the water first on re-entry.

Tip Keep your head as flat as possible, with eyes looking up to the ceiling, to minimize drag in the water.

Below: An efficient breathing technique is crucial for a good performance in strokes such as the butterfly.

Breaststroke

For an effective breaststroke, it is essential to get the timing of your legs and arms right in order to cover the maximum distance with the least amount of effort. Start by pushing your arms out in front of you to create a forward glide as your legs kick back. Cup the water and press your hands against the water laterally, arms slightly bent, then sweep your hands in toward your chest and start the upward leg movement in preparation for the kick. To complete the stroke, thrust your hands forward to the straight-arm position as the leg kick starts.

Breathing

When you are swimming, breathing correctly takes practice. You should decide which method of breathing works best for you: trickle breathing or explosive breathing. Trickle breathing involves slowly breathing out when your head is down in the water, and then taking a breath in on the recovery as your head comes out of the water. Explosive breathing requires you to hold your breath while your head is in the water, then quickly breathing out and back in as you lift your head out of the water in the recovery.

Warning

Breaststroke can be bad for you if you have a weak lower back, hips or knees, as it involves a strong kicking action in an awkward position.

Getting started

A good swim session should be structured as follows: a good warm-up, main set and cool-down. Doing the technique drills before the main set will remind you what the correct technique should feel like. Before you start, warm-up with 5 minutes of easy swimming.

Below: Good aerodynamic technique is essential to cut through the water in backstroke.

Boxercise

Tense, stressful day at the office? Boxercise is just what you need to work it out of your system. And you don't have to get into the ring to enjoy the benefits of this popular sport. Many sports centres now run boxing-based exercise classes.

Boxercise is a sport that will improve your endurance, speed, power and core stability. It will also strengthen and tone your arms, legs and abdominals. The satisfaction of landing a correct punch will help to alleviate the stress induced by a long day pounding a keyboard or sitting through yet another meeting. It is also a great way to burn up to 500 calories per hour, so it's time to get the gloves on.

Technique

To get the correct stance, stand with your feet just over shoulder-width apart, with one foot slightly in front of the

Muscles used in boxing

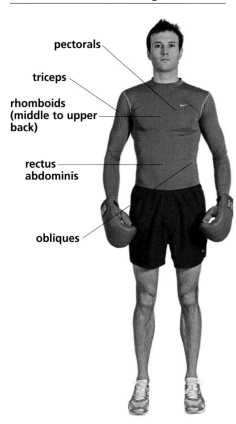

pectorals

triceps

rhomboids
(middle to upper
back)

rectus
abdominis

obliques

The muscles illustrated represent those that are mainly used in boxercise. Some muscles will be used to make the punch while other muscles stabilize the rest of the body making the punch even more powerful.

Above: The correct stance when you are ready to attack is feet balanced, with hands raised to protect the face.

other. If you are right-handed, place your right foot slightly behind the line of the left foot, and vice versa if you are left-handed. If you are right-handed, your left hand should be in front. If you are left-handed, your right hand should be in front.

Getting started

Warm up with 5 to 10 minutes of cardiovascular exercise, such as running or rowing, and some light stretches and core exercises to prepare your muscles. You will need a pair of boxing gloves for yourself and pads for your training partner. To avoid injuries, your partner should, ideally, be someone of a similar size to you.

Begin by learning the three different punches – jab, hook and uppercut. Once you have mastered these, slowly build

High intensity

The level of intensity for boxing is high. Expect to be in Level 3 and 4 for the actual movements of the workout. Between punching combinations, try to take some deep breaths and lower the intensity to Level 2 so that you can recover sufficiently to get enough oxygen to cope with the demands of the next set of combinations.

up combinations to try to make it an exciting workout. Next, you can add some leg exercises, such as squats, lunges and side lunges as you do the boxing combinations to raise the heart rate further and make your legs work harder.

It is important to remember that this is not a contest to see who can hit the hardest. It is, instead, a good way to increase your heart rate to improve your fitness levels and burn calories. To get the most from your muscles, focus on mastering the technique, then you can go on to add speed and power.

Below: When sparring, always hit across at your partner's opposite hand.

Jab

Though not a particularly hard punch, the jab can be made more powerful by stepping into the punch with a short forward step. To maintain a high heart rate, use the jab more frequently than any other punch.

Watchpoint It is important to control your breathing, especially with long combinations of punches. Experiment to find the best breathing method for you. Try breathing out as you land every third punch, and in before the fourth punch.

1 *Stand with your feet shoulder-width apart, holding both hands up in front of your face to act as a guard. Your training partner holds the pads out in front of him, at your eye height, his arms slightly bent to absorb the punch.*

2 *With your right arm almost fully extended, throw a quick punch, straight and forward, to make contact with your partner's right pad. Your hand should finish in a horizontal position, the back of your hand facing upward.*

Hook

Aim to get a good follow through with this punch. Use your abdominal muscles to produce a powerful rotation of the body to add extra weight to the punch, and keep them tight to control the follow-through. If your follow-through is too big, you will risk overstretching other muscles, which can cause lower-back problems.

Watchpoint To help prevent wrist injuries, keep your wrists, elbows and shoulders in line at the same height for the jab and the hook punches.

1 *Hold a hand up in front of your face to act as a guard. Your training partner holds the pads out to the side with his palms (face of the pad) facing in toward each other.*

2 *Take your right arm back round to the side of your body and then throw it back around in a semicircle to hit your partner's right pad, with your knuckles pointing forward.*

Uppercut

This is a powerful punch. Due to starting in a lower squatting position, you will use more muscle mass and momentum, so your partner should expect a big impact. Hit upward hard to raise your partner's hand.

1 *Hold a hand up in front of your face to act as a guard. Squat down slightly by bending both knees. Your training partner stands close to you with the face of the pads facing the floor. Keep your balance throughout the movement.*

2 *From a bent-arm position, straighten your arms as you straighten your legs, and throw the punch up toward your partner's right pad. Make contact with your knuckles facing away from you.*

Combination punches

Experiment with different combinations of punches. For example, try two jabs with the left hand and then a hook with the right. Having mastered that, try four jabs then a squat, four hooks, a lunge, four uppercuts and a side lunge.

RESISTANCE TRAINING

The benefits of resistance training include weight loss, a faster-acting metabolism and improved body shape. It is particularly good for people who struggle with sustained cardiovascular training. This chapter outlines the muscles involved, and the exercises and techniques that work them effectively and safely. Before you begin, familiarize yourself completely with the exercises and the equipment. To challenge your body and make training fun, make sure to include a variety of exercises in your resistance-training plan.

Above: Alternate your time in the gym with fun exercise in the open air.
Left: Correct resistance training will build your strength for different forms of exercise.

Benefits and Principles of Resistance Training

After the age of 30, your metabolic rate starts to decrease every year. Resistance training involves applying resistance to a movement that will not only increase your metabolic rate, but also give you greater strength and more energy.

Resistance training will build muscle and can even reverse the inevitable decline in your metabolic rate. The afterburn (calories expended after exercise) of resistance training will burn far more calories than the afterburn of a cardiovascular session. Knowing that you are still burning calories when you are sitting at your desk, several hours after your training session, is a real bonus.

Resistance training and health

You can build and tone over 600 of your muscles using resistance training; it will help reduce the risk of injury, especially lower back injury, by promoting good balance, co-ordination and posture.

Sports that involve contact, such as rugby or American football, will take their toll on your body. The correct resistance training, however, will give you the strength you need to withstand the impact of the tackle or of falling to the ground. Endurance sports such as running require your muscles to

Below: Press-ups are one of the oldest resistance exercises, but they are still just as effective as ever.

Above: For any sports involving impact, such as American football, resistance training is essential to build muscle.

contract over and over again for long periods of time; resistance training will help give your muscles the strength they need to prevent overuse injuries. Changing your body shape through resistance training will give you improved self-esteem and will motivate you to keep up your training. There are also medical benefits to resistance

training. It will strengthen your bones and reduce the risk of bone degenerating disease such as osteoporosis. Resistance training will also help to lower your blood pressure, lower your resting heart rate, decrease the risk of diabetes, decrease the chance of certain cancers and promote an increase in high-density lipid (HDL) cholesterol, or good cholesterol.

Technique

Start by only using weights that are up to 75 per cent of your One Repetition Maximum (ORM). Each set should consist of at least 12 repetitions and at the end of each set you should feel as if you could do two more repetitions. Do no more than three sets of each exercise to avoid overtraining a muscle

---

Increase metabolic rate

Having muscle means having more living tissue that is available to burn calories; just in the same way a car with a big engine will burn more fuel than a car with a small engine.

Above: Get your trainer or training partner to check your technique while you are exercising.

partner to help you force out another two to three repetitions by adding just enough force to help you lift the weight.

Descending sets Lift a weight to failure and then quickly lower the weight so that you can continue with the set. Using a training partner to do this type of training is best, as it will reduce the time taken to decrease the weight during sets.

Burns Lift a weight to failure using full range of movement and correct technique, then do two to three further repetitions using a shorter range of movement.

Negative repetitions Resist the weight in the negative phase of movement, for example, loading the bench press with 100kg/220lb when your ORM is only 80kg/176lb and then resisting the bar as it lowers down to your chest. You may require a training partner to do this, as you will be using a weight that is greater than your ORM. If you don't have a training partner use safety catches to prevent injury.

Below: Cable machines are a very versatile training aid.

group. To avoid muscle imbalances and promote good co-ordination, rotate your routine so that you use all your body parts in the week's training. Do not move on to other resistance training methods until you have completed six weeks of basic weight-training. Try to find a training plan that fits in with your goals.

Supersets These will help you to increase the intensity of your workout by decreasing the rest between exercises. This technique involves two exercises with just 5 seconds' rest between each exercise, followed by a 60–90 second rest at the end of a set before repeating.

Exercise opposing muscle groups, such as chest and back, hamstrings and quadriceps or triceps and biceps. This type of supersetting is great if you want to have an express workout or want to maintain a high heart rate to get cardiovascular benefits and to lose weight.

Pre-exhaustion supersets You may find that when you are working muscles in your upper body, your smaller muscles fatigue before you have worked the bigger muscles; for example, your triceps fatigue before you can work your pectorals hard enough. To combat this employ pre-exhaustion supersets using minimal rest. For example, to work the pectorals superset cable flies and bench presses. Only allow 5 seconds between each exercise so that the pectorals don't get a chance to recover.

Cheating repetitions Lift a weight to failure and then 'cheat' for a further two to three reps. For example, do a set of bicep curls to the point where you can't do another rep using the correct form and then try to do a further cheating rep swinging your upper body to help curl the weights up.

Forced repetitions Lift a weight to failure and then get your training

The Muscular System

Many people want to increase their muscle size. However, before you can even begin to think about effective training to achieve that goal, you need to understand how each of your muscles works to enable you to isolate the muscles you want to use.

Muscles are made up of bundles of fibres which are held in place by protective sheaths called fascia. The fibres are then subdivided into myofibrils. They contract when chemically stimulated by the nervous system and extend when the stimulation stops. Weight-training makes muscles grow by increasing the size of the myofibrils, which in turn increases the volume of blood flow to the muscle, the number of nerves that stimulate the muscle and the amount of connective tissue within the muscle cells. Myofibrils are divided again into bundles of myofilaments which are made up from chains of sarcomeres. As you reach the point of fatigue during resistance training, you will get small tears (microtears) in the myofilaments.

Below: The leaner you are, the easier it is to see the muscles you are working during resistance exercise.

During recovery after exercise your body will repair these small tears by giving the fibres nutrients which will also make these small fibres grow in size. The more exercise you do and the harder the intensity becomes, other

adaptations occur in the muscles. Muscles are able to store more glycogen which will enable the muscles to work even harder in the next workout. This also helps the muscles to slightly increase in size. As you lift a weight and

The muscles of the body

Pectorals these are used to push and pull the arms across the body.

Deltoids these are used to control the movement of the arms, taking them above the head, out to the side, in front and behind.

Biceps these are used to bend the arms at the elbow to bring the hands up toward you.

Obliques these are used to bend to the side and to control the twisting of the upper body.

Rectus abdominis these are used to bend the top half of the body forward.

Hip flexors these are used to lift the upper legs forward and upward.

Adductors these are used to pull the legs inward, toward the body.

Quadriceps these are used to extend and straighten the upper legs.

Tibialis anterior these are used to pull your feet upward, toward your shins.

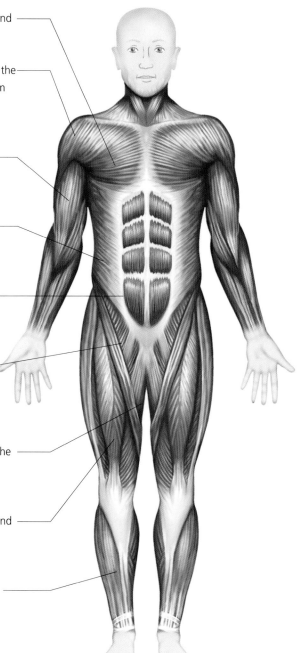

Visualization
Think about what is going on inside your muscles to help you focus on keeping perfect technique throughout your training session.

cause tension in a muscle, more blood is transferred to that muscle, giving the muscle more oxygen and nutrients to provide energy for hard work.

The muscular nervous system

As you lift a weight and put your muscles under tension your nervous system sends a signal to the sheaths protecting the muscle fibres. This results in the muscle fibres contracting and the weight being lifted. It is important to use good technique in all your resistance training from the start, otherwise your nervous system will adopt an incorrect sequence of movement, which long-term could lead to you sustaining an injury – and you won't get the desired results from your training. However, if your training is done correctly your nervous system will become even more efficient at telling your muscles when to work. Muscle recruitment is the key to getting stronger.

Right: The more toned you are, the more motivated you will feel about your workouts.

The muscles of the body

Neck muscles (semispinalis capitis muscle) these are used to move the head in a semi-circle from side to side, forward and backward.

Trapezius these are used to lift the shoulders upward and backward.

Rhomboids these are used for pulling movements; they help protect the spine.

Triceps these are used to push and to fully extend the arms.

Latissimus dorsi these are used to pull the arms into the body when there is resistance.

Abductors these are used to pull the legs outward, away from the body.

Gluteus maximus provide strength in powerful movements that involve most of the body. They maintain a connection between the legs and upper body.

Biceps femoris (hamstrings) these are used to bend the legs at the knees and lift them behind.

Gastrocnemius these are used to extend the feet when the legs are straight.

Soleus these are used to extend the feet when the legs are bent at the knee.

Muscular contractions

There are three types of muscular contractions:

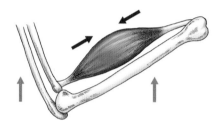

Concentric contraction
The arrows show a decrease in joint angle and muscle shortening. An example of this would be shortening your bicep muscle to bring your hand up toward you.

Eccentric contraction
The arrows show an increase in joint angle and muscle lengthening. An example of this would be lengthening of your bicep muscle as it lowers under resistance.

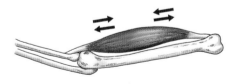

Isometric contraction
The arrows show no change in joint angle and muscle length under constant tension. An example of this would be tensing the abdominal muscles to stay in a fixed plank position.

Muscle Types

Now you know what the muscles of the body are called and where to find them. However, before you head straight to the gym, it is also important that you know what type of muscle you need to help you to achieve your goals.

Your body is made up of more than 250 million muscle fibres. Some muscle fibres consist of a high number of motor units per muscle fibre, such as muscles in the eye, which control small, precise movements. Other muscles, such as the quadriceps, need fewer motor units per muscle fibre, as they control bigger movements.

There are essentially two types of muscle fibre: Type I and Type II. Your genetic make-up does, to some extent, determine your muscle fibre type, but with the correct training and nutrition, you can change the percentage of each type. For endurance sports such as running and cycling, resistance training will give the muscles the strength they need.

Type I

These are also known as slow-twitch muscle fibres. They are red in colour as a result of their high myoglobin (a protein

Below: Long-distance marathon runners require Type I muscle fibres so they can sustain an effort for a long time.

Above: Cyclists who ride for long distances need Type I muscle fibres so they can keep going for long periods.

found in heart and skeletal muscles) content and have a high concentration of mitochondria (the 'power plant' of our cells, which use oxygen fat and sugar to release stored energy). A person with this type of muscle fibre is best at long-distance events such as Ironman triathlons or cross-country skiing. People with slow-twitch muscle fibre are likely to be smaller and have an ability to keep going for long periods of time. Type I muscle fibres contract more slowly than Type II muscle fibres, so people with this type of muscle are less good at movements such as throwing a ball fast or throwing a hard, fast punch.

Type II

These are also known as fast-twitch muscle fibres. They are white in colour due to a low myoglobin content and have a low concentration of mitochondria. People with this type

Which type of muscle fibre does your sport require?

This table shows the ratio of Type I muscle fibres to Type II muscle fibres that different athletes are likely to have, and also their VO2 max (ml/kg/min) as an indicator of the level of aerobic capacity they are likely to need for their sport.

Type of activity	Ratio of Type I to Type II	VO2 max ml/kg/min
Cyclist	60–40	60–75
Swimmer	55–45	55–65
Elite distance runner	80–20	70–80
American footballer	40–60	45–55
Ice hockey player	40–60	50–60
Cross-country skier	85–15	75–85
Rower	75–25	50–65
Sprinter	35–65	50–60

Above: Track cyclists need a higher percentage of Type II muscle fibres to pedal faster for short distances.

of muscle fibre are good at shorter athletic events because the muscle fibres contract faster. Power lifters and sprinters need a greater percentage of this type of muscle fibre. People with Type II muscle fibre appear bigger and have a larger amount of muscle mass. Type II muscle fibres can be split further into two subdivisions: IIa and IIb.

Type IIa is similar to a Type I muscle fibre in that it has adapted from being a Type II fibre to be able to assist in endurance events, such as cross-country skiing and marathon running. It is still able to contract fast but also has a well-developed capacity for both aerobic (the body's use of oxygen to generate energy) and anaerobic (without oxygen) energy transfer. This fibre type is more dependent than the others on a ready supply of oxygen.

Type IIb has the ability to work totally anaerobically, or without oxygen, and this athlete is capable of fast contractions using only anaerobic energy transfer.

Training the muscle types

It is possible to train muscle fibre to be of better use to you. For example, if you are a marathon runner, the more long-distance running you do, the better trained your Type I muscle fibre becomes. It is harder to train Type II muscle fibre.

Experiment with low-repetition weight-training on or close to your personal best, or sprint training with short recoveries.

One of the most effective ways of recruiting the fast-twitch muscle fibres is plyometrics training, because it activates the stretch-reflex mechanism of the muscle with an eccentric contraction. Plyometrics uses the acceleration and deceleration of body weight and includes exercises such as jumping and bouncing to enhance neuromuscular co-ordination of muscular movement.

In some sports it is hard to set training plans. For example, tennis requires lots of aerobic training to produce slow-twitch muscle fibres to give the player the endurance to last the entire match. However, this

steady cardiovascular training can interfere with the demand for high power output (fast-twitch muscle fibres) in the actual tennis strokes. Boxing is the same – being able to move around the ring constantly requires lots of endurance training and use of slow-twitch muscle fibres but the ability to give powerful punches means training your fast-twitch muscle fibres.

You should plan out your training sessions carefully, always being clear in your mind which type of muscle you want to train in each session.

Below: Sprinters require a higher percentage of Type II muscle fibres, which contract faster.

Resistance Training Safety

Every weight room in every gym should have on display a set of rules and regulations pertaining to safety. Make sure that you are fully aware of these rules and don't deviate from them. If you can't see one, ask a member of staff to point you in the right direction.

It is important that you always use the correct technique in all of your workout sessions. Do not copy the bad habits of other gym users who may be taking short cuts to make the training easier. Poor technique is a waste of time and effort because you will not be exercising the right muscles. Good technique, on the other hand, will help to prevent injuries, enabling you to train regularly and achieve your goals sooner. Use lighter weights than you think you might be capable of to start with in order to get your muscles used to the correct movements. Always make sure that you breathe in the correct way; holding your breath during a repetition will cause your blood pressure to rise and, in extreme cases, you could even pass out.

Training partner

If possible, train with another person. Your training partner can monitor and comment on your technique, and help you with heavier weights. If your partner is going to spot for you, make sure that you are both aware of what signal you will give when you are struggling. Your training partner will also need to know

Below: Your trainer or training partner can check your position to ensure that you are exercising safely.

where to stand if he is going to spot for you. For example, in a seated dumbbell shoulder press, he needs to stand behind you and give support to your elbows to help you press the dumbbells up when you are struggling. In an Olympic bar bench press, your partner should stand behind your head, with both hands moving up and down close to the bar, ready to take the bar at any moment; or to help with the press when you start to struggle on the last few repetitions.

Equipment

Wear the correct clothing so that your body temperature does not go down after the warm-up. Have all the equipment you will need for the next few sets ready so that you are not waiting to go from one piece of equipment to the other. This way, you will stay in the right training zone, physically and mentally. Be safe when you are using the equipment – always use collars on the end of barbells and make sure racks have safety catches if you are training on your own. Put the equipment away after you have used it to avoid people tripping up – dumbbells rolling around on the floor are a safety hazard, and safety catches not fully engaged may cause severe injury. Always look to see what condition the equipment is in. Common problems include: dumbbells not screwed together correctly; bench press safety stoppers missing or not aligned correctly; loose foot supports; fraying cables; broken or loose seat supports; loose cable attachments; and slippery floors.

Warm-up

During resistance training, most injuries are caused by an inadequate warm-up and by attempting to lift weights that are too heavy. Warming up lubricates the tissues between the joints and

Above: Using a rowing machine is a good way to prepare your body before doing resistance training.

increases the oxygenated blood supply to the muscles you want to work. It is essential to warm up correctly in order to prepare your muscles and joints for action in your exercise session. Wear a

Below: Shoulder press movements are a good way to warm up the upper body before training.

number of layers in the gym to help maintain your body's temperature after the warm-up. You may need three to four layers in cold gyms or winter months. A good warm-up is an indispensable part of your routine for safe training and should never be skipped – even if it means that you have to cut your weight-lifting exercises short.

Below: To prepare for a session in which you will use your legs, stretch the quadriceps beforehand.

Warm-up procedure

Start with a light aerobic exercise such as jogging, cycling or rowing, depending on the body parts that you intend to use in the session. For example, do rowing if you are going to do a heavy session on the back muscles, or cycling if you are going to do a leg weights session.

Exercise for 5 minutes, then build the intensity for a further 5 minutes until your heart rate is up and you start to sweat and you begin to feel slightly short of breath.

For the next stage of the warm-up, simulate the movements you are going to be doing in the workout. For example, do three sets of ten squats if you are planning a leg exercising session, or three sets of ten shoulder presses with no weights if you are planning a shoulder workout.

Follow these exercises with some light stretches on the muscles you want to use, for example a quadriceps stretch for a leg workout and a cross-body shoulder stretch for a shoulder session. Hold each for 30 seconds at a time.

To finish the warm-up, use light weights and high repetitions on the first exercise that you want to do. Do one set of at least 20 repetitions before you move on to heavy weights.

Below: Stretch the shoulders to warm up the upper body in preparation for resistance training.

Leg Exercises for Beginners

There are more than 200 muscles in the lower half of the body, so it is no surprise that there are a great number of different leg exercises. To build up your leg muscles safely and effectively, start with these beginners' exercises.

Your legs are five times stronger than your arms because they have to support the body. To get real results from training your legs, you must be prepared to work hard. Take 2 to 3 seconds for each movement. Breathe in at the start of the movement and out as you return to the start position.

Static squat

Muscles used Quadriceps – rectus femoris, vastus lateralis, vastus intermedius

Squat with your back flat against the wall, feet in front of you, knees directly above your ankles, and thighs parallel to the floor. Hold for 60 seconds. When 60 seconds gets easy, make it harder by holding dumbbells.

Beginners' leg exercises	
Exercise	**Sets and repetitions**
Leg press	5 x 8–12
Dumbbell squat	5 x 8–12
Static squat	5 x 20 second holds

Dumbbell squat

Muscles used Quadriceps – rectus femoris, vastus lateralis, vastus intermedius; gluteus medius and maximus

1 Stand with your feet shoulder-width apart. Hold a dumbbell in each hand, with your palms facing inward.

2 Bend your knees until your thighs are almost parallel to the floor. Pause for a second, then push back up.

Barbell front squat

Muscles used Quadriceps – rectus femoris, vastus lateralis, vastus intermedius; gluteus medius and maximus

1 With a barbell across your shoulders (front), squat as for a dumbbell squat.

Wide-leg power squat

Muscles used Quadriceps – vastus medialis, rectus femoris, vastus lateralis and intermedius; gluteus medius and maximus; abductor magnus

1 With a barbell across your shoulders (back), squat with your toes at 45 degrees.

Machine hack squats

Muscles used Quadriceps – vastus medialis, vastus lateralis, rectus femoris

1 *Make sure that your back, shoulders, neck and head are fully supported. Place your feet shoulder-width apart in front of you.*

2 *Release the weight with the handle and squat down, keeping your back flat. With your feet shoulder-width apart, your knees won't go forward of your feet.*

3 *Once your thighs are parallel with the floor, pause for one second, then push the weight back up by straightening your legs.*

Leg press

Muscles used Quadriceps – vastus medialis, rectus femoris, vastus lateralis, vastus intermedius; gluteus maximus; biceps femoris – short head, long head

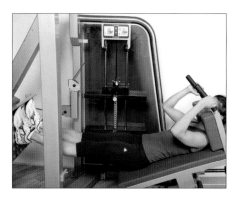

1 *Lie on the machine with your back resting against the back support. Place your feet hip-width apart against the foot support. Focus on tensing the abdominals so that you feel the burn more in that area. Push your weight through the heels to make the quadriceps work harder.*

2 *Carefully release the handle and slowly bend your legs, allowing the weight to come back toward you, until your legs are bent at 90 degrees at the knee. Push firmly down through the heels to get the quadricep muscles working really hard. Try to keep the head and neck relaxed, without any tension.*

3 *Pause for one second and then push the weight back away from you by extending your legs and pressing through your heels. To work your quadriceps, place your feet farther back on the foot plate. To work the hamstrings and gluteus maximus, place your feet farther up the plate.*

Leg Exercises: Quadriceps

The quadriceps are the large group of muscles at the front of your thighs. Leg extensions are the best way of isolating the quadriceps – and you can fully expect to feel as if your legs are on fire with the following leg extension exercises.

For each exercise, take 2 to 3 seconds for each movement. Breathe in at the start of the movement, and out as you return to the start position.

Basic leg extension

Muscles used Quadriceps – rectus femoris, vastus lateralis, vastus intermedius, vastus medialis

1 *Sit on the machine and tuck your legs behind the pad, which should rest just on the bottom of your shins. Sit upright, arms at the sides, and hold the handles to help keep your hips still.*

Machine single-leg extension

Muscles used Quadriceps – rectus femoris, vastus lateralis, vastus intermedius, vastus medialis

Exercises to build strong quadriceps

Carry out these exercises in pairs and superset them so that you have just 5 to 10 seconds' rest between each set.

Exercise	Sets and repetitions
Machine hack squat	5 x 8–12
Wide-leg power squat	5 x 8–12
Machine leg extension	5 x 8–12
Medialis leg extension	5 x 8–12

Sit comfortably, positioning yourself as you would for a basic leg extension. Lift the weight up by fully extending just one leg. Leave the other leg in the start position. Once the leg is horizontal, pause for 1 second and then slowly lower the weight back down. Keep the core tensed to prevent the body from twisting. This is an efficient way to make sure you get equal strength in both legs; it is also useful for rehabilitation purposes after an injury or an accident.

Medialis leg extension

Muscles used Quadriceps – vastus medialis, rectus femoris, vastus lateralis, vastus intermedius

2 *To lift the weight up tense your quadricep muscles and fully extend the legs. Pause for 2 seconds, then slowly lower the weight back down. Get your legs back under you as far as possible.*

1 *Position yourself as you would for a basic leg extension, hips still and legs tucked behind the pad, which should rest on the bottom of your shins. This extension aids knee injuries.*

2 *With your feet outward at 45 degrees, extend your legs to lift the weight. When your legs are straight, pause for 2 seconds, then slowly lower the weight. Emphasis is on the vastus medialis.*

Cable single-leg extension

Muscles used Quadriceps – rectus femoris, vastus lateralis, vastus intermedius, vastus medialis

1 *Attach the cable to the back of your lower leg. Stand facing away from the cable machine. Bring your knee up in front of you so that your leg is bent at 90 degrees. Keep your body still to keep the workload isolated on the quadriceps.*

2 *Tense your quadriceps and extend your leg until it is straight. Pause for 1 second and then slowly bend your knee back to the start position. Use a light weight to isolate your quadriceps or else the momentum will help to lift the weight.*

Cable hip flexor

Muscles used Tensor fascia lata; pectineus

1 *Attach the cable to the back of your lower leg, just above the ankle. Stand with your feet hip-width apart and your back to the cable machine. Tense your core muscles to keep your spine in neutral. Lift the leg that has the cable attached off the ground.*

2 *Bring your leg up in front of you, stretching it as far as it can go. Pause for 1 second then slowly lower the leg back down to the start position. Give the abdominals a good workout at the same time by tensing your abdominals to prevent your body from moving.*

Leg Exercises: General

The following exercises use the majority of the leg muscles; they simulate the same muscular movements that you make when you are running, walking or cycling. For athletes wishing to excel, these exercises should play a significant part in your training routine.

You don't have to be a highly competitive athlete to benefit from these exercises. These are also the exercises to do if you simply want to have firm buttocks. The human body – like many large, powerful animals – needs large gluteus muscles (buttocks) to provide power and speed. You don't actually need your gluteus muscles when you are just walking, but as soon as the intensity of the exercise increases, for example when you walk uphill or run, you need them to help extend your hip and keep an upright torso.

The exercises described here will help to train your gluteus muscles and work them in conjunction with your trunk and other lower-body muscles, which will improve your physical performance in your chosen sport.

Many people have weak gluteus muscles because of their sedentary lifestyle. They sit on these muscles but never use them. By putting one foot in front of the other, these exercises simulate everyday sporting movements, especially as they require balance that forces your smaller muscles to act as stabilizers and work in tandem with your core muscles. If the stabilizers around your trunk and lower-body muscles are inactive, you will be prone to injury as the intensity of your exercise increases.

For each exercise, take 2 to 3 seconds for each direction of the movement. Breathe in at the start of the movement, then breathe out as you return to the start position.

Exercises to build powerful buttocks	
Exercise	Sets and repetitions
Step-up	5 x 8–10
Bench drop lunge	5 x 8–10
Side lunge	5 x 8–10
Side step-up	5 x 8–10

Step-up

Muscles used Quadriceps – vastus medialis, rectus femoris, vastus lateralis, vastus intermedius; gluteus medius and maximus

1 *With a dumbbell in each hand, place one foot on the aerobics step (or bench). The slower you carry this out, the harder you work the quadriceps.*

2 *Step up to your full height. Hold the opposite foot in the air to work your leg harder. Pause for 1 second then slowly step back down.*

Side step-up

Muscles used Quadriceps – rectus femoris, vastus lateralis, vastus intermedius, vastus medialis; adductor – longus, magnus; gluteus medius and maximus

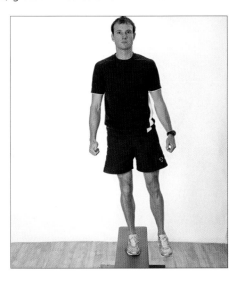

1 *Stand side-on to a bench (or aerobics step), with your arms by your side. Place the near foot on the bench.*

2 *Step up to your full height, pause, then slowly lower yourself back down, using your quadriceps to control the fall.*

Static lunge

Muscles used Quadriceps – rectus femoris, vastus lateralis, vastus intermedius, vastus medialis; gluteus maximus

1 *Stand with one foot in front of the other, roughly 60cm/2ft apart, with both feet facing forward, and your body weight suported evenly between your feet. Your back heel will be raised off the floor. Hold a dumbbell in each hand. Keep your hips level, your back straight and your shoulders back.*

2 *Slowly lower yourself by bending both legs until the thigh of your front leg is parallel with the floor. Pause for 1 second, then slowly push back up to the start position. Keep your chest out to help isolate the legs during the lunge.*

Bench drop lunge

Muscles used Quadriceps – rectus femoris, vastus lateralis, vastus intermedius, vastus medialis; gluteus maximus

1 *Standing with your back to a bench, with a dumbbell in each hand and your feet roughly 60cm/2ft apart, place one foot up on the bench behind you, with the top of the foot downward.*

2 *Slowly lower yourself by bending both legs until your front leg thigh is parallel with the floor. Try to get your back knee as low as possible for the best stretch. Pause for 1 second, then push back up.*

Side lunge

Muscles used Quadriceps – rectus femoris, vastus lateralis, vastus intermedius, vastus medialis; gluteus maximus and medius; adductor – longus, magnus; gracilis; pectineus

1 *Stand with your feet wide apart and your back straight. Keep your arms straight, your hands just touching the tops of your thighs. Hold a dumbbell in each hand. Keep your abdominals tensed all the time.*

2 *Lunge sideways, shifting your weight behind the bent leg, tensing the abdominals to support the lower back. With the thigh of the lunging leg parallel to the floor, pause for 1 second, extend the leg, then push yourself back to the start position.*

Leg Exercises: Hamstrings

The hamstrings are the group of muscles at the back of the thigh. Their function is to tip the pelvis back (posterior rotation) and straighten the pelvis when the pelvis is locked by isometric contraction – when the muscle exerts force but does not change in length.

Hamstrings are shortened by some exercises, such as cycling, and can often cause other muscles, such as those in the back and gluteus, to tighten. Hamstring injuries are also common. In runners, the hamstrings need to be long and stringy to allow a full range of movement. To achieve this, regular stretching when training hamstrings is essential. Take time to stretch after every set of hamstrings exercises to keep the muscles as long as possible.

If you get hamstring tears, stretch the muscle as soon as the pain has subsided to reduce the effect of the scar tissue, and re-educate the muscle to work with light hamstring exercises.

Sedentary lifestyles – which so many people lead today – make the hamstring muscles shorten, which leads to a curve in the lumbar region of the spine, making you prone to injury. If you have been sitting all day, make sure that you have at least 10 minutes of cardiovascular exercise and spend some time stretching to prepare your hamstrings for resistance training. Sportsmen and women often neglect their hamstrings, and the demands placed on them lead to muscle imbalances between the quadriceps and the hamstrings. The following exercises mainly work the hamstrings. Whatever your goal, you should try to train your hamstrings at least once a week.

For each exercise, take 2 to 3 seconds for each direction of the movement. Breathe in at the start of the movement, and breathe out as you return to the start position.

Exercises to build indestructible hamstrings	
Exercise	**Sets and repetitions**
Machine leg curl	5 x 15–20
Seated leg curl	5 x 15–20
Lunge	5 x 15–20
Cable leg kickback	5 x 15–20

It can be difficult to recruit the hamstrings without using other muscles in the lower back. To prevent the lower back from working, tense your buttocks and pull in the abdominal muscles. If you suffer from lower back pain, your hamstrings may be too tight and the abdominals cannot support your back. Try using lighter weights to prevent the muscles in your lower back recruiting.

Machine leg curl

Muscles used Biceps femoris – short head and long head; semimembranosus; semitendinosus

1 *Lie face down on the leg-curl machine with your legs tucked under the leg pad. Grip the handles and tense the core muscles to help maintain a still body and a neutral spine. Relax your head over the end of the bench or rest it to one side. The slower you do this exercise, the harder your hamstrings will have to work.*

2 *Gripping the handles firmly, curl the weight up until your legs are bent at 90 degrees. Tense your buttocks throughout the movement to help isolate your hamstrings and buttocks. Pause for 1 second in this position, then slowly lower the weight back down to the starting position.*

Seated leg curl

Muscles used Biceps femoris – short head, long head; semimembranosus; semitendinosus

1 *Sit on the leg-curl machine with your back pressed firmly against the back pad for support. Tuck your legs under the top pad and rest them on the lower pad. Tense your core muscles to help maintain a still upper body, keeping your spine in neutral and your head facing forward, in line with your spine. Slightly point your toes to make the hamstrings work harder.*

2 *Pull up on the handles to keep the hips down in the seat. Curl the weight under you until your knees are bent at 90 degrees. Pause for a second, then return to the start position. Return to the start slowly so that your knees do not take all the weight, causing them to hyper-extend at the end of the movement.*

Cable single-leg curl

Muscles used Biceps femoris – short head, long head; semimembranosus; semitendinosus gastrocnemius – lateral head, medial head

1 *Face the cable machine with a strap around one ankle. Tense your core muscles to keep your spine in neutral, and keep your head facing forward in line with your spine. Hold the machine handles to help keep your torso still.*

2 *Curl the weight back behind you by bending at the knee until your leg is bent at 90 degrees. Pause for 1 second, then slowly straighten your leg to lower the weight back down to the start position.*

Cable leg kickback

Muscles used Gluteus maximus; gluteus medius; tensor fascia lata; biceps femoris – short head, long head.

1 *Take up the same start position as for the cable single-leg curl (above) and tense your core abdominal muscles as much as possible to prevent your lower back from doing any of the work. Hold the machine handles for balance and to keep the torso still. The difference with this exercise is that it places more emphasis on your buttock muscles.*

2 *Tense your buttocks and kick the leg attached to the pulley back out behind you to 45 degrees. Pause for 1 second, then slowly return the leg to the start position. This is a great exercise for people who have weak buttocks, especially for runners or athletes who do not recruit their buttock muscles properly.*

Leg Exercises: Thigh Muscles

Whenever you start to accelerate with a longer stride or to lunge to one side, you are using your inner and outer thigh muscles. These muscles, which are known as the adductors and abductors, help to stabilize your body. For example, if you run and you have lots of lateral movement in the hips, it may cause a snaking effect in your spine, which can lead to back pain. In any case, you want to transfer all your power into going forward, not sideways. When riding a bike, you want all your leg power to go down through the chain to give you more forward speed. When hitting a golf ball, you want good hip stability to allow you to rotate and strike it with as much power and speed as possible.

The following exercises work a number of inner and outer thigh muscles together. There is no time for them to relax – when one is working, the other is acting as a stabilizer. While training these muscles, always contract your core muscles to help isolate the inner and outer thigh muscles you want to work. Be careful when starting your adductor and abductor routine. Begin with a light weight and work up. Don't ignore pain when training these muscles, as you could injure yourself.

For each exercise, take 2 to 3 seconds for each direction of the movement. Breathe in at the beginning of the movement, and breathe out as you return to the start position.

Exercise plan for abductor/ adductor strength and toning	
Exercise	**Sets and repetitions**
Lunge	3 x 20
Side lunge	3 x 20
Cable abduction	3 x 20
Cable adduction	3 x 20
Machine abduction	3 x 20
Machine adduction	3 x 20

Cable hip abduction

Muscle used Gluteus medius

1 *Stand side-on to the cable machine with feet hip-width apart. Attach an ankle strap to the outside leg. Keep the emphasis on the sides of the buttocks throughout the movement.*

2 *Slowly raise the outside leg as far out to the side as possible. Pause for a second, then slowly lower it back down. Doing the exercise slowly ensures that the gluteus is working hard.*

Cable adduction

Muscles used Adductor – longus, magnus; pectineus; gracilis

1 *Stand on one leg side-on to the cable machine. The other leg is raised in the air, attached to the cable by an ankle strap. Keep your upper body as still and upright as possible by tensing the abdominals.*

2 *Adduct the attached leg until the legs are together. Pause then lower the weight by taking your leg back out to the start. Start with a weight that is lighter than you think you can manage and then work your way upward.*

Machine abduction

Muscles used Gluteus – medius and maximus

1 Place your legs against the leg pads. Hold on to the handles to keep yourself firmly positioned in the seat. If you change the angle of your upper torso by adjusting the back pad angle you can focus the exercise on different muscles.

2 The more vertical the back pad, the more your gluteus maximus will work, and the more angled the back pad, the greater the emphasis on the gluteus medius. Tense your gluteus and spread the legs as far apart as comfortable. Pause for 2 seconds, then slowly bring your legs back together, while resisting the weight.

Machine adduction

Muscles used Adductor muscles – brevis, longus, magnus; pectineus

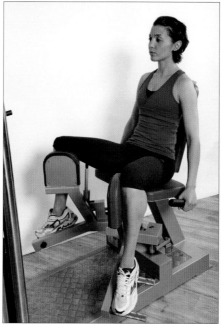

1 Place your legs into the leg pads and tense your core muscles to keep your torso motionless. Hold the handles to keep yourself in the seat while you do the exercise. Take this exercise slowly to begin with.

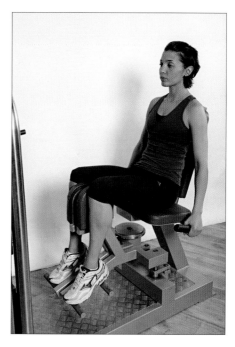

2 Push in your legs until they meet. Pause for 2 seconds, then slowly allow them to be pulled back out, still tensing your muscles to create resistance. If you have never worked these muscles before, it will take some time to build them up.

Elastic abduction

Muscles used Gluteus – medius, maximus

1 Lie on your back with the legs bent up at 90 degrees and your feet flat on the floor in front of you. Place an elastic strip around your knees and tie it in a secure knot. Tense your abdominals so that you can keep your back flat on the floor.

2 In this exercise, to make your buttocks work even harder, do a hip raise before you move your legs apart. Tense the gluteus muscles and spread the knees as far apart as possible. Pause for 2 seconds, then slowly return to the start position, keeping the abdominals tense.

Leg Exercises: Calf Muscles

Every time you step forward, you use your calf muscles. For faster activities, such as running and sprinting, strong calf muscles are essential. They maintain your forward motion and provide good strength and stability for the other muscles in your legs.

People often skip calf-strengthening exercises because they think they are dull. This is a mistake – you will not perform at your best with weak calves. Also, you will be prone to injury, particularly Achilles' injuries. Bodybuilders often say they can't be bothered with training their calves because they believe they can't build them up. The main reason for this is that calf muscles are small and it takes a lot of patience to see the gradual improvements in size and definition through the appropriate training. If this is the case for you, take time in your workout and make your calves a priority – even try putting calf exercises at the start of your workout for a few weeks.

Training the calf muscles

There are three muscles that flex and extend the foot to make up the calves. These are: the tibialis anticus, which runs down the front of the shin and contracts to flex the toes toward the knee; the gastrocnemius, a long, wide muscle that connects the bottom part of your upper leg to your heel (it flexes to extend your toes when your leg is straight and contracts to flex all of the muscles in the back of the leg); and the soleus, a shorter muscle that connects to the upper part of the shin and the heel, and works mainly when the leg is already bent at 90 degrees.

If you have been training your calves and seeing no improvement, try changing your routine. To get a better training effect, change the repetition range each time you train them. One day, do 6–10 reps with a heavier weight and, on another day, do 20–30 reps on a lighter weight. Try holding the weight for 3 seconds at the top of each peak contraction to make the calf muscles work even harder. But don't overtrain them and leave at least a day's rest between calf

sessions – otherwise your progress will come to a halt. Also, be careful not to train the calf muscles first if you also want to include bigger leg-muscle exercises in your routine. You need your calf muscles to be fresh if they are to provide enough support and stability when your bigger muscles are working.

Always stretch your calves to prevent them becoming tight and affecting the Achilles' tendon. If you do suffer from tight calves, do some regular stretching and have them massaged before this leads to injury. Stretching the calves can actually make them

Exercise plan for stronger calf muscles	
Exercise	**Sets and repetitions**
Double-leg calf raise	3 x 20
Calf press	3 x 20
Seated single-leg calf raise	3 x 20

bigger and give them a more ripped look. For each of these exercises, take 2 to 3 seconds to carry out each direction of the movement. Breathe in at the start of the movement, then breathe out as you slowly return to the start position.

Double-leg calf raise

Muscles used Triceps surae – gastrocnemius medial head, gastrocnemius lateral head, soleus

 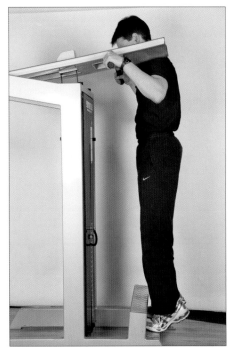

1 *Stand on the edge of a step on the balls of your feet. Hold on to the handles for balance. Tense your core muscles and the tops of your legs to keep your body in a straight line. Lower your heels below the line of the step.*

2 *Pause for a second, tense your calf muscles as much as possible and raise your heels as high as you can above the step. Pause for 2 seconds in this position, then lower yourself back down to the start position.*

Calf press

Muscles used Triceps surae – gastrocnemius medial head, gastrocnemius lateral head, soleus

1 *Sit in the calf-press machine, with the back straight and head in line. Hold the handles and place the balls of your feet up against the edge of the leg press plate. To put emphasis on the calf muscles, keep the whole leg as straight as possible and tense your core muscles to keep your back flat.*

2 *Keeping your calf muscles tense, press the plate away from you. Pause for 2 seconds, then slowly relax your calves. Repeat the exercise six to ten times. To make this exercise more demanding and to make sure you have equal strength in both legs, try using one leg only.*

Seated single-leg calf press

Muscles used Triceps surae – gastrocnemius medial head, gastrocnemius lateral head, soleus

1 *Sit in the calf-press machine, with the back straight. Hold the handles and place the balls of your feet up against the edge of the leg press plate. Straighten your legs and tense your core muscles to keep your back flat.*

2 *Take one leg off the plate, straighten the other, tense your core muscles and your calf muscle, and press the plate away from you. Pause for 2 seconds and slowly relax your calf. If you can do 50 repetitions, you have good calf strength.*

Chest Exercises: Bench Press

The chest muscles are large muscles that cover the upper section of your ribs called the pectorals. They help to drag the upper arm forward via a tendon extending from the side of the upper arm bone to the pectoral muscle.

Bench pressing is the most common chest exercise and is a good exercise for building a bigger chest. There are several variations of the bench press that will help to tone and shape your pectorals. Bench press exercises, however, will only help build the lower and outer edges of the pectoral muscles.

To get the inner and upper parts of your chest working well, and give you good symmetry, you will need to do other exercises.

Top bodybuilders believe bench presses are the key to developing a strong, well-developed chest. There is no doubt that they do bring out the size in the chest and so it is no surprise that they are often referred to as the 'meat and drink' of all upper-body exercises.

Don't try to take the bar too low when doing the bench press or else other muscles will have to work, not just your chest muscles in isolation. Taking your elbows just past the line of your body is enough. As you press the weight back to the top, try to keep your chest as big as possible and force your pectorals to contract as much as possible.

Changing the angle of the position you are pressing from will help to work different parts of the chest. Putting the bench into an incline position will isolate the top part of the chest. It will also make the front of your shoulders work hard to create a strong connection between your chest and shoulders. Putting the bench into a decline bench position will work the lower part of your chest and your upper-back muscles, forcing a good connection between the chest and back muscles. If the bench press is going to be the biggest upper-body exercise in your routine, do it first, so that all your stabilizing muscles are fresh and can help support your chest muscles. Make sure it has been at least 48 hours since you last trained your triceps, because they can tire fast when you are doing bench presses.

For each exercise take 2 to 3 seconds for each direction of the movement. Breathe in at the beginning of the movement, and breathe out as you return to the start position.

Bench press exercises for bigger chest muscles	
Exercise	**Sets and repetitions**
Incline press	5 x 6–8
Decline press	5 x 6–8
Bench press	5 x 6–8
Incline press	3 x 20+ less than 60 seconds' rest between sets
Decline press	3 x 20+ less than 60 seconds' rest between sets
Bench press	3 x 20+ less than 60 seconds' rest between sets

Bench press

Muscles used Pectorals major; anterior deltoid; triceps brachii – medial head and long head

1 Lie on a bench with the head back and the feet on the floor. Grip the bar in both hands and hold it above you, in line with the middle of the chest. Grip it with your hands slightly wider than shoulder-width apart, palms facing outward. Keep the bar in line with your chest and not your shoulders or you might cause yourself an injury.

2 With straight arms, lower the bar down to your chest, bending your elbows to the side. Keep lowering until your elbows are at 90 degrees. Pause for 1 second, then raise the bar to the start position, keeping your abdominals tense. The bar should come down low enough to work your chest, and as you press it back up, push your chest out to make it work harder.

Narrow grip bench press

Narrow grip bench press is a variation of the bench press. This involves holding the bar with your hands no more than 15cm/6in apart; this will work the inner pectorals and triceps.

Incline press

Muscles used Pectorals major; anterior deltoid; triceps brachii – medial head and long head

1 *Adjust the bench to a 45-degree incline. Lie on it and grip the bar, your palms facing your feet. Keep your feet flat on the floor. Hold the bar vertically above the top half of your chest. Rest your head on the bench and keep your back flat.*

2 *Lower the bar, taking your elbows out to the side until they are at 90 degrees. Pause for a second, then raise the bar to the start position. Tense your abdominals throughout the movement to help maintain a flat back.*

Decline press

Muscles used Pectorals major; triceps brachii – medial head, long head

1 *Adjust the bench to a 30-degree maximum decline. Lie on it with your legs hooked over the end to prevent sliding. Grip the bar with your palms facing toward your feet, your hands slightly wider apart than shoulder width. Hold the bar vertically above the lower half of your chest. Rest your head on the bench. This exercise is good for outlining the bottom of the chest. Keep the bar in line with the bottom of the chest and don't allow the shoulders to take over.*

2 *Gripping the bar firmly, lower it toward your chest, taking your elbows out to the side until they are at 90 degrees. Pause for 1 second, then raise the bar to the start position. Tense your abdominals throughout the movement to help maintain a flat back. Try to prevent your shoulders from rising up, which has the effect of tensing your neck muscles. In this way you will be able to place greater emphasis on your chest muscles.*

Chest Exercises: Dumbbell Presses

Dumbbell chest press exercises are similar to bench presses using the same muscles. However, you can go lower with dumbbells because there is no bar directly in front of the chest, thus providing a longer range of movement and a more intense workout for your chest.

The movement involved in dumbbell presses also enables the weight to progress from straight above the chest and out to the sides, making it a more effective exercise to develop the entire set of pectoral muscles.

Many bodybuilders believe they get faster results when they use dumbbells. Because dumbbells have to be balanced to carry out chest press exercises, this involves having to recruit all your stabilizing muscles so that you can control the movement of the dumbbells. As a result, your stabilizing muscles will develop better.

Always have a training partner with you when you are doing heavy dumbbell presses, as you can never tell when you may suddenly weaken, especially as one

arm might prove to be stronger than the other. (The dumbbells will reveal if one side of your body is weaker than the other.) Avoid big increases in weights to prevent injury and always be in control of the movement.

For each chest exercise, take 2 to 3 seconds for each direction of the movement. Don't forget your breathing: breathe in at the beginning of the movement and breathe out as you return to the start position.

Chest building session for beginners

Try doing supersets: pair up two exercises and switch from one exercise to the other with only 5–10 seconds' rest between sets. To get a really good workout, try doing the sets and repetitions twice weekly.

Exercise	Sets and repetitions
Bench press	3 x 8–12
Dumbbell chest press	3 x 8–12
Incline bench press	3 x 8–12
Decline dumbbell press	3 x 8–12

Dumbbell chest press

Muscles used Pectoralis major; triceps brachii; anterior deltoid

1 *Sit on the end of the bench with your feet firmly on the floor in front of you. Hold a dumbbell in each hand, resting on top of your thighs, palms facing toward each other. Keep the dumbbells in line with the middle of the chest. Slowly lie back, taking the dumbbells with you. Tense your abdominals to maintain a flat back.*

2 *Hold the dumbbells with straight arms above your chest, your palms facing your feet. Keep your feet on the floor, on the bench or in the air, with your legs at 90 degrees. Relax your head and rest it on the bench. Work the chest harder by pushing it out on the return phase. If you need to, rest in between chest presses.*

3 *Lower the weights, taking your elbows out to the side until they are at 90 degrees. To prevent injury, and isolate the chest and triceps, don't let your elbows go lower than 90 degrees. Raise the dumbbells to the position in step 2. The forearms should always be perpendicular to the ground. Continue with your planned repetitions.*

Incline dumbbell chest press

Muscles used Pectoralis major; triceps brachii – long head, medial head; anterior deltoid

1 *Adjust the bench to a 20- to 60-degree incline. Sit on the end of the bench with your feet on the floor. Hold a dumbbell in each hand, resting on your thighs, your palms facing toward each other. Tense your abdominals throughout the movement to help keep your back flat.*

2 *Lie back, placing your head on the bench, and hold the dumbbells with straight arms above the top half of your chest, with your palms facing your feet. The raising movement here should be slightly rounded as if you are hugging a tree. Your back should be flat against the bench.*

3 *Lower the dumbbells, taking your elbows out to the side, keeping your forearms perpendicular to the ground, until your elbows are at 90 degrees. Pause for 1 second, then raise the dumbbells to the position in step 2. Keep them in line with the upper half of the chest for emphasis on the pectorals.*

Decline dumbbell chest press

Muscles used Pectoralis major; triceps brachii – long head, medial head

1 *Adjust the bench until it is at a 20- to 60-degree decline. Sit on the end of the bench with your feet placed firmly on the floor. Hold a dumbbell in each hand, resting on the top of your thighs, your palms facing toward each other. Lower yourself down slowly into the decline to give you an opportunity to work your abdominals.*

2 *Hold the dumbbells with straight arms above the lower half of your chest, with your palms facing your feet. Place the head against the bench and hook your legs over the end of the bench, or keep your legs straddling the bench, so that the feet are on the floor. Slowly raise the dumbbells upward above the upper chest so that the arms are straight.*

3 *Lower the dumbbells, taking the elbows out to the sides. Keep your forearms perpendicular to the ground, until your elbows are bent at 90 degrees. Pause for 1 second, then raise the dumbbells to the position in step 2. At the end of the movement, for more emphasis, squeeze the bottom of your pectorals up and together.*

Chest Exercises: Strength and Power

The following exercises will give you a strong powerful chest. They will also work the muscles that surround the chest and work alongside the pectorals. However, to get the results you want, you will need to do a range of chest exercises, not just one or two.

These exercises will work your chest muscles in conjunction with other surrounding muscles to make you more powerful for your chosen sport. Pullovers will make your abdominals and latissimus dorsi work hard to assist the chest muscles. It is also important to train your core muscles to recruit at the same time as your pectorals. If you are lifting heavy weights and your core strength is not working for you, you will be more prone to injuries and your chest will be useless in sporting movements.

Correct technique

Most of the following exercises force your arms to work independently and also engage your core so that you can actually do the exercise. The muscles surrounding your chest will work during these movements, give them the strength and tone to work in unison with your chest, and also improve your posture. It is easy to do other chest exercises with poor technique and get away with it. However, poor technique will quickly become apparent in these chest exercises because, quite simply, you won't be able to do them.

When you do your chest workout, concentrate and ensure you apply the correct muscles. Use a suitable weight when you do chest exercises. For each exercise, take 2 to 3 seconds for each direction of the movement. Breathe out at the start of the movement, and in as you return to the start position.

Chest stabilizing exercises	
Exercise	**Sets and repetitions**
Dumbbell chest press	3 x 12
Dip	3 x max
Dumbbell pullover	3 x 12
Machine pullover	3 x 12
Single-arm cable chest press	3 x 12
Medicine ball throw-down	3 x 12

Machine pullovers

Muscles used Pectoralis major; latissimus dorsi; teres major; serratus anterior; triceps brachii – long head

1 *Sit in the pullover machine with your back against the back pad. Put your head flat against the back pad and tense your abdominals to keep your back flat.*

2 *Pull the handles over your head and out in front of you, bringing your hands level with your abdomen. Pause for 1 second, then return to the start position.*

Dumbbell pullovers

Muscles used Pectoralis major; latissimus dorsi; teres major; serratus anterior; triceps brachii – long head

1 *Lie with your shoulders resting on a bench, your feet on the floor, just over hip-width apart, and knees, hips and chest level with the bench. Hold a dumbbell above your chest with straight arms. Tense your core muscles throughout.*

2 *Lower the weight with straight arms until you feel the stretch in your chest. Don't make your back work, focus on the chest. Pause for 1 second, then return to the start. Keep your abdominals tight to maintain a straight body.*

Dips

Muscles used Pectoralis major; anterior deltoid; triceps brachii – long head, lateral head and medial head

1 *Grip the handles and hold yourself up, with arms straight. Tense your core muscles to maintain a good position. Angle your head forward and down. To prevent the shoulders from rising upward, put greater emphasis on your chest.*

2 *Slowly lower your weight by bending your elbows out to the sides at 45 degrees, keeping them in line with your chest until your shoulders are level with your elbows. Lean slightly forward as you lower yourself. Once at 90 degrees pause for 1 second, then slowly return to the start position.*

Single-arm cable chest press

Muscles used Pectoralis major; latissimus dorsi; teres major; serratus anterior; triceps brachii – long head

1 *Face forward, core muscles tense, feet just wider than hip-width apart. Pull the handle forward until your elbow is at 90 degrees and in line with your body.*

2 *Pull the handle forward until your arm is straight and your hand is in front of your chest. Pause for 1 second, then return to the start position.*

Medicine ball throw-down

Muscles used Pectoralis major; latissimus dorsi; teres major; serratus anterior; triceps brachii – long head, medial head

1 *Stand with feet shoulder-width apart. Hold the medicine ball vertically above your head with straight arms.*

2 *Bring the medicine ball down in front of you to hit the floor fast enough to bounce back up above knee height.*

Chest Exercises: Pectorals

The inner and outer pectorals are possibly the hardest areas of the chest to work, and this usually involves pressing a weight above the chest at different angles. Some of the exercises described here use cables for a more effective workout.

Well developed pectoral muscles result from good upper and lower pectoral development.

More effective training

By using cables and changing the pressing action into a pulling action, you can make the training more effective for the inner and outer regions of the pectoral muscles. The cables provide a consistent tension through the entire range of the exercise, unlike a machine or free weights, which cannot work the chest in the same way. Instead of the weight attacking the chest muscle with gravity as, for example, in a chest press, with the cables the resistance is coming from the side of the chest.

People often find it difficult to get their chest to work to its full potential because they have weak triceps, which have to work with the chest in the pressing movement. But with these exercises, you hardly use your triceps. You can use these exercises at the start of your routine to pre-fatigue the pectoral muscles. Then you can do the other chest exercises with fresh triceps able to cope with the weights needed to make the chest burn – without the triceps weakening and letting you down. You can use dumbbells and the pec deck to similar effect – still not using your triceps. Take 2 to 3 seconds in each direction for each exercise. Breathe in as the weight is lowered, and out as you return to the start position.

Training plan for a ripped chest	
Exercise	**Sets and repetitions**
Dumbbell chest press	3 x 12
Dumbbell flies	3 x 12
Lying cable flies	3 x 12
Lower cable crossover	3 x 12
Pec deck	3 x 12

Dumbbell flies

Muscle used Pectoralis major

1 *Lying back on the bench, with your feet on the floor, hold a dumbbell in each hand above your chest, with arms straight and your palms facing each other. You can keep your feet on the floor or on the bench. Push the chest out throughout to make it work harder.*

2 *Slowly lower the dumbbells to your sides in an arc, keeping your arms almost straight and in line with your chest. Once the dumbbells are level with the line of the body pause for 1 second, then slowly return to the start position.*

Incline dumbbell flies

Muscles used Pectoralis – major and minor

1 *With the bench inclined upward at a 30–60-degree angle, lie back, holding a dumbbell in each hand, with straight arms, above your chest, palms facing each other. Your feet can be on the floor or on the bench.*

2 *Slowly lower the dumbbells to the side of your body in an arc, keeping your arms almost straight and in line with the chest. Once the dumbbells are level with the line of the body, pause for 1 second, then return to the start position.*

Low cable crossover

Muscles used Pectoralis – lower; triceps; biceps

1 *Stand with your feet facing forward, one behind the other. Grip the handles with palms facing forward and arms out at your sides at 180 degrees. Keep your core muscles working to maintain a still body position.*

2 *Keeping your arms almost straight (don't let the arms bend by more than 10 degrees), slowly pull your hands together and downward so that they meet in front of your chest. Pause for 1 second, then slowly let the weight pull your hands back to the start position, squeezing the lower part of the chest as you return to the start position.*

Lying cable flies

Muscles used Pectoralis – major, minor

1 *Lie on the bench and grip the handles with your palms facing each other. Keep your arms straight and in line with your chest.*

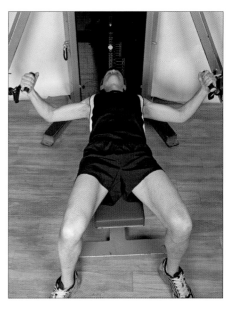

2 *Slowly let the weight pull your arms apart until your elbows are level with your chest. Pause for 1 second, then slowly return to the start position.*

Pec deck

Muscle used Pectoralis major

1 *Sit with your back flat against the support, feet on the floor, elbows and forearms resting against the pads, elbows at 90 degrees, in line with the bottom of your chest. Start with your arms out in front, the pads almost touching. Keep your head in line with your spine. Try to keep a relaxed grip throughout.*

2 *Slowly let the weight pull the arms back until they are level with your body. Pause for 1 second before pulling your arms back to the start position, pushing through your elbows and forearms to work the chest. Tense the abdominal muscles to maintain a flat back throughout the movement.*

Chest Exercises: Body Weight-training

There are a variety of chest exercises you can perform using just your body weight. The principal advantage is that you can retain the firm chest you developed in the gym even when you are on holiday or travelling on business.

It is possible to work your chest muscles without going to the gym, and simple press-ups are very effective. Press-ups from different angles work different parts of the pectoral muscles and can be incorporated into outdoor workouts using park benches. To work the stabilizing muscles surrounding your chest harder, use fit balls and medicine balls.

For each exercise, take 2 to 3 seconds for each direction of the movement. Breathe in at the start of the movement and out as you return to the start position.

Press-up

Muscles used Pectoralis major; anterior deltoid; triceps brachii – medial head, long head

1 *Place your hands on the floor, just over shoulder-width apart, your feet behind you, hip-width apart, elbows in line with your chest. Tense your core muscles and keep your head in line with your spine.*

2 *Keeping your abdominals tight, lower yourself toward the floor, taking your elbows out to the side until your chest is one fist from the floor. Pause for a second, then return to the start position.*

Decline press-up

Muscles used Pectoralis major; triceps brachii – medial head and long head

1 *Place your hands on the floor, just over shoulder-width apart, core muscles tense, feet behind you on the bench, hip-width apart, elbows in line with your chest. Keep your head in line with your spine.*

2 *Lower yourself toward the floor, taking your elbows out to the side until your chest is one fist from the floor. Pause for a second, then return to the start position.*

Incline press-up

Muscles used Pectoralis major; anterior deltoid; triceps brachii – medial, long head

This is a simple variation on the standard press-up. The start position is exactly the same except that you place your hands on an aerobic step instead of on the floor. Then lower yourself toward the step, taking your elbows to the side. Pause for 1 second, then return to the start position. To make sure that your chest does the work, don't push back behind you, and keep your chest up above the bench. Keep the core muscles tensed to hold the straight body position throughout the movement.

Knee press-up

If you haven't done press-ups before, don't press up completely from your arms, start by doing them balancing on your knees. Gradually increase the angle at the back of your knees as you get stronger and can support yourself fully on your arms. This method is recommended for women.

Fit ball press-up

Muscles used Pectoralis major; anterior deltoid; triceps brachii; serratus anterior; abdominals; gluteus

1 Place your hands on the fit ball. Keep your arms straight, your feet behind you, hip-width apart, and your head in line with your spine. Tense your core muscles to keep your body straight. Turn your hands outward at 45 degrees to avoid wrist injuries.

2 Slowly lower your weight, taking your elbows out to the side until they are bent at 90 degrees. Pause for 1 second, then return to the start. Take extra care, or avoid this exercise if you have weak wrists.

Chest exercises with little equipment

Exercise	Sets and repetitions
Double-hand medicine ball press-up	3 x 10
Single-hand medicine ball press-up	3 x 10
Decline press-up	3 x 10
Press-up	3 x max
Incline press-up	3 x max

Single-hand medicine ball press-up

Muscles used Pectoralis major; triceps brachii; abdominals

1 Place one hand on the ball and one hand on the floor, just wider than shoulder-width apart. Your wrist should be in the middle of the top of the ball to prevent wrist injuries. Support your weight on straight arms, your feet out behind you, hip-width apart. Keep your elbows in line with your chest. Use your core muscles to maintain this position. Your head should remain in line with your spine throughout the movement.

2 Keeping the core muscles switched on to maintain good balance and posture, slowly lower your body weight, taking your elbows out to the side until they are at 90 degrees. Pause for 1 second before returning to the start position. Keep your abdominal muscles tight throughout the movement to maintain a straight body. As you get stronger, transfer more weight onto the side with the medicine ball so your muscles work harder and improve your stability.

Double-hand medicine ball press-up

Muscles used Pectoralis major; triceps brachii – medial, long and lateral heads

1 Place both hands on the ball. Support your weight on straight arms, and keep your feet out behind you, hip-width apart, with the toes on the floor and the heels raised. Keep your elbows in line with your chest. Switch on your core muscles to maintain good balance and posture. Your head should remain in line with your spine throughout the movement.

2 Keeping your core muscles tense, slowly lower yourself, taking your elbows out to the side until they are at 90 degrees. The angle of the elbows changes the emphasis of the exercise. The closer your elbows are to your ribs the more the triceps will work, the farther away, the harder the chest muscles will work. Pause for 1 second before returning to the start position.

Back Exercises: The Lats

Your back is one of the strongest areas of your body but one that is often neglected by gym users. This may be because it is difficult to see the back muscles, which makes it harder to monitor them, and therefore to stay motivated to train them.

The following exercises work the large muscles called latissimus dorsi, which are situated on the widest part of the upper back. For each exercise, take 2 to 3 seconds for each direction of the movement. Breathe out at the beginning of the movement, and breathe in as you return to the start position. Try using forced repetitions, when you have done as many reps as possible. Get your training partner to help you do two to three more reps.

Exercises to build stronger back muscles

The back muscles are large, so it takes hard work to train them.

Exercise	Sets and repetitions
Overhand chin-up	5 x max
Lat pull-down, wide grip	3 x 12
Lat pull-down, underhand grip	3 x 12

Lat pull-down, underhand grip

Muscles used Latissimus dorsi; teres major; biceps brachii; brachialis

1 *Sit on the bench, with your feet shoulder-width apart, between you and the machine. Hold the bar with a close underhand grip. Lean back slightly and keep your head in line with the spine.*

Lat pull-down, wide grip

Muscles used Latissimus dorsi; teres major; biceps brachii; brachialis

1 *Hold the bar using a wide overhand grip. Sit on a seat, bench, fit ball or floor. Place your feet on the floor between you and the machine, shoulder-width apart. Lean back slightly and keep your head in line with your spine. Keep your body fixed in one position with your abdominals tensed.*

2 *Pull the bar toward the bottom of your chest, your elbows going out to the side and behind you. When the bar is close to the chest, pause for 1 second, then slowly return to the start position. Push your chest out as the bar is pulled in. Focus on using your lat muscles and don't let your shoulders rise up in the movement.*

2 *Pull the bar toward the bottom of your chest, chest out, elbows out to the side and behind you. When the bar is close to your chest, pause for a second, then slowly return to the start position.*

Overhand chin-up, wide grip

Muscles used Latissimus dorsi; teres major; rhomboid – minor, major; biceps brachii; brachialis

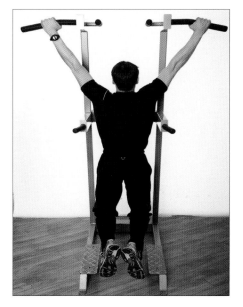

1 *Grip the outside of the chin-up bar with an overhand grip so that your palms are facing away from you. Hang from the bar with straight arms and tense core muscles. Keep your head facing forward and in line with your spine. Your legs should be hanging straight under you in line with your body.*

2 *Slowly pull your body weight up, with your elbows going out to the sides until your chin is over the top of the bar. Pause for 1 second, then return to the start position. Keep the core muscles tensed at all times, and let your arms go almost straight between repetitions.*

Rope pull-down

Muscles used Latissimus dorsi; teres major; biceps brachii; brachialis

1 *Hold the rope using a wide overhand grip. Place your feet on the floor, shoulder-width apart, between you and the machine. Lean back slightly and keep your head in line with your spine. Don't let the weight drag you forward and round your shoulders.*

2 *Pull the rope toward the bottom of your chest, chest out and elbows to the side and behind you. Push your hips slightly forward and tense your core muscles to emphasize your lats. When the rope is close to your chest, pause for a second, then slowly return to the start.*

Straight arm cable pull-down

Muscles used Latissimus dorsi; teres major; triceps brachii – long head

1 *Face the cable machine with feet shoulder-width apart. Hold the bar in front of you at eye level, with straight arms. Tense the core muscles during the exercise. Keep your head in line with your spine during the movement.*

2 *Pull the bar down to below the waist. Keep the grip relaxed so the back, abdominals and triceps work harder. Pause for 1 second, then return to the start. Push the chest out and keep the head facing forward throughout.*

Back Exercises: The Spine

The following exercises will work all the major muscles of your back, but with greater emphasis on the muscles close to the spine. These are excellent exercises to strengthen your back for sports such as rowing and sailing.

Many people avoid training their back muscles because it is so energy intensive. But back muscles, alongside thigh and buttock muscles, are the largest in the body, so it is worthwhile training them properly. You should feel breathless at the end of a set of back exercises because these large muscles use a lot of oxygen.

Most back exercises involve pulling a weight toward you and demand a certain amount of bicep and forearm strength. To get the best training effect, do your back exercises first and arms later – otherwise your arm muscles will not be able to support the heavy weights you need to work the back muscles hard.

For each exercise, take 2 to 3 seconds during each direction of the movement. Breathe out at the beginning of the movement; breathe in as you return to the start position.

Exercises for a wider, V-shaped back	
Exercise	Sets and repetitions
Overhand chin-up, wide grip	3 x max
Lat pull-down, wide grip	3 x 12
Seated cable row	3 x 12
Single-arm dumbbell row	3 x 12
Single-arm cable row	3 x 12

Single-arm cable row

Muscles used Latissimus dorsi; teres major; rhomboid major; trapezius; posterior deltoid; biceps brachii; brachialis; brachioradialis

1 *Stand firm, with one foot in front of the other, 60cm/2ft apart. Keep your body square on, to isolate the muscles that should be used. Reach down, grip the handle and pull it up with a straight arm to the start position. Lean forward, toward the machine, placing your spare hand on the machine to help keep your body still.*

2 *Do not use a weight that is so heavy that your back has to twist to help your arm pull it in. Pull the handle toward your armpit, allowing your elbow to pass close to your ribs, and back behind you. Do not let your shoulder rise up in the movement. Pause for 1 second, then slowly let the handle return to the start position, keeping your feet firmly in place.*

Single-arm cable row, high to low

Muscles used Latissimus dorsi; teres major; rhomboid minor; rhomboid major; biceps brachii; brachialis; brachioradialis

1 *Stand with one foot in front of the other, 60cm/2ft apart, to establish a good base. Reach down and grip the handle and pull it up with a straight arm to the start position. Single-arm rows are one of the best exercises for the shoulder and upper back.*

2 *Stand up and lean slightly backward, with your pelvis pushed slightly forward. Start with the cable in a higher position and pull it down with your elbow, brushing past your ribs. Repeat the exercise using the other arm. This exercise helps if there is poor posture as a result of weakness of the muscles at the back of the shoulders and upper back.*

Single-arm dumbbell row

Muscles used Latissimus dorsi; teres major; rhomboid major; trapezius; posterior deltoid; biceps brachii; brachialis; brachioradialis

1 *Place your left knee and left hand on a flat bench. Keep your right foot on the ground, with your leg straight, and position yourself with your back parallel to the bench. Grip the dumbbell in your right hand with a straight arm. Tense your core muscles to maintain this position. Keep your core muscles working hard to stop your back twisting.*

2 *Pull the weight up, allowing your elbows to pass close to your ribs, and back behind the line of your body, until your hand is just under your armpit. If your body can't stay square-on to the bench, then you know the weight is too heavy. Pause for 1 second, then slowly lower the weight back to the start position.*

Seated cable row

Muscles used Rhomboid major; teres major; latissimus dorsi; trapezius; erector spinae; posterior deltoid; biceps brachii; brachialis; brachioradialis

1 *Sit on the floor, legs almost straight out in front of you, your feet up against the machine or foot rests. Keeping both arms and your back straight, and abdominals tensed, pull the handles back with both hands. Keep the chest pushed out throughout the movement so that the shoulders stay behind the line of the chest.*

2 *Pull the handles toward you, allowing your elbows to pass close to your ribs until the handles are near to your armpits. Pause for 1 second, then let the handles slowly return to the start position. Tense the core muscles and don't let your shoulders get dragged forward as the weight returns to the start position.*

Back Exercises: Back Muscles

For these exercises, you will need you to recruit your core muscles more than ever, as they form a strong connection between the upper and lower body. If you want to build body mass and pure lifting strength, these are the right exercises for you.

The following exercises work all the back muscles. They may be of particular use to you for lifting heavy weights and in contact sports such as rugby and American football. These exercises are exhausting, as you use a massive amount of muscle. So, practise getting your breathing right to ensure you are getting enough oxygen to your muscles, especially as you are trying to tense the core muscles as much as possible throughout the movements.

Make sure that you do at least 10 minutes' cardiovascular exercise and some stretching before you start these exercises, to get good blood flow to the muscles and avoid injury. Practise without any weight to get the correct technique before adding weights.

For each exercise, take 2 to 3 seconds for each direction of the movement. Breathe out at the beginning of the movement, and in as you return to the start position.

Exercises to build mass for your back	
Exercise	**Sets and repetitions**
Olympic bar deadlift	3 x 8–10
Single-arm dumbbell row	3 x 8–10
Bent-over barbell row	3 x 8–10
Underarm barbell row	3 x 8–10
Seated cable row	3 x 8–10

Olympic bar deadlift

Muscles used Trapezius; rhomboid major; latissimus dorsi; gluteus maximus; semitendinosus; semimembranosus; biceps femoris – long head and short head; vastus lateralis, medialis; rectus abdominis

1 *Stand with your feet shoulder-width apart. Bend your knees until your thighs are nearly parallel with the floor, the upper body leaning forward, bending at the hip. Arch your lower back slightly and tense your core muscles as much as possible. They must remain tight throughout this exercise in order to prevent your back from becoming rounded. A rounded back could result in severe spinal disc problems. Look straight ahead, keeping your head in line with the spine.*

2 *Grip the Olympic bar with an overhand grip, with palms facing backward. The hands should be shoulder-width apart, arms straight. Pull the weight up by straightening your legs, with the bar passing close to your shins and over the knees in a smooth, continuous movement. Straighten your upper body until you are completely upright. Pause for 1 second, then slowly reverse the movement back to the start position.*

Bent-over barbell row

Muscles used Latissimus dorsi; teres major; rhomboid major; trapezius; posterior deltoid; biceps brachii; brachialis; brachioradialis

1 Grip the bar with an overhand grip, hands just wider than shoulder-width apart. Bend your hips at just 90 degrees. With your feet shoulder-width apart, legs straight and core muscles tensed, push your hips back and arch your lower back slightly to maintain good body position. The bar should hang, from straight arms, perpendicular to the ground.

2 Pull the bar toward your chest, with your elbows going out to the sides until the bar is against your chest. Pause for 1 second, then lower the weight back to the start position.

Bench barbell row

Muscles used Latissimus dorsi; teres major; rhomboid major; trapezius; posterior deltoid; biceps brachii; brachialis; brachioradialis

Lie face down on the bench with your abdominals tensed to provide a stable base. Grip the bar using an overhand grip just over shoulder-width apart. Pull the bar up toward you with the elbows passing your ribs at the sides. Once at the top pause for a second and then slowly lower the bar back down. Keep arms straight to work the back muscles through a range of movement.

Bent-over T-bar row

Muscles used Posterior deltoid; teres – minor, major; trapezius; infraspinatus; rhomboid; latissimus dorsi; erector spinae; brachialis; brachioradialis

1 Stand with your legs either side of the T-bar, shoulder-width apart. Grip the bar with an overhand grip, slightly bend your knees and bend your upper body at the hips, keeping your torso very still.

Underarm barbell row

Muscles used Latissimus dorsi; teres major; rhomboid major; trapezius; posterior deltoid; biceps brachii; brachialis; brachioradialis

The start position is the same as for the bent-over barbell row (left), except you grip the bar with an underhand grip, hands just wider than shoulder-width apart. Bend the hips at 90 degrees. With your feet shoulder-width apart, legs straight and core muscles tensed, push the hips back and arch your lower back slightly to maintain good body position. The bar hangs perpendicular to the ground.

2 Pull the bar in toward your body, with your elbows bending out to the side, behind the line of your body. Once the bar is close to your ribs, pause for a second, then return to the start position.

Shoulder Exercises: General

Many people want wider shoulders. Although you can't increase the actual bone size of the shoulder, you can, with the right exercises, increase your shoulder muscle, which will make your shoulders appear much broader.

For most people, changing the width and depth of their shoulders makes them appear different and can have a dramatic effect on their body shape. Wider shoulders make it much easier to give your torso a great V-shape. Hanging clothes on wide shoulders can make you look more athletic and slimmer.

There are a number of shoulder exercises that you can use to build the depth and increase the width of your shoulder muscles.

To build strong shoulders, you need to use three types of movement: pressing, pulling and raising. It can take a long time to develop really strong shoulders because there are a number of different muscles surrounding a complex joint, and these are not necessarily muscles you use in everyday life.

Your deltoid is the primary muscle in your shoulder and is split into three parts: the anterior deltoid, medial deltoid and posterior deltoid. Depending on the movement you are performing, one part of the deltoid will work more than the others. In most movements, however, two parts of the deltoid will work together, or even all three parts. Make sure that you use the correct weight and warm up sufficiently in order not to damage the smaller muscles in the shoulder (rotator cuff).

When you start training your shoulders, it is important that you use basic pressing exercises to make your shoulder muscle active before moving on to exercises better suited for isolating the different areas of the shoulder. Otherwise, you might injure yourself.

Make sure your lower back is well supported during any pressing movements. As soon as you feel your body starting to twist while trying to do shoulder exercises, your shoulders are fatigued and you should rest. For every exercise, take 2 to 3 seconds for each direction of the movement. Breathe out at the beginning of the movement and in as you return to the start position.

Exercises to build stronger shoulders for beginners	
Exercise	**Sets and repetitions**
Olympic bar front shoulder press	3 x 12
Dumbbell shoulder press	3 x 12
Alternate dumbbell shoulder press	3 x 20

Olympic bar front shoulder press

Muscles used Deltoid – middle, anterior, posterior; triceps brachii – medial head, lateral head and long head

1 *Sit on the bench with your back pushed against the pad and put your feet out in front of you, shoulder-width apart, for support. If possible, put your feet up against a wall or dumbbell rack to help keep your back flat. Grip the bar firmly with both hands using an overhand grip. Always have someone there to spot for you for this exercise.*

2 *Lift the bar from the rack up above your head and hold it in a straight-arm position. Slowly lower the bar down, with the elbows going out to the sides, until the bar is in front of your head at eye level. Pause for 1 second, then press the bar back up to the start position. Take care, the shoulders can fatigue, so that you struggle to get the bar back on the rack.*

Dumbbell shoulder press

Muscles used Deltoid – middle, anterior, posterior; triceps brachii

1 *Sit on the bench with your feet in front of you, shoulder-width apart, to make a firm base. Slowly lift the weights up above your shoulders until they are straight up above head height, out to the sides. Try not to let your neck tense, and keep your shoulders working equally.*

2 *Slowly lower the weights, with your elbows going out to the sides to 90 degrees, the weights level with your ears. Pause for 1 second, then press the weights back up to the start position.*

Alternate shoulder press

Muscles used Deltoid – middle, anterior, posterior; triceps brachii – medial head, lateral head and long head

1 *Sit on the bench, feet out in front of you or pressed up against a wall or dumbbell rack, at least shoulder-width apart, to make a firm base. Keep your core muscles tight throughout the movement. With one arm, lift one weight above your shoulders until it is straight up above head height, out to the side. Move slowly, without jerking, so you don't damage any muscles.*

2 *Slowly lower the weight, with your elbow going out to the side, until it is at 90 degrees and the dumbbell is level with your ears. Pause for 1 second, then press the weight back up to the start position. Repeat with the other side. Wait for one arm to complete the press before you start to press the dumbbell up with the other arm.*

Body weight shoulder press

Muscles used Deltoid – middle, anterior, posterior; pectoralis major; triceps brachii – medial head, lateral head, long head

1 *Assume the decline press-up position with your feet up behind you on a bench. Pike at the hips and bring your hands back closer toward you, palms flat on the floor. Avoid this exercise if you have weak wrists.*

2 *Lower yourself down by bending your elbows until your head is almost touching the floor. Try not to let your back arch. Pause for 1 second, before pressing back up to the position in step 1.*

Shoulder Exercises: Rotational Strength

The following exercises will work the shoulder muscles as well as some of the muscles surrounding them. The range of movement involved will make your core and stabilizing muscles work harder, giving you the benefits of good rotational strength.

Most sports require some rotation at the shoulder joint. Throwing movements use all the muscles in the deltoid and make you over-dominant in one arm, which can lead to muscle imbalances and injury. So it is important that you work both shoulder muscles equally. In these rotational movements, many shoulder muscles have to work together. The rotator cuff, often the site of shoulder injuries, is the main stabilizer during any shoulder movement to keep the ball of the upper arm central. If it is not centred, this can put abnormal stress on the surrounding tissue, making tendonitis, rotator cuff tears and shoulder impingement likely.

As you get older, the tendons in the rotator cuff lose elasticity, making injury more likely. With age, too, comes a gradual decline in the muscle bulk that surrounds the shoulder. The following exercises will help to counteract the effect of aging, allowing you to continue with your chosen sport for longer.

The rotator cuff is made up of three parts: the supraspinatus, located at the top of the shoulder, which adducts the shoulder (raises the upper arm and moves it away from the body); the subscapularis, at the front of the shoulder, which internally rotates the shoulder; and the infraspinatus and teres, at the back of the shoulder, which externally rotates it. The following exercises work all three.

Generally, take 2 to 3 seconds for each direction of the movement. Breathe out at the beginning of the movement, and in as you return to the start position.

Variation: single-arm cable shoulder press

Muscles used Deltoid – middle, anterior, posterior; triceps brachii – medial head, lateral head and long head

Start by holding one handle of the cable shoulder press above your head until your arm is straight. Pause for 1 second then slowly lower the weight back to the start. Repeat with the other arm.

Cable shoulder press

Muscles used Deltoid – middle, anterior, posterior; triceps brachii – medial head, lateral head and long head

1 *Stand with your feet shoulder-width apart, one foot in front of the other and hold the handles at shoulder height.*

2 *Press the handles above your head until your arms are straight. Pause for a second, then slowly lower the weight back down.*

Exercises to build rotational strength of shoulders

Try some forced sets on the final exercise by getting your partner to help you with the lat two reps after you have already fatigued.

Exercise	Sets and repetitions
Arnie shoulder press	3 x 12
Cable shoulder press	3 x 12
Single-arm shoulder press	3 x 12
Olympic bar front shoulder press	3 x 8–12

Seated reverse dumbbell shoulder press, with rotation

Muscles used Deltoid – middle, anterior, posterior; pectoralis major; triceps brachii – medial head, lateral head and long head

1 *Sit on the bench, with core muscles tense. Bring the dumbbells up in front of your shoulders, palms facing you and your elbows as close together as possible.*

2 *Press the dumbbells upward, palms facing you and elbows as close together as possible. As the dumbbells reach eye level, start to rotate them so that they have rotated through 180 degrees by the time they reach the straight-arm position above your head. Pause at the top, then slowly lower the weights, rotating back to the start position.*

Arnold shoulder press

Muscles used Deltoid – middle, anterior, posterior; pectoralis major; triceps brachii – medial head, lateral head and long head; biceps brachii; brachialis; brachioradialis

1 *Use a lighter weight than you think you need to keep the emphasis on the deltoids. Stand with the feet shoulder-width apart. Hold one dumbbell in each hand, your arms by your sides, your hands just below hip level.*

2 *Slowly bicep-curl the dumbbells by bending the elbow until the dumbbells are at shoulder height, with your elbows squeezed into your ribs. Keep your head and back straight and avoid arching the back.*

3 *Keeping your palms facing toward you and your elbows close together, press the dumbbells up to eye level before rotating them through 180 degrees to complete the press-up above your head. At the top, pause for a second before slowly lowering the dumbbells, and gradually rotating them through 180 degrees.*

4 *As you complete the 180-degree rotation on the way back down, reverse-curl the dumbbells to the start position. For this exercise, take 4 to 5 seconds in each direction. Don't let the back arch during this exercise. Keep your abdominals tensed throughout the entire movement. If you feel your upper torso twisting, stop immediately.*

Shoulder Exercises: Connecting the Muscles

To make the connection between your deltoids, trapezius and other upper back muscles stronger, these exercises are essential. For the deltoids, the main emphasis will be on the anterior and medial deltoid muscles.

As these exercises require you to lift your shoulders upward, it is important to keep your neck relaxed to prevent injury and to keep the emphasis on the appropriate muscles. If you are involved in contact sports, these exercises are essential to provide the strength you need in the shoulders, upper back and neck. For combat sports, such as boxing, exercising these muscles should also be a priority.

The deltoids move the upper arm in a number of directions and are split into three parts called heads: the anterior head at the front of the shoulder; the medial head in the middle of the shoulder; and the posterior head at the rear of the shoulder. If you look at a bodybuilder from above, you should be able to see all three parts clearly defined like strips of muscle wrapped around the shoulder. Depending on the direction of the shoulder movement, one of the heads of the shoulder will work harder than the others to achieve the correct movement.

If you raise your arm up in front of you from down by your side, you will make the anterior head work the hardest. Raising your arm out to the side will work the medial head the hardest. Pulling your arm back behind you will work the posterior head. Most movements will work two of the heads – and sometimes three.

Be careful with the following exercises not to use your body weight to move the weights. It is easy to arch your back or bend the legs in the last few reps to make lifting the weights easier. Upright rowing exercises greatly exert the upper back and the trapezius muscles, which is good as long as your lower back is not doing the work. If you find it hard to prevent your body arching backward, try positioning yourself with one foot in front of the other to create a more stable platform, and tense your core muscles to restrict how far you can lean back.

For each exercise, take 2 to 3 seconds for each direction of the movement. Breathe out at the beginning of the movement, and in as you return to the start position.

Exercises for shoulder muscles	
Exercise	**Sets and repetitions**
Dumbbell shoulder press	3 x 12
Arnie shoulder press	3 x 12
Upright cable row	3 x 12
Upright dumbbell row	3 x 12
Dumbbell shoulder shrug	3 x 12

Upright cable row

Muscles used Trapezius; deltoids – anterior, posterior

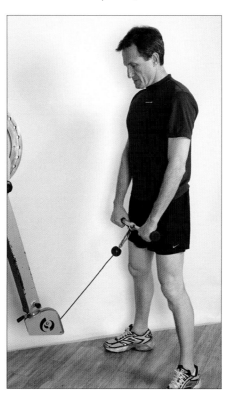 

1 *Stand 60cm/2ft from the cable machine, with your feet shoulder-width apart. Grip the bar with an overhand grip, with hands thumb-width apart. Tense your core muscles to help keep your back straight throughout the movement. Try to keep your neck relaxed throughout the movement.*

2 *Pull the bar up toward your chin, and take your elbows out to the sides, keeping them above the wrists throughout the movement. Once the bar is at chin height, pause for 1 second, then slowly lower the bar back down to the start position. Try not to lean backward as you start to fatigue.*

Above: With a contact sport such as boxing, shoulder exercises are necessary for strength in the neck, shoulders and upper back.

Upright dumbbell row

Muscles used Trapezius; deltoids – middle, anterior, posterior

1 *Stand with feet shoulder-width apart. Grip the dumbbells with an overhand grip, with palms facing backward. Hold the dumbbells with your arms straight down in front of you. Tense your core muscles to keep your back straight. Your head should be in line with your spine. Ask your training partner to monitor your technique and make sure that you are not tensing your neck.*

2 *Pull the dumbbells up, taking your elbows out to your side until the dumbbells are level with your chin. Keep hands close together throughout the movement. Keep the elbows above your wrists at all times. Try to keep the neck relaxed to help isolate the shoulders. Once you reach chin level, pause for 1 second then lower the dumbbells back down to the start position.*

Dumbbell shoulder shrug

Muscles used Trapezius; deltoids – middle, anterior, posterior

1 *Stand with your feet shoulder-width apart and your arms hanging straight by your sides to just below hip level. Grip one dumbbell in each hand, with your palms facing inward. Try to avoid tensing your neck.*

2 *Keeping your arms as straight as possible, lift the outside of the shoulders up to raise the dumbbells just a few centimetres. Pause for 1 second, then lower the weights back down to the start position.*

Shoulder Exercises: The Anterior Deltoids

The exercises here train the front of the shoulders (anterior deltoids), with little strength coming from other parts of your deltoids. These muscles give you toned shoulders and are essential for exercises, especially those involving pressing big weights above the chest.

The anterior deltoid muscles are involved in stabilizing the muscles during chest presses and are heavily involved when a chest exercise is done on an incline. The high usage of this muscle makes it susceptible to injury. It is a mistake to try to work these muscles using shoulder exercises in the same routine as chest presses or even on the day after. You must try to avoid overtraining the anterior deltoids, so have a day's rest between exercises that involve using them.

All these exercises involve raising movements, so there will be no real help from your triceps. People often choose to work the anterior deltoids harder than other parts of the deltoids because it is easy to see the muscle in the mirror. But this often leads to muscle imbalances and can make the anterior deltoids over-dominant in the movement of the shoulder press exercises, causing the weight to be dragged forward. Your posture will also be affected in that your shoulders will be dragged forward, creating a more rounded upper back. Make sure you balance this out by using the other parts of the deltoid. If you

have poor posture, you need to pay more attention to exercising the medial and posterior deltoid in your workouts. It is worth considering omitting specific exercises for these muscles from your routine, because they will be worked with the chest press exercises anyway.

When planning your routine, make sure that you use each arm equally to prevent one getting stronger than the other. To help isolate the muscle, try

sitting down for some of the exercises in order to prevent your body getting into too much of a swinging motion. You may need to use a lighter weight than you think you need so that you will be able to activate the muscle correctly.

For each exercise, take 2 to 3 seconds for each direction of the movement. Breathe out at the beginning of the movement, and in as you return to the start position.

Exercises to build powerful shoulders

Superset each exercise with the one below, with only five to ten seconds' rest between sets.

Exercise	Sets and repetitions
Olympic bar shoulder press	3 x 8–12
Arnie shoulder press	3 x 8–12
Upright dumbbell row	3 x 8–12
Upright cable row	3 x 8–12
Single-arm dumbbell frontal raise	3 x 8–12
Cable frontal raise	3 x 8–10

Single-arm dumbbell frontal raise

Muscles used Deltoids – middle, anterior, posterior; pectoralis major

1 *Stand with your head up but relaxed, and your feet shoulder-width apart so that you feel stable and balanced. Take hold of a dumbbell in each hand and hold them close together in front of your thighs, with your arms hanging straight down and the palms facing behind you.*

2 *Pull one arm forward, keeping it straight, until it is in front of you at eye level. Try not to let momentum take over. Pause for 1 second, then slowly lower the weight back to the starting position. Repeat with the other arm. Only lift the weight once the other arm has returned to the start position.*

Cable frontal raise

Muscles used Deltoids – middle, anterior, posterior; pectoralis major

1 *Stand with your feet shoulder-width apart, 60cm/2ft from the cable machine. Hold the bar with an overhand grip, with hands just less than shoulder-width apart. Focus on the front of your shoulders. Don't let your back arch.*

2 *Beginning with arms straight down in front of the body, pull the bar up, with your arms straight out in front of you, until it is at eye level. Keep the neck relaxed. Pause for 1 second, then slowly lower it back down to the start position.*

Single-arm cable frontal raise

Muscles used Deltoids – middle, anterior, posterior; pectoralis major

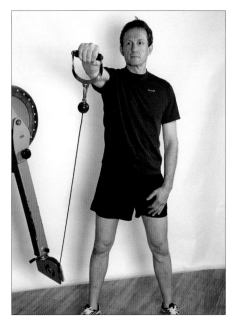

1 *Stand with your feet shoulder-width apart, side-on on to the cable machine. Using one hand, hold the bar with an overhand grip, with the palm facing backward. Stay in a position that is square-on to the machine. Focus on the front of the shoulder that is doing the exercise.*

2 *Keeping your arm straight out in front of you, pull the cable up until it is at eye level. Pause for 1 second, then, without jerking, slowly lower it back down to the start position. Keep the shoulders level and don't let your back arch. Don't hold your breath; keep breathing throughout.*

Bench frontal raise

Muscles used Deltoids – middle, anterior, posterior; pectoralis major; rectus abdominis

1 *Lie face down on a 30-degree incline bench with your arms straight down in front of you just above floor height. Place the balls of your feet on the floor behind you, and out to the sides of the bench. Hold a dumbbell in each hand. Check that the dumbbells are the right weight for you.*

2 *Lift the dumbbells up in front of you with straight arms, keeping the arms as close to each other as possible. Do not allow your lower back to arch. Once your hands are up to almost shoulder level, pause for 1 second, then slowly lower the weights back down to the start position.*

Shoulder Exercises: Stability

The exercises given here use raising movements to place emphasis on the posterior deltoid and middle deltoid muscles – the muscles that provide much-needed stability for a range of movements involved in many sports.

If you want wider, toned shoulders, include the following exercises in your routine. If you have poor posture, use these exercises to prevent rounded shoulders. The exercises will pull your shoulders back and force your back muscles to work in conjunction with your shoulders. They will also help improve your posture. There are many stabilizers in the shoulders, one of which, the scapular (shoulder blade), helps the rotator cuff to stabilize the shoulder joint while in motion. The scapular must be stable – if not, the pressure on it caused by lifting heavy weights may cause injury to the rotator cuff.

These exercises will give you strength with the full range of movement and help to stabilize your shoulder at the same time. Concentrate especially on not using your lower back to help lift the weights. If you are suffering from shoulder injuries, consult your physician before you do these shoulder exercises. While they will help with shoulder stability, your shoulder needs to be sufficiently stable in the first place before you attempt them.

Unless stated otherwise, for each exercise, take 2 to 3 seconds for each direction of the movement. Breathe out at the beginning of the movement, and in as you return to the start position.

Exercises to give wider, toned shoulders	
Exercise	**Sets and repetitions**
Reverse dumbbell shoulder press	3 x 12
Single-arm dumbbell frontal raise	3 x 20
Upright dumbbell row	3 x 12
Bent-over cable lateral raise	3 x 12
Windmill	3 x 12
Single-arm dumbbell lateral raise	3 x 12

Bent-over cable lateral raise

Muscles used Deltoids – middle, anterior, posterior; teres minor; rhomboid; trapezius

1 *Stand between the two arms of the cable machine, with feet just over shoulder-width apart. Take hold of the handle so that your arm is across your body. Bend the upper body at the hips so that your back is parallel to the floor.*

2 *Pull the handle back across your body with a straight arm until it is out to the side, level with your body like the wing of an airplane. Pause for 1 second, then slowly lower the weight back to the start position.*

Bent-over dumbbell lateral raise

Muscles used Deltoids – middle, anterior, posterior; teres minor; rhomboid; trapezius

1 *Sit on the end of a bench with your feet on the floor and legs bent at 90 degrees. Lean forward so that your chest is almost resting on your knees. Hold a dumbbell in each hand.*

2 *Pull the dumbbells out to the sides in an arc, arms almost straight, until the weights are level with the line of your shoulders. Pause for a second, then slowly lower your arms back to the start position.*

Windmill

Muscles used Deltoids – middle, anterior, posterior; rhomboid; trapezius

1 *Stand with your feet shoulder-width apart, arms straight, a dumbbell in each hand in front of you.*

2 *Take your arms out to the side until they are at shoulder level. Pause in this position for 1 second.*

3 *Continue the movement until the weights are above your head. Once they are above your head, slowly lower them back to shoulder level as in step 2, pause for a second, then continue to lower them back to the start position. For this exercise, take 3 to 4 seconds for each direction of the movement.*

Dumbbell lateral raise

Muscles used Deltoids – middle, anterior, posterior

1 *Stand with your feet shoulder-width apart, looking straight ahead, keeping your neck straight. Hold one dumbbell in each hand, with your palms facing toward each other and your elbows tucked in tight against your ribs.*

2 *Keeping your elbows at the same angle, take your arms out to the sides until your upper arm, elbow, forearm and wrist are all level with your shoulders. Pause for a second, then slowly lower back to the start position.*

Single-arm dumbbell lateral raise

Muscles used Deltoids – middle, anterior, posterior

1 *Stand with feet shoulder-width apart, hold a dumbbell in one hand by your side. Let the other hand hang straight and loose by your side to hip level. Tense the core muscles to stop movement and to isolate the deltoid muscle.*

2 *Lift your arm to the side, keeping it straight, until your wrist, forearm and elbow are level with your shoulder. Pause for 1 second, then slowly lower the weight back down to the start position. Repeat with the other arm.*

Biceps Exercises: Powerful Arms

Your biceps make up only 30–40 per cent of your upper arm – the triceps account for most of it – but biceps exercises are probably the most popular upper-body weight-training exercise because, quite simply, many people believe that big biceps look good.

There are two muscle groups in the front of your upper arm. The largest group is the biceps brachii and the smallest is the brachialis. This small area of the body requires a variety of different exercises. It is important to change your bicep routine regularly to get the most from each session. Many gym users use bad technique to lift the heaviest weights they can. The following exercises will ensure that you stick to the correct technique to put the emphasis on your biceps.

For each exercise take 2 to 3 seconds for each direction of the movement. Breathe out at the beginning of the movement, and in as you return to the start position.

Standing barbell bicep curl, wide grip

Muscles used Biceps brachii – long head, short head; brachialis

1 *Stand with your feet shoulder-width apart so that you feel well balanced and stable. Grip the barbell close to the thighs, with an underhand grip so that your palms are facing forward, your arms straight and your hands just over shoulder-width apart. To prevent any part of your body other than the biceps from working, keep the upper torso still by tensing your core muscles.*

2 *Keep your elbows at your sides, locked in to your ribs, and curl the bar up to the shoulders. Prevent your elbows from moving forward and backward: imagine a pin going through your elbow into your ribs; rotate on this axis. Stand side-on to a mirror and glance at it in the middle of each set to check your elbow is in the right place. Pause for 1 second, then slowly return to the start position.*

Reverse dumbbell bicep curl

Muscles used Brachioradialis; biceps brachii – long head, short head; brachialis; extensor carpi; radialis – longus, brevis; extensor digitorum; extensor digiti minimi; extensor carpi ulnaris

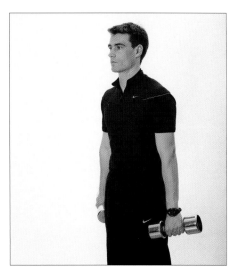

1 *Stand with feet shoulder-width apart. With an overhand grip, hold a dumbbell in each hand, close to your thighs.*

2 *Keeping your elbows locked in to the ribs, curl the dumbbells up to your shoulders. Pause for 1 second, then slowly return to the start position.*

Exercises to build big biceps for beginners		
Exercise	Sets and repetitions	Comments
Barbell bicep curl	3 x 12	Put these exercises into
Dumbbell bicep curl	3 x 12	pairs and superset them to
Concentration curl	3 x 12	really work your biceps.
Hammer curl	3 x 12	

Standing dumbbell bicep curl

Muscles used Biceps brachii – long head, short head; brachialis

1 Stand, feet shoulder-width apart, a dumbbell in each hand, close to your thighs, using an underhand grip. To prevent your forearms from overworking, don't grip the dumbbells too tightly.

2 Keeping your elbows locked in to your ribs, curl the dumbbells up to your shoulders. Pause for a second, then slowly return to the start position. Keep your palms facing in the same direction. Don't let the weight of the dumbbell twist them, especially on the way back down.

Dumbbell hammer curl

Muscles used Brachioradials; biceps brachii – long head, short head; brachialis

1 Stand with your feet shoulder-width apart, your elbows tucked into your ribs. With an underhand grip, hold one dumbbell in each hand, close to your thighs. Concentrate on the arms doing the work.

2 Keep the elbows close to the ribs. Curl the weights up to the shoulders, turning the angle of the forearms by 90 degrees. At the top of the curl, pull the elbows back, pause for a second, then return to the start position.

Concentration curl

Muscles used Biceps brachii – long head, short head; brachialis

1 Sitting on a bench, take hold of the dumbbell and rest your elbow against your inner thigh. The palm of your hand should be facing away from you. Try to focus on isolating your bicep.

2 Keeping your elbow firmly up against your inner thigh, curl the dumbbell up to your shoulder. Use control to get a good burn. Pause for a second, then lower it down to the start position.

Biceps Exercises: Strong Lower Arms

Most upper-body exercises will help to work your lower arms but you should also regularly use specific lower-arm exercises. Changing the angle of the wrist when doing biceps curls will make the different parts of the bicep work more effectively.

Forearms need to be strong to give you the support to do other exercises, especially when you need to grip hard and pull weights to work the back muscles.

There are three types of forearm muscle structure and function: forearm supinator, a large muscle on the outer part of the forearm, which can be trained with reverse curls and hammer curls; forearm flexor, a small muscle on the inside of the forearm used to close your fist, which can be trained with barbell wrist curls; and forearm extensors, small muscles on the outside of the forearm, which straighten the fingers after your hand has been clenched, and bring your wrist back toward the arms.

There is virtually no sport which doesn't require strong lower arms. You can adapt your resistance exercises to your chosen sport. If you want stronger arms and wrists for mountain biking do more reps and less sets for greater endurance. Hovering with your fingers over the brakes and hands wrapped around the bars for hour after hour will take its toll if you don't do enough of these exercises. Even if a boxer's lower arms and wrists are heavily wrapped, the muscles must still be able to stand up to the impact and maintain stability to keep throwing punches.

Breathe out when you begin each exercise; then breathe in as you return to the start position.

Exercises to tone and strengthen lower arms	
Exercise	**Sets and repetitions**
Cable bicep curl	3 x 12
Single-arm cable bicep curl	3 x 8
Lying-down cable bicep curl	3 x 12
Wrist curl	3 x 15–20
Reverse wrist curl	3 x 15–20
Hammer wrist curl	3 x 15–20

Cable bicep curl

Muscles used Biceps brachii; brachialis

1 *Stand up straight, arms straight down in front of you, core muscles tense, feet shoulder-width apart, 30cm/1ft from the machine. Grip the bar using an underhand grip, so that the bar rests against the tops of your legs.*

2 *Curl the bar up to the shoulders keeping your elbows tucked into your ribs and your feet shoulder-width apart. Pause for 1 second at the top and then slowly return the bar to the start position.*

Lying-down cable bicep curl

Muscles used Biceps brachii; brachialis

1 *Lie down flat on your back, with your feet close to the cable machine. Hold the bar attached to the cable with an underhand grip, with your hands shoulder-width apart.*

2 *Place the bar down by the front of your legs and curl it up toward your shoulders, keeping your elbows tucked against your ribs. Pause for 1 second then slowly lower it back down.*

Single-arm cable bicep curl

Muscles used Biceps brachii; brachialis

1 *Stand with your feet shoulder-width apart, 30cm/1ft from the cable machine. Grip the bar, with one hand, using an underhand grip, so that it rests against the top of your thigh. Keep your other hand close in by your other thigh. Stand up straight with your core muscles tense. Try to keep the rest of your torso as still as possible.*

2 *Curl the bar up to the shoulder, keeping your elbow tucked in to your ribs. Focus on getting a good full range of movement. Pause for 1 second at the top, then, keeping the core muscles tense, slowly return the bar to the start position. Repeat the same movement on the other side.*

Wrist curl

Muscles used Flexors – carpi ulnaris, digitorum, carpi radialis; palmaris longus

1 *Stand or sit with a barbell in each hand, using an underhand grip, hands shoulder-width apart, elbows at 90 degrees.*

2 *With forearms out in front of you, to isolate the forearm and wrist muscles, curl the weight up as far as possible. Pause for 2 seconds.*

Reverse wrist curl

Muscles used Extensors – carpi radialis longus, carpi radialis brevis, carpi ulnaris, indicis, digitorum

1 *Stand or sit with a dumbbell in one hand, using an overhand grip, elbow bent at 90 degrees to help isolate the forearm and wrist.*

2 *Curl the weight up as far as possible, using just the wrist and forearm muscles, and pause for 2 seconds. Repeat with the other arm.*

Hammer wrist curl

Muscles used Extensors – carpi radialis longus, carpi radialis brevis, carpi ulnaris, digitorum

1 *Stand or sit holding the dumbbell in a hammer position, then gradually allow the weight to tilt your wrist away from you.*

2 *Keep the forearm and arm still and use the muscles in the wrist to tilt the dumbbell back up toward you. Pause for a second then lower to the start position.*

Triceps Exercises

All upper-body resistance training that involves pressing movements will also involve the triceps. If you want to build bigger upper arms or press heavier weights, triceps exercises need to be part of your regular routine.

There are three parts to the triceps muscle: the medial head, lateral head and long head. These muscles are positioned at the back of your upper arm and are responsible for extending your upper arm. Always do your chest or shoulder exercises first before training your triceps. If you have a good session on the triceps, and then try to press weights to work your chest or shoulders, you will not achieve very much. Your triceps will be fatigued long before your chest or shoulders have had a good workout. Compared to the chest or shoulder muscles, the triceps are small muscles, so be strict in your technique to ensure that you are working your triceps only and not other larger muscles.

You need to work hard to get bulging triceps. Remember that roughly 70 per cent of your upper arm mass is made up of the triceps. Once you are strong enough, try to include one or two triceps exercises that involve using your body weight as these are often some of the most effective, and can be of most use to you in everyday life and for your sport.

Remember good technique; if your technique is poor you will be recruiting other muscles such as your chest and shoulders, which will not develop the triceps. For each exercise, take 2 to 3 seconds for each direction of the movement. Breathe out at the beginning of the movement, and breathe in as you return to the start position.

Exercises to build bigger triceps	
Exercise	**Sets and repetitions**
Triceps dip	5 x max
Triceps bench dip	5 x max
Cable push-down	3 x 8–10
Reverse cable push-down	3 x 10
Overhead cable triceps extension	3 x 10

Triceps bench dip

Muscles used Triceps brachii – long head, lateral head, medial head; anconeus

1 *Grip the edge of the bench, with the back of your hands facing forward at your sides, arms fully extended to suspend your body weight. Keep your feet flat on the floor in front of you.*

2 *Lower your body toward the floor, bending your elbows behind you, at 90 degrees. Pause for 1 second, then return to the start position. As you get stronger, take feet farther away from you.*

Triceps dip

Muscles used Triceps brachii – long head, lateral head and medial head; anconeus; pectoralis major

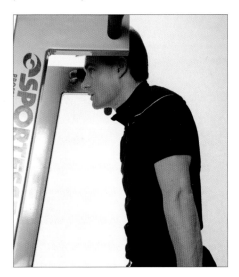 

1 *Grip the handles of the machine, with an overhand grip, your legs hanging under you. Keep your elbows tucked in to isolate your triceps. Fully extend your arms to suspend your body weight from the machine.*

2 *Lower your body toward the floor, bending your elbows behind you at 90 degrees. If your elbows are wide apart, you will work the pectorals. Pause for a second, then push yourself back up to the start position.*

Cable push-down

Muscles used Triceps brachii – long head, lateral head and medial head

1 *Use a lighter weight than you think you need to isolate and work the triceps. Grip the bar with an overhand grip, with hands just less than shoulder-width apart, and your arms bent at 90 degrees. Tuck your elbows in against your ribs. Don't let your shoulders rise up.*

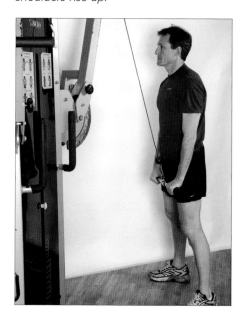

2 *Fully extend your arms, keeping the elbows locked in to your ribs, until your hands are down in front of your legs. Pause for 1 second, then slowly bend your arms, allowing the bar to raise. Open your grip at the bottom of the movement when your arms are in full extension to work your triceps harder.*

Reverse cable push-down

Muscles used Triceps brachii – long head, lateral head and medial head; anconeus; extensors – carpi radialis brevis, digitorum, carpi ulnaris and carpi radialis longus

1 *Grip the bar with an underhand grip, with your hands just less than shoulder-width apart, and arms bent at 90 degrees. Tuck your elbows in closely against your ribs throughout the whole movement.*

2 *Fully extend your arms until your hands are down in front of your legs. Pause for 1 second, then slowly bend your arms, allowing the bar to raise. Pause for longer at full extension to get a good burn on the triceps.*

Overhead cable triceps extensions

Muscles used Triceps brachii – long head, lateral head and medial head

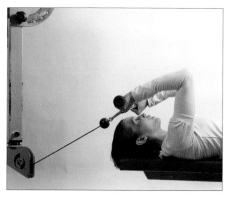

1 *Lie on the bench and grip the bar from behind your head with an overhand grip. Pull it forward so that your arms are bent at 90 degrees and the bar is roughly in line with the front of your head. Your elbows should be facing forward and in a fixed position.*

2 *Bring the bar forward in front of you by fully extending your arms, keeping your elbows as close together as possible. Pause for 1 second on full extension and then bend at the elbow to allow the bar to return to the start position.*

Specific triceps exercises

Many bodybuilders in the past have not used specific triceps exercises and have managed to get away with it because the triceps are involved in so many other exercises, especially chest presses and shoulder presses. Now, however, most bodybuilders do exercises specifically to isolate the triceps and give them that ripped look. The danger is that the triceps can easily be overtrained, especially as they are much smaller than other pressing muscles such as the chest and shoulders. So, avoid making the mistake of thinking that your triceps need to be trained more than your biceps because they make up a bigger percentage of the overall size of your arm when so many exercises work the triceps anyway.

The triceps are a three-headed muscle complex that originates in the shoulder and attaches to the forearm after passing over the top of the elbow. Their function is to straighten your arm from a bent position. They can be worked by moving your arm in an arc in front of you until it is straight down by your side, and also function during pressing movements above the chest or the shoulders.

For really ripped triceps, focus on isolation exercises and spend time on cables, which provide continuous tension throughout the entire movement. It is important to feel the muscle you are isolating, yet many people cheat on triceps exercises by allowing their elbows to move back and forth, making their shoulders and back do the work instead of their triceps. You may need to use a lighter weight than you think you need to achieve proper isolation of the muscle.

For each exercise, take 2 to 3 seconds for each direction of the movement. Breathe out at the beginning of the movement; breathe in as you return to the start position.

Exercises to isolate triceps

Exercise	Sets and repetitions
Triceps press-up	5 x max
Overhead triceps extension	3 x 8–10
Lying-down triceps extension	3 x 8–10
Single-arm cable triceps push-down	3 x 8–10

Single-arm cable triceps push-down

Muscles used Triceps brachii – long head, lateral head and medial head; anconeus

1 *Hold the cable handle in one arm using an overhand grip, with your arm bent at 90 degrees and forearms out in front of you. Keep your elbows close to your ribs. Your other arm should rest at your side. Don't let your shoulders rise up in the movement – keep them level and don't let your body twist to help with the movement.*

2 *Fully extend your arm in a downward direction until your arms are straight and the handle is by your side. Pause for 1 second then slowly allow the arm to bend back up to the starting position at 90 degrees. Hold the full extension for more than 1 second if you want to get even better recruitment of all the tricep muscles.*

Triceps press-up

Muscles used Triceps brachii – long head, lateral head and medial head; anconeus

1 *Assume the standard press-up position, with hands on the floor, just less than shoulder-width apart, and fingers facing forward. Hold your body up with straight arms. The toes should touch the floor with heels raised.*

2 *Bend your arms to lower your body, keeping your elbows tucked in close to your ribs. Once the elbows are at 90 degrees pause for 1 second, then press back up extending the arms. This isolates the triceps by using your own body weight.*

Overhead triceps extension

Muscles used Triceps brachii – long head, lateral head and medial head

1 *Hold a dumbbell, with an interlocking grip. Slowly take the dumbbell over the top of your head, fully extending your arms. Hold the dumbbell in this position for a few seconds then go on to do step 2. Don't forget to co-ordinate your breathing with the movement and ensure that you are standing in a comfortable position and well balanced.*

2 *Slowly lower the dumbbell behind your head until your arms are bent at 90 degrees. Keep your elbows as close together as possible. Once your elbows go out to the side, you are at the lowest point your flexibility will allow you to go or the weight is too heavy. Pause for 1 second, then push the dumbbell back up above your head by fully extending your arms.*

Lying-down triceps extension

Muscles used Triceps brachii – long head, lateral head and medial head; anconeus

1 *Lie on your back on a flat bench so that your back, shoulders, neck and head are supported. Hold a barbell with an overhand grip, hands no more than shoulder-width apart, up above your shoulders, straight arms, elbows facing forward.*

2 *Keeping your back flat and your feet on the floor, slowly lower the barbell toward your face until your arms are bent at 90 degrees. Pause for 1 second then extend the arm back to the starting position.*

Abdominal Exercises: General

The abdominals are possibly the most important muscles to train in your body. The following exercises, along with the correct techniques to use, provide an effective workout for the full range of abdominal muscles that you need to exercise.

The abdominals, which cover a large area of the mid-section of your body, enable your torso to bend forward and sideways, and to twist. Before you start lifting heavy weights, you need sufficient abdominal training to prevent lower-back injuries. To benefit fully from your training, change the exercises regularly.

These exercises mainly work the rectus abdominis, a large, flat muscle covering the entire front of the abdomen between the lower ribcage and the hips. It contracts to flex your body at the waist and tenses as soon as you start to bring your shoulders and head forward. Sit-ups and leg-raising exercises work the rectus abdominus throughout the entire movement.

For each exercise, take 2 to 3 seconds for each direction of the movement. Breathe out at the beginning of the movement, and breathe in as you return to the start position.

Below: Rectus abdominis, external and internal obliques and the transverse abdominis are the abdominal muscles that support the trunk and hold the organs in place.

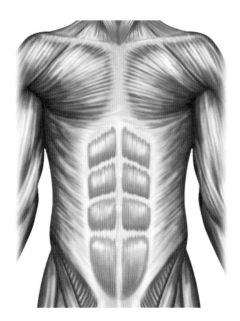

Sit-up

Muscles used Rectus abdominis; obliques – external and internal

1 *Lie on your back and bend your knees to 90 degrees and place your feet flat on the floor. Put your hands behind your head and elbows back out to the sides.*

2 *Tense your abdominals and raise your head, shoulders and upper back off the floor. Pause for 1 second, then lower yourself back down. Keep the abdominals tense throughout.*

Sit-up technique
• Keep your feet on the ground or get your training partner to hold them on the floor. Or, put dumbbells on top of your feet.
• If your neck is weak, tuck your chin in to your chest so it does not move during the exercise.
• Keep your elbows back out to the sides to make the exercise harder.
• You do not need to sit-up – if your abdominals are working, a small movement is enough.

Sit-up with Russian twist

Muscles used Rectus abdominis; obliques – external and internal.

1 *Lie on your back and bend your knees to 90 degrees and place your feet flat on the floor, with your arms up vertically in front of your chest.*

2 *Tense your abdominals and raise your head, shoulders and upper back off the floor. As you sit up, twist your upper body to one side, pause for 1 second, then twist back to straight before slowly returning to the start position. Keep your elbows back out to the sides so that your abdominals will be made to work harder during the movement.*

Exercises to build abdominals for beginners

Exercise	Sets and repetitions
Sit-up	3 x 10
crunch	3 x 10
Sit-up with Russian twist	3 x 10
Reverse crunch with alternate legs bent	3 x 20

Crunch

Muscles used Rectus abdominis; obliques – external and internal

1 *Lie on your back and bend your knees to 90 degrees, lifting the feet off the floor. Put your hands behind your head and your elbows back out to the sides. Tense your abdominals.*

2 *Crunch your knees in and raise your head, shoulders and upper back off the floor. At the top of the crunch pause for 2 seconds, then return to the start position, abdominals still tense.*

Reverse crunch with bent legs

Muscles used Rectus abdominis; external oblique; tensor fascia lata

1 *Lie on your back. Keeping your abdominals tense, pull your legs in toward your abdomen until they are bent at 90 degrees.*

2 *Lower your legs until they are almost parallel to the floor, pause for a second, then return to the start position.*

Reverse crunch with alternate legs bent

Muscles used Rectus abdominis; external oblique; tensor fascia lata

1 *For the starting position, lie on your back and raise your legs, keeping your abdominals tense. Place your hands, palms facing down, flat on the floor, out to your sides in line with your hips.*

2 *Pull one leg in toward your abdomen until the lower part is almost parallel to the floor. Pause for 1 second, then return to the start. Repeat with the other leg. In this way, both sides of your abdominals are working equally.*

Abdominal Exercises: Bodybuilding

For bodybuilders, the abdominals are probably the most important part of their physique. In bodybuilding competitions, judges pay most attention to the contestants' abdominals, looking to see if they are tight, well built and clearly defined.

Great abdominals are a sign of good preparation and dedication to training regularly and appropriately. People often see abdominals as a key indicator of just how fit someone actually is. However, more importantly, abdominals play a crucial role in supporting other working muscles in the body and provide the central support to the back. Many lower-back injuries can be prevented if the abdominals are strong enough to take the stress away from the back. If you do have a back injury, you can reduce back pain through abdominal exercises. Making the abdominal muscles recruit and support your back also massively reduces the work your back has to do.

For each exercise, take 2 to 3 seconds for each direction of the movement. Breathe out at the beginning of the movement, and breathe in as you return to the start position.

Hanging leg raise with twist

Muscles used Rectus – abdominis, femoris; tensor fascia lata; iliopsoas – psoas minor, psoas major and iliacus; obliques – external and internal

1 *Grip a chin-up bar. Hang from the bar, with arms and legs straight to work the abdominals. Tense your abdominals.*

2 *Pull your legs up toward your chest, twisting them to one side to work the abdominals. Pause, then lower them.*

Hanging leg raise

Muscles used Rectus – abdominis, femoris, tensor fascia lata; iliopsoas – psoas minor, psoas major and iliacus

1 *Grip a chin-up bar (any grip). Hang from the bar with your arms and legs straight. Tense your abdominals.*

2 *Crunch your legs up until your thighs are parallel to the floor. Keep your abdominals tensed. Pause for a second, then lower your legs back down.*

Session to build pronounced abdominals	
Exercise	**Sets and repetitions**
Hanging leg raise	3 x 10–20
Crunch	3 x 20–30
Reverse crunch	3 x 20–30
Rope crunch with twist	3 x 20–30
V-crunch	3 x 20–30

Tense abdominals
During both of these hanging leg raises with twist exercises, be aware of how your body moves. It should not swing at any point during the movement. If it does swing, it means that your abdominals are not sufficiently tensed to do their job properly.

Rope crunch

Muscles used Rectus abdominis; external oblique

1 Kneel down, facing the cable machine. Hold the rope and pull it down until it is in front of you at eye height. Lock your arms in this position. Keep the pace of the movement slow so that momentum doesn't take over.

2 Tense your abdominals to keep your back straight and bring the rope down in front of you as far as your abdominals will let you go. Try not to let any part of your body move to help the rope down. Make your abdominals do all the work. Pause for 1 second, then, keeping your abdominals tense, slowly return to the start position.

Rope crunch with twist

Muscles used Rectus abdominis; obliques – external and internal

1 Get down on your knees facing the cable machine. Hold the rope and pull it down until it is in front of you at head height. Lock your arms in this position. Tense your abdominals to keep your back straight.

2 Bring the rope down in front of you as far as your abdominals will let you, twisting to one side to make your oblique muscles do the work. Pause for a second, then slowly return to the start position, abdominals still tense.

V-crunch

Muscles used Rectus abdominis; tensor fascia lata; external oblique

1 Lie on your back with your legs straight up in the air and your feet apart, creating a wide V-shape. With your arms straight, hold your hands together out in front of you, fingers fully extended. You do not need to raise your upper body far off the ground to work your abdominals.

2 Tense your abdominals to bring your head, shoulders and upper back off the floor, pushing your hands between your legs. Keep the crunch slow – don't use your lower back muscles to gather momentum. Pause for 1 second at the top of the crunch, then slowly return to the start position, abdominals still tense.

Abdominal Exercises: The Sides

The following exercises will make you use the sides of your abdominals. To bend to the side and rotate your torso in relation to your hips, you use your oblique muscles, which are made up of the internal obliques, transverse obliques and external obliques.

When you are performing these exercises, stay focused on your abs and be careful to avoid any lateral movement in the hips, because this takes the emphasis away from the abdominal muscles.

If you find it hard to avoid the movement in the hips, try sitting with your legs either side of a bench.

This will prevent your hips moving. Or, you can sit on a fit ball and try to keep the ball as still as possible when you bend to the sides.

For each of these exercises, take 2 to 3 seconds for each direction of the movement. Breathe out at the beginning of the movement, and breathe in as you return to the start position.

Exercises to build side abdominals	
Exercise	**Sets and repetitions**
Side crunch	3 x 20–30
Oblique crunch	3 x 20–30
Dumbbell side bend	3 x 20–30
High cable side bend	3 x 20–30

One-leg crossed crunch

Muscles used Rectus abdominis; external oblique

1 *Lie on your back, with your arms out to the sides, your fingers touching the sides of your head. Cross your left leg over your right leg so that your left ankle rests on your right knee. Keep the movement slow, and focus on the abdominals.*

2 *Tense your abdominals and crunch up toward your knees. At the top of the crunch, twist to one side so that you are facing your left knee. Pause for a second, then slowly lower back down. Repeat the movement with the left leg crossed over the right leg. To put emphasis on the obliques, keep the elbows back and hands relaxed. Look the way you are turning to help the rotation.*

Side crunch

Muscles used Rectus abdominis; obliques – external and internal

1 *Lie on your right side, with your legs slightly bent, your left hand behind your head, and your right arm tucked across your body. Stay as side-on as possible to make the crunch more effective.*

2 *Tense your abdominals, keep your feet firmly together and crunch up sideways as far as you can go. Keep your left hand slightly behind your head and your right arm tucked across your body throughout. Turn over and repeat the movement with the opposite side. As long as the obliques are working, the range of movement can be small to begin with.*

Dumbbell side bend

Muscles used Rectus abdominis; obliques – external and internal

1 *Stand with your legs shoulder-width apart and your right hand behind your head. Hold a dumbbell in your left hand, down at your side.*

2 *Keeping your abdominals tense and staying side-on, bend at the hips to lower down to the side that holds the dumbbell. Once the dumbbell is level with your knee, pause for 1 second, then raise your body back up to the start position. Repeat with the other side. As you stretch down, you will be lengthening your abdominals, and on the way back up, you will be contracting them to make them work harder.*

High cable side bend

Muscles used Rectus abdominis; obliques – external and internal

1 *Stand side-on to the cable machine, feet shoulder-width apart. Take hold of the pulley with one hand and hold it at shoulder height, with your arm bent. Let your other hand hang by your side. Keep the arm holding the cable as still as possible to ensure that it is only the abdominals that are doing the work.*

2 *Tense your abdominals and crunch down to the side. Try holding the position at the bottom of the bend for longer to really isolate the correct muscles. Pause at the bottom for 1 second, then slowly come back up to the start position. Repeat the movement on the other side.*

Oblique crunch

Muscles used Rectus abdominis; obliques – external and internal

1 *Lie on your back with your legs bent and over to the left side, your feet placed firmly together. Try to keep your shoulders on the floor and your legs as far over to one side as possible. Place your hands behind your head with your elbows out to the side, with your fingers, fully extended, touching the sides of your head.*

2 *Tense your abdominals and crunch up, keeping your upper body as square-on as possible. Pause for a second at the top of the crunch and then, keeping your abdominals tense, slowly return to the start position. To make the abdominals work harder, tense them equally on the way back to the start as you did on the way up. Repeat on the other side.*

Abdominal Exercises: Rotational

It is important to use abdominal exercises that simulate the types of movements you need to do in everyday life and for your sport. The following exercises involve rotational exercises. Virtually every sporting activity calls for good rotational strength.

You should always maintain your abdominal muscles in tension throughout any exercise. If you can practise this in your strength workouts, you will start to use these muscles without having to make any conscious effort to do so. Get in touch with your abdominal muscles mentally – you need to learn how to recruit them and how to isolate the different abdominal muscles with various exercises.

When you train your abdominals, you should feel a burn and as you train harder, the burn should intensify. As your abdominal muscles get stronger, you will feel the burn even more as they work that bit harder. Your abdominals should feel pumped up after a workout, just like any other body part you have been training.

Be careful not to attempt too many repetitions. If your abdominal muscles get tired, you will start to use your lower back, which can lead to back injuries and overdevelopment of the lower-back muscles. To avoid using your lower back, always keep your abdominals tensed as you return to the start position in any abdominal exercise. The negative phase of the movement can make a massive difference in your abdominal development.

For each of these exercises, take 2 to 3 seconds for each direction of the movement. Breathe out at the beginning of the movement; breathe in as you return to the start position.

Excercises to tone and build rotational strength	
Exercise	**Sets and repetitions**
Hanging leg raise with a twist	3 x 10–20
Broomstick twist	3 x 30–40
Kneeling cable rotation	3 x 30–40
Alternating leg crunch	3 x 20–30

Alternating leg crunch

Muscles used Rectus abdominis; obliques – external and internal; tensor fascia lata; quadriceps

1 *Lie on your back, with your arms out to the sides, your fingers touching the sides of your head. Raise both legs up in the air at 90 degrees so that your calves are parallel to the floor. Keep your feet firmly together. Ensure that the movement is slow and under control to make your abdominals do all the work.*

2 *Straighten your right leg and crunch up with a twist, bringing your right elbow toward your left knee. When your elbow touches your knee, pause for 2 seconds, then return to the start position. Repeat with the other side. To make this exercise harder, try performing it on a slight incline.*

Leg criss-cross

Muscles used Rectus abdominis; obliques – external and internal; tensor fascia lata; quadriceps

1 *Lie on your back with your legs on the floor stretched straight out in front of you. Put your hands by your sides, with your palms flat on the floor, for added stability. Press your back flat against the floor throughout the movement.*

2 *Lift your legs into the air and criss-cross them, alternating right over left and left over right. Keep your hands by your sides. To check that your lower abdominals are working, put your fingers under your lower back. You will feel it pushing against your fingers.*

Kneeling cable rotation

Muscles used Rectus abdominis; obliques – external and internal

1 Kneel on the floor, side-on to one side of the cable machine. Keeping your arms straight and together in a V shape and your lower body straight from the abdomen down, grip the handle firmly with both hands.

2 Tense your abdominals and rotate at the waist, taking your arms from one side to the other in a semicircular movement. When you have rotated through 180 degrees, pause for 1 second, then return – again through a semicircular movement – to the start position.

Machine trunk rotation

Muscles used Rectus abdominis; obliques – external and internal

1 Sit on the machine and wrap your arms around the supports to keep yourself facing forward. Emphasize the abdominals throughout the movement.

2 Tense your core muscles and rotate from one side to the other, keeping the movement smooth. Try not to move the hips and shoulders too much.

Broomstick twist

Muscles used Rectus abdominis; obliques – external and internal

1 Stand with your feet shoulder-width apart so that you feel well balanced. Hold a broomstick or similar lightweight pole behind your head, across the back of your shoulders.

2 Keeping your feet firmly shoulder-width apart, rotate your upper body from one side to the other, keeping your hips as still as possible so that you can put more emphasis on the obliques.

FLEXIBILITY AND INJURIES

Pre-exercise and post-exercise stretches are essential to avoid exercise-related injuries, to keep your muscles long and relaxed after training, and to allow them to recover for your next training session. This chapter combines flexibility exercises for all parts of the body with a self-help guide to common training injuries. It is not, however, a substitute for medical advice. When injured, always see a doctor. Include a variety of flexibility exercises in your routine to stretch your muscles from different angles.

Above: Even with the maximum body protection, some sports are liable to cause more injury.
Left: Injuries can occur at any time and any place.

The Importance of Flexibility

Flexibility training is one of the most frequently ignored and least understood areas of most fitness routines. You should, however, treat it with all the seriousness and commitment that you would accord any other part of your training routine.

There are a number of reasons why flexibility is essential. If, to give one example, your calf muscles are tight before you start a 10km/6.2-mile race or training session, then you are far more likely to suffer from cramps and muscle tears. If you play contact sports, such as American football or rugby, and you go hard into a tackle, your neck may be vulnerable if you don't have a good range of movement – a stiff neck will put the muscles and tendons under significant pressure.

If you are a swimmer with limited mobility around the shoulder joint, the result will be poor technique, a weak performance and likelihood of injury.

Stretching to remain flexible is not a new concept for your body. Everyone is born with great flexibility but as we get older we become less and less flexible due to lack of activity, sitting for long periods of time, and injuries from everyday life and sport. Everyone needs to be flexible.

What is flexibility?
You may often hear the word 'flexibility' used in relation to fitness training, but what is it? It is the range of mobility around a joint and the muscles that surround it. Flexibility training should: reduce the risk of injury; create a good range of movement (especially as a muscle reaches its outer limits of movement); improve the movement around a joint; reduce muscular ache; increase co-ordination; increase blood flow circulation; break down scar tissue from general and overuse injuries; and equip the body to cope with the demands of a specific type of training or sport.

Sit and reach
The most commonly used test of flexibility is the sit and reach test. Thanks to the ample amount of research that has been carried out on the subject, it is fairly easy to compare yourself with other people. As a test, it illustrates the level of flexibility in your hamstrings and lower back. Studies show that there is direct correlation between flexibility in the hamstrings and the lower back, with muscular pain in the lower back, gait limitation and the risk of falling in older adults. (American College of Sports Medicine 1998.)

Use a sit and reach test box or simply make your own using a box and a solid ruler. Place the soles of your feet up

Left: The sit and reach test assesses the flexibility of the back and the hamstrings, at the back of the thigh.

Below left: To keep muscle flexibility during your training, stop now and again to do some stretches.

Sit and reach test
This simple test is a reliable measure of the flexibility of the hamstrings and the lower back.

	Male	Female
Very poor	−20cm/−7¾in	−15cm/−6 in
Poor	−19 to 9cm/−7½ to 3½in	−14 to 8cm/−5½ to 3in
Fair	−8 to 1cm/−3 to ⅓in	−7 to 0cm/−2¾ to 0in
Average	0 to 5cm/0 to 2in	1 to 10cm/⅓ to 4in
Good	6 to 16cm/2⅓ to 6¼in	11 to 20cm/4⅓ to 7¾in
Excellent	17 to 27cm/6⅔ to 10½in	21 to 30cm/8¼ to 12in
Superior	27cm+/10½in+	30cm+/12in+

Flexibility test

Before you undertake a stretching programme in your warm-up and cool-down, you should test your flexibility so that you are aware of areas of particular weakness.

against the box and then, with your arms out in front of you and your legs straight, slowly reach forward along the ruler. After three attempts at stretching forward, you should be at your farthest point. The point where your fingers touch the ruler or box is your score (if you don't make it beyond your toes, you receive a negative score). The ruler should read zero where the soles of your feet are in contact with the box. Compare your score with the data in the box to see how flexible you are. Be aware that warm-up will make a massive difference to your flexibility, so always use the same warm-up before you do the test. About 5 minutes of cardiovascular exercise would be suitable.

When to stretch

You should try to stretch before and after every training session or competition. Before you begin any activity, warm up

Below: After you have completed your training programme, do some stretches to aid recovery.

first with some cardiovascular exercise to promote blood flow and heat in the muscles. For example, if you intend going for a 10km/6-mile run, do 5 minutes' fast walking. Follow this with 5 minutes of stretches, paying particular attention to your hamstrings, quadriceps and calf muscles. After the run, do static stretches in your cool-down. If you are intending to lift heavy weights, do 5 minutes' easy warm-up on the

Below: Stretching is beneficial to everyone, whatever their level of fitness or their age.

Above: When you begin any major training, always include stretches in your warm-up.

rowing machine before you do dynamic or proprioceptive muscular facilitation stretches (PMF stretching), paying particular attention to the muscle regions you may use. For example, before a chest weights session, stretch the pectorals, triceps and lower back. After the weights session, do static stretches to help lengthen the muscles back to full movement and decrease the risk of injury.

Educate yourself to avoid injury

Most muscular injuries are caused by lack of flexibility and poor core stability. When you are injured, take time to seek professional advice and learn as much as possible about the injury to ensure it doesn't happen again. Follow the basic RICES principle for all your sporting injuries to help get you back to full fitness as soon as possible:

R = Rest
I = Ice
C = Compress
E = Elevate
S = Stabilize

Types of Flexibility

The different types of stretching that should be included in you training programme are static active stretching, static passive stretching, ballistic stretching, isometric stretching and proprioceptive muscular facilitation.

Everyone wants to achieve greater flexibility in the shortest time possible, with minimum pain and risk, so that they can get on with their fitness training programme. The good news is that you can – and you don't need to get yourself into bizarre contortions as if you were auditioning for the circus in order to do so.

There are a number of different types of stretches that are suitable for inclusion in your training programme. First, though, you need to understand how the following types of stretches can help you, when it is appropriate to do them, and what exactly is meant by terms such as 'static active stretching', 'static passive stretching', 'dynamic stretching', 'ballistic stretching', 'isometric stretching' and 'proprioceptive muscular facilitation stretching' (PMF stretching).

When deciding which technique to use, think about the range of movement you are trying to achieve, and always use a variety of stretches to improve your flexibility. It is important to remember that stretching should not be painful. Simply getting into the correct stretching position and starting to feel the tension in the right muscle is enough. Some types of stretching are more aggressive than others, for example dynamic stretching or ballistic stretching. Before you do any of these types of stretches, make sure you warm up for at least 10–15 minutes in order to get adequate blood flow and heat in the muscles.

When not to stretch?

In some situations it may be best not to do any stretches. If you feel any discomfort in the muscle from an injury, leave the injury for at least 48 hours and consult a physician to determine whether it is safe to begin stretching the muscle. Avoid stretching areas that are suffering from muscular and ligament strains or areas of recent fractures. If you are at all unsure, get expert advice.

Static active stretching

This is a method of stretching muscles with minimal movement. An example would be placing one leg on a step and holding it there for 30 seconds. This is the best form of stretching for a cool-down after your training to help re-align the muscles and promote good blood flow. This type of stretch uses the opposing muscles to hold the stretch.

Static passive stretching

This stretch will increase the range of movement of a muscle. Unlike static active stretching, you will need to use an external force to stretch the muscle. Static passive stretching is best used after training or competition to realign the muscle fibres. It is often used for the rehabilitation of torn muscles.

> **Build in flexibility**
> To get the most out of exercise, it is important to get an understanding of which stretches and types of flexibility are going to be good for you.
>
> Flexibility is as necessary as any other training. Without a good programme of flexibility exercises, you will be more prone to injury. Injuries mean less training, or even no training as a result. So there are no excuses – make flexibility a vital part of your fitness training programme.

Hold a towel around your foot to pull it up by stretching your hamstrings. Hold the stretch for 20 to 30 seconds.

Dynamic stretching

This is a good way to warm up – but not after injury, as it could cause further damage. It uses training movements, such as lunges and squats, to warm up and stretch the muscles you will use in the activity. Your body's movement and momentum create the stretch. Ensure that your heart rate has been elevated for at least 10 minutes for sufficient blood flow and heat in the muscles.

Proprioceptive muscular facilitation (PMF) stretching

This is commonly used in sports that require a larger range of movement, such as ballet and gymnastics. It involves a muscle being stretched by a partner. It is perhaps one of the most advanced forms of stretching and can often promote the best results. When contracting the muscles being stretched, do so for only 5 to 6 seconds, then stretch again for 10 seconds.

This lunge with rotation has some momentum to get a good dynamic stretch. Maintaining your balance while stretching is important.

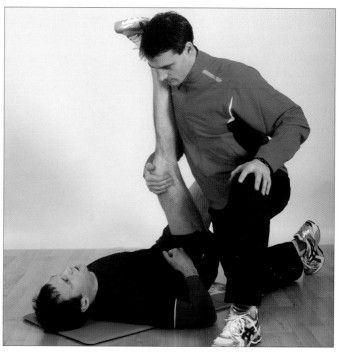

Have your training partner stretch your hamstrings until they reach stretching point. Resist by contracting your hamstrings to try to force your partner's arm back.

Isometric stretching

This uses the contraction of the muscle to stretch muscle fibres that are not being stretched in a normal passive stretch. Following the stretch, allow the quadriceps to contract for 3 to 5 seconds to wake up any fibres that are not being stretched. This creates a greater stretch response in the muscle fibres. When a muscle is contracted during exercise, not all the fibres are contracting; some are at rest. When a muscle is being stretched, some muscle fibres are elongated and some are not. During an isometric contraction, the muscle fibres will be pulled from both ends by the contracting muscles, so the resting fibres are stretched.

Lie on your front and have your training partner bend your leg up behind you to stretch your quadriceps muscles.

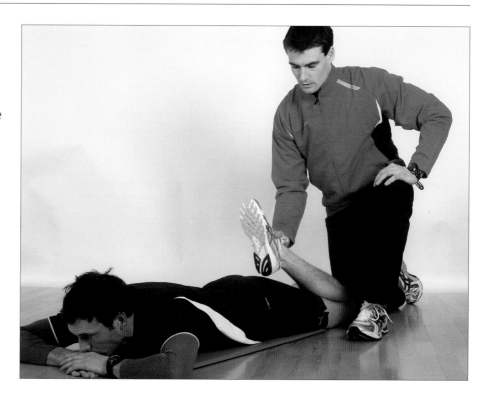

Shoulders

The shoulder joint has many moving parts, with muscles pulling from every direction, making it susceptible to injury. Because it has a large range of motion, and tends to be unstable, tears and inflammation can easily occur.

The shoulder joint is supported by ligaments, tendons and muscles. If these tissues are underused, overused or injured during a sporting activity, it is likely to affect your range of movement. The position of the shoulder may seem different to normal. There are many types of shoulder injury, the common ones are rotator cuff injury, impingement syndrome, frozen shoulder syndrome and winged scapular.

Rotator cuff injury

There are two different types of rotator cuff injuries. One is an acute sudden tear and the other is a chronic tear that happens over a longer period of time. The sudden tear might be from throwing a baseball or a fast punch. The chronic tear will begin as a dull pain that gradually worsens. The pain may start in the shoulder and gradually go down the arm, perhaps preventing you from moving your arm out to the side or above your head.

Impingement syndrome

This type of shoulder injury is commonly known as swimmer's shoulder or thrower's shoulder because it is often triggered off by the overuse of the shoulder in front crawl swimming or overhead throwing activities. The tendons of the rotator cuff become inflamed and don't have enough room for proper movement as they go through a narrow space called the subacromial space. Weak stabilization of the shoulder is the cause of impingement syndrome, and the best form of rehabilitation involves exercises for stabilizing the shoulder. Using a thera band is a good way to start rehabilitating a shoulder injured in this way. For both of these injuries, you should stretch your shoulder at least five times a day to help maintain the shoulder's full range of movement.

Common shoulder injuries

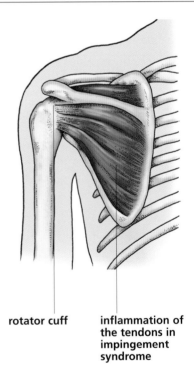

rotator cuff

inflammation of the tendons in impingement syndrome

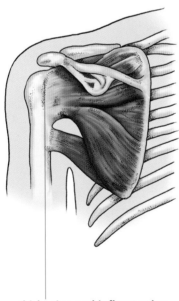

thickening and inflammation of the capsule causing pain and lack of movement

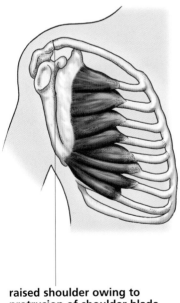

raised shoulder owing to protrusion of shoulder blade

Impingement syndrome

Site of rotator cuff and impingement syndrome. The rotator cuff is vital for shoulder stability. Impingement syndrome is inflammation of the tendon, usually caused by overuse of the shoulder such as throwing a ball or swimming. Exercises using a thera band can help the injury.

Frozen shoulder

In the condition of frozen shoulder, the shoulder capsule thickens and eventually it is difficult to get any movement. Frozen shoulder can be extremely painful and movement in the shoulder is restricted. Regular stretching a few times a day can increase the range of movement.

Winged scapular

In the condition called winged scapular, the shoulder blade sticks out at the back causing the top of the shoulder to be elevated. The cause is usually an accident that damages a nerve that keeps the shoulder stable. Strength training and thera band exercises will help to remedy the problem.

Frozen shoulder syndrome

Despite years of medical research, there is, as yet, no specific explanation for the painful frozen shoulder syndrome. Internally, the lining of the shoulder capsule may thicken and cause scar tissue to form, which will then restrict the movement of the top of the arm bone. It is more common in men over 40, and in women generally. Poor posture and rounding of the shoulders may be a contributing factor. Eventually the pain in the shoulder will restrict sideways movement of the arm and any movements above the head, hence the term 'frozen shoulder'.

Rehabilitation will involve thawing out the shoulder in order to regain a full range of movement, which could take more than 12 months. Stretch the shoulder five times a day to maintain the range of movement in the shoulder.

Winged scapular

This is a visible injury – your shoulder blade will protrude at the back and cause the top of your shoulder to be elevated. This type of injury is most likely to be caused by sudden aggressive movements or accidents. The scapular becomes winged because the long thoracic nerve, which supplies the serratus anterior muscle, is damaged and can no longer hold the muscle in the correct position. This can be a painful condition, for example, there may be pressure on the scapular from the back of a chair. Also there can be limited elevation. In most cases, once the nerve has settled down, strength training is required, with back exercises to stabilize the scapular, such as single-arm cable rows, single-arm dumbbell rows, and bent-over rows. Use a thera band initially, working up to using cables and dumbbells.

Stretching and flexibility

Your shoulder muscles carry the weight of your arms all day and are therefore prone to fatigue and tightness. In addition to having to hold your arms up, the shoulder joint has to be able to rotate through 360 degrees, so flexibility in the muscles surrounding the shoulder joint is essential. Your shoulders should be pulled back for correct posture and to prevent problems with the rotator cuff inside the muscle. Also, pushing your shoulders back promotes even deeper breathing. Sitting all day with poor core-stability muscles and hands held forward on computer keyboards drags your shoulders up and forward, so do regular shoulder stretches throughout the day to prevent this.

Most gym users want to work their chest muscles, which normally involves some pressing exercises above the chest. This movement also contracts the muscles at the front of the shoulders and pulls them forward. Always stretch the shoulder muscles after these types of movements to counteract muscle shortening and keep it at optimum length.

Testing for flexibility

To test your shoulder flexibility, stand upright with your arms down by your sides, then slowly raise one arm, keeping it straight and your palm facing inward until it is beside your head. You should be able to take your hand through 180 degrees for good shoulder flexibility.

Cross body stretch

This stretches the outside of the shoulder and arm. Repeat three to four times at regular intervals. If you feel pain, stop doing the excercise and try again at a later date.

Place the left arm straight across your chest and, with your right hand on the elbow, pull it across your body. Hold the position for 10 seconds. Repeat with your right arm.

Overhead shoulder stretch

Repeat this stretch three to five times to get a good stretch around the shoulders and upper back.

Hold your hands together with your arms straight above your head, pushing upward and backward. When your arms are at full stretch, hold the position for 10 seconds, then slowly bring your arms back down in front of you.

Swimmer's shoulder stretch

This stretch is a test of shoulder flexibility. Repeat three to five times for a good stretch. You can also do it against a wall.

Stretch your arm and place the palm of your hand flat against the floor. Press as close to the floor as possible – your armpit should almost be touching the floor. Hold for 10 seconds, then release.

Neck

Tight muscles in the back of your neck can cause your chin to push forward, while tight muscles in the front of the neck and top of the chest will drag your head forward and downward. Flexibility is important to help avoid overuse injuries and sports injuries.

Hands-up stretch

1 *Stand, with your feet hip-width apart, and your back flat against the wall, and position your arms up at 90 degrees, in a shoulder press position, with the back of your arms and hands flat on the wall.*

2 *Try to push your arms upward, keeping them against the wall all the time. Do not tense your neck. At maximum stretch, hold the position for 10 seconds, then slowly release.*

Thera band stretch

1 *Thera bands help you to follow a program using a suitable resistance level. Wrap the band around your hand.*

2 *Gently pull toward you and behind you. After a shoulder injury, use a thera band to strengthen the muscles.*

Sedentary lifestyles – such as those that involve staring at computer screens all day and overusing your neck muscles to hold your head in one position for long periods of time – will give you strong neck muscles but may put your head in the wrong position. The neck muscles then become stronger than they should be. While lifting heavy objects, the brain tells the body to recruit the neck muscles first before other muscles. If this happens, try to do more exercise and regular neck stretches to prevent the neck from tightening under muscular strain, and to keep it at optimum length.

Use these flexibility exercises to lengthen your neck muscles and position your head so that it is aligned with your pelvis to give you correct posture. At work, change your position regularly and ensure that you take time to do these neck flexibility exercises.

To check neck flexibility, stand upright, holding your arms down at your sides, with the shoulders back and down. Turn your head to look over your shoulder as far as possible before it starts to get uncomfortable.

Forward neck stretch

Keeping your back straight, slowly lower your chin toward your chest and hold the position for 10 seconds then slowly bring your head back up.

Sideways neck stretch

Take 4 to 5 seconds for each direction of the movement and repeat five to ten times. For a greater stretch, lean your head to one side, then raise the opposite shoulder up, then slowly down.

1 *Stand upright, head straight and your arms hanging down by your sides.*

2 *Slowly lean your head over to one side and hold for 10 seconds before slowly bringing the head back up to the straight position.*

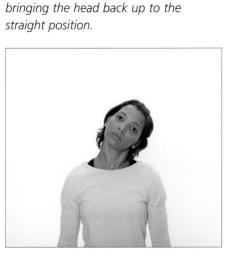

3 *Slowly lean your head over to the other side and hold for 10 seconds before slowly bringing the head back up to the straight position.*

Neck rotation

If possible, have your training partner massage your neck as you are doing this rotation. This should create a better stretch, as your muscles will feel much more relaxed.

1 *Stand upright, head straight and your arms hanging down by your sides.*

2 *Very slowly rotate your head so that you are looking over your left shoulder, hold for 5 seconds. Keep the movement smooth, without jerking the head.*

3 *Slowly rotate back through the start position to the other side, and hold again for 5 seconds. Repeat five to ten times to each side.*

Neck and shoulder stretch

With this exercise, you can get your training partner to hold your arms back to achieve a greater stretch. You could also adopt the PMF stretch principle for this stretch.

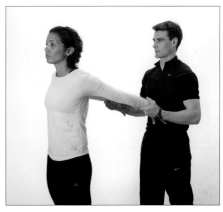

1 *Hold your arms straight by your side, with your training partner behind you.*

2 *Let your partner take your arms back behind you and hold them gently until you can feel the front of your shoulders being stretched.*

3 *After 10 seconds, your partner should let go of your arms, allowing them to return to the start position. Repeat five to ten times.*

Back

The muscles in your back are some of the strongest in your body but you still need to look after them. The following exercises will help you to keep them flexible, allow them to recover from regular exercise and avoid injury.

Cross-hand hanging reach

This is one of the most relaxing stretches you can do. Repeat three to five times.

1 *Keeping your arms straight, and your feet firmly on the floor, hip-width apart, grip the frame of a weight machine with your hands crossed over.*

2 *Push your hips out behind until you feel the stretch in your upper back muscles. Hold for 10 seconds before slowly bringing yourself back up to the bar.*

Reaching forward stretch

Repeat three to five times.

Grip your hands together, then stretch your arms straight out in front of you at chest height, rounding your upper back. Hold the position for 10 seconds.

Single-arm back stretch

This isolates the muscles of one arm and one side of the back. Repeat three to five times.

1 *Holding all your weight with one arm, and your feet hip-width apart, grip a weight machine.*

2 *Lean back. When you feel the stretch in your upper back, hold the position for 10 seconds, then slowly straighten up.*

Bent-forward stretch

Repeat three to five times.

Bend at the hip toward the floor until you feel the stretch in your lower back and hamstrings. Hold for 10 seconds. Repeat.

Hanging stretch

This stretch will not only stretch out your lower back but also your arms and abdominals. Repeat three to five times each side.

1 *Hang from a chin-up bar, gripping with both hands. Hold the position for about 10 seconds, then relax.*

2 *Gently rotate, twisting to the left, holding the stretch for 5 to 10 seconds. Relax for a few seconds then repeat.*

3 *Twist back to the right, holding the stretch for 5 to 10 seconds. Relax for a few seconds then repeat.*

Common back conditions

The back is prone to painful conditions as a result of overuse or muscular imbalances in other areas of muscle.

Lower back muscle pain

This may be the result of overuse, such as rowing twice as far as normal or a massive increase in weight-bearing exercise. Sometimes, sudden movements can cause lower back pain when the muscles in the lower back are not warmed up, for example, bending over to bathe a baby. The baby may not be heavy but the muscles that need to recruit in the lower back are not switched on.

Your back is very strong but, occasionally, if you make it work too hard, and don't have the necessary abdominal and core strength, your back will respond by going into spasm. These spasms may also be the result of poor posture or poor technique – if a spinal joint is injured, the muscle surrounding the joint goes into spasm as a natural response to stop the injured joint moving. When you experience lower back pain, consult a doctor for treatment to relieve the pain. Once the pain has started to subside, do stretches every 2 hours. When you are pain free, do abdominal exercises to prevent the injury recurring.

Scoliosis

This is a curving of the spine, which is often caused by overuse of one side of the body. Participation in sports such as rowing, racket sports and throwing sports are the main causes. For example, if you hit a ball all day with a tennis racket in your right hand, the muscles on that side of the body will become much stronger and more developed than the muscles on the other side of the body. This will make the spine form into an 'S' shape and will cause pain in the back muscles. Do regular stretches on both sides of the body to prevent the muscles getting tight and pulling the spine in one direction. To help prevent the injury in the first place, or prevent it from happening again, do the sporting activity using the opposite side of the body to keep the muscle balance. For example, throw the baseball with your non-throwing arm, or row on the left side of the boat instead of the right.

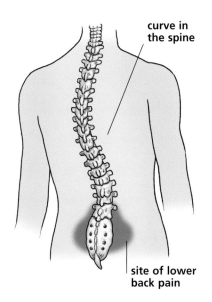

curve in the spine

site of lower back pain

Above: Overuse of one side of the body causes scoliosis, a curving of the spine. Muscles in spasm cause back pain.

Floor rocks

This is a great way to help the spine relax and release muscular tension in the vertebrae. Repeat three to five times.

Lie on the floor on your back, take hold of your knees with both arms and pull them into your chest. Gently rock forward and backward ten times, keeping your abdominals tense all the time.

Back roll-up

Straighten your legs and take them over the head to create a strong stretch. Repeat three to five times.

Lie on your back with your arms flat to the floor, palms down, and lift your legs up above your head until you feel the stretch in your lower back. Hold the position for 10 seconds, then gently lower your legs to the floor.

Common back injuries

If you suffer from a back injury, it can refer pain to other muscular areas, such as the back of the legs or the pelvis, affecting pelvic alignment.

Sciatica
Pain referred from the lower back into the legs is called 'sciatic'. Usually, the pain goes down the back of the thigh. If the lower back injury is across the whole back, the pain may be in both legs but in severe cases, it can go farther down the back of

Below: The illustration shows the areas around the pelvis and lower back that may be injured in piriformis syndrome.

the leg. The tingling, burning pain is caused by pressure on a nerve in the lower back. Keep stretching the back of the leg and the lower back to maintain as much movement as possible. Once the pain has gone, start a core workout routine to prevent a recurrence of the injury.

Sacroiliac joint inflammation
These joints are based at the bottom of both sides of the back. If you injure them you may feel an aching or sharp pain that can restrict your movement on one side, due to the pelvis having become twisted. The core muscles surrounding the pelvis may not be strong enough or may have

become too relaxed; this is often the case after childbirth. Often in endurance sports, especially running, the impact and tiredness in the muscles will cause the pelvis to slide forward, while the twisting effect can cause inflammation in the sacroiliac joint. Stretch the lower back and tops of the legs to keep the range of movement. The pelvis may twist back into place on its own, or you may need a specialist to fix the problem. Do lots of core strengthening work to prevent this problem recurring.

Piriformis syndrome
This is more commonly known as pain in the buttocks. The piriformis is a lump of muscle deep inside the buttocks, which the sciatic nerve runs alongside. If the muscle gets tight, it puts pressure on the sciatic nerve, which causes pain down the back of the leg. Overuse of the adductor muscles in the inside of the thigh causes the piriformis to overreact and tighten. Massage and lots of stretching are essential to prevent this syndrome. To regain full strength, do regular stretches for the buttocks, and strengthen the muscles of the buttocks and adductors.

sacroiliac joint

piriformis

location of sciatica

Sitting on heels stretch

Many athletes suffer from lower back pain, which could be prevented by regular stretching to prevent a build-up of tension in the muscles. Repeat three to five times.

Kneel on the floor, then gradually lower your weight backward until you are sitting on your heels and you can feel the stretch. Keep your arms straight and hold them as low as possible, as if they were being pulled to the ground through your armpits. Hold for 10 seconds, then release.

Lying one-leg, cross-over stretch

This is a great way to stretch the lower back and buttocks and assess the difference in flexibility between one side and the other. Repeat three to five times.

Bend one leg and pull the knee in to the chest using the opposite hand. As it gets pulled in, pull it across toward your opposite shoulder, allowing your lower back to twist slightly. Hold the position for 10 seconds before repeating.

Bend sideways stretch

This stretches the sacroiliac area and the obliques. Repeat three to five times.

Standing upright, with your arms hanging straight by your sides, lean over to one side as far as possible. Hold for 10 seconds.

Trunk rotation

This is ideal for sports such as golf and tennis. Repeat three to five times.

Stand and rotate round to your side as far as you can without moving your hips. Hold for 10 seconds.

Chest

Upper-body strength training, many sports, and simply sitting with poor posture, can all lead to a lack of flexibility in the chest. Regular stretching will help you to maintain good chest flexibility and avoid injury.

A tight chest will pull your arms closer together, giving the impression of a concave chest, and drag your shoulders forward. This has the effect of producing a poor posture.

Most arm movements take place in front of the body, so it is no surprise that the muscles in the chest get tight. Sports such as golf require you to hold your hands close together, causing your chest muscles to shorten. Golfers and all other sportsmen and sportswomen should regularly stretch their chest muscles and spend some time doing back exercises to counteract the effect of the chest muscles shortening. People who want to build muscle in the gym normally spend a lot of time doing chest exercises because the chest is a large muscular area in which it is easy to see improvements in size and definition.

If training the chest is a major part of your routine, then make sure you do flexibility exercises for your chest between sets of chest exercises.

To test your chest flexibility, stand with your back to a wall with 60cm/2ft between the back of your heels and the wall. Keep your feet where they are and lean back so that your shoulders and back are against the wall. Next, bend your arms at 90 degrees against the wall, with your elbows at shoulder height and palms facing outward. If the flexibility in your chest is good, you should be able to get your forearms, upper back and head to touch the wall all at the same time, without feeling any discomfort.

Make sure to do regular chest stretches to improve and maintain the flexibility in your chest muscles.

Bent arm assisted stretch

Use isometric stretching for better results. As you feel the stretch, contract your chest muscles to resist it for 4 to 6 seconds, then release. Repeat three to five times.

Get your training partner to hold your elbows and slowly push them together behind your back. Hold for 10 seconds.

Rupture of pectoralis

This injury is likely to be caused by heavy weight training, using exercises such as bench press or flies. It often occurs following a sudden increase in the weights that are being used. Always make sure your weight-training technique is correct and arrange to have a training partner to help you in case of a sudden injury. Activities that involve throwing, such as javelin and discus, are also common causes, as they require very explosive power across the chest muscle.

The pain is usually felt at the insertion of the pectoralis major with the humerus (top of the arm), but there will be effects over your whole upper body. You will notice an immediate loss of power when you try to sweep your arm across your body, your chest and upper arm will be painful to move or touch and there may be swelling and bruising. Rest for 4 to 6 weeks then do lots of stretching exercises. Start rehabilitation using a thera band: pull it across your body, then resist the tension on the way back. When you can do these exercises without feeling pain, you can return to weight training, starting with light weights.

Left: This illustration shows the area (shaded in red) affected by a rupture in the chest muscle (pectoralis). The rupture usually occurs at the junction of the pectoralis and the top of the arm. This injury causes loss of power, and rehabilitation can take several weeks.

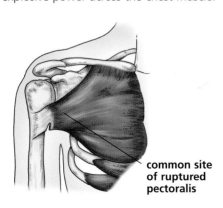

common site of ruptured pectoralis

Above: Once you are completely free of any pain after an injury, use a thera band with a suitable resistance to build the pectoralis muscle.

Fit ball chest stretch

To get an effective chest stretch, you can't just lean forward. You will need either some apparatus or a training partner. Repeat three to five times.

Get on all fours. Place one arm out to the side and rest it on the top of a fit ball. Lower your body until you feel the stretch in one side of your chest. Hold the position for 10 seconds before repeating.

Bend and hold chest stretch

If you don't have someone around or apparatus to help you, a stretch like this can be done in conjunction with a core exercise to make good use of your warm-up.

Bend at the hip and push your chest down toward the floor, keeping your arms straight out to the sides. Hold the position for 10 seconds before repeating.

Lying down assisted stretch

Use isometric stretching for a longer stretch. As you feel the stretch, contract your chest muscles to resist it for 4 to 6 seconds before release. Repeat three to five times.

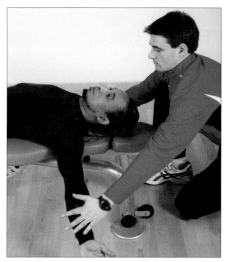

Get your training partner to stand behind you, to hold your forearms and push your arms toward the floor. Hold for 10 seconds before repeating.

Door frame chest stretch

This is one of the few exercises in which you can use your body weight to lean into a stretch. Keep your body straight from head to toe to promote a better stretch. Repeat three to five times.

Place your hands on either side of the door frame. Lean forward through the door frame until you feel the stretch in your chest. Hold the position for 10 seconds before repeating.

Upper Leg: Hamstring Stretches

The backs of the legs are used to control everyday movements and to provide power to go forward. The intense use of a large amount of muscle requires lots of stretching. If your hamstrings become tight, other parts of your body may also suffer.

Tight hamstrings can affect other parts of the body and cause problems with your pelvis and lower back. They will cause your pelvis to tilt and pull at your lower back, possibly leading to back pain and even sciatica.

Your pelvis needs to remain upright and aligned with the arches of your feet. Farther down the body, tight hamstrings can produce pain in the back of the knee and could also affect the calf muscles in the back of the lower leg, so that they tighten, thus preventing them from functioning normally.

Many people focus on exercising the fronts of their thighs in training because it's easy to see the muscles working and appreciate the developments in size and strength. This, however, can lead to poor balance between the muscles, hamstring tightness and possibly injury.

Hamstring injury

This is a common injury for those who participate in any form of explosive sport; it can also occur following excessive running, cycling or other cardiovascular activities. However, you are unlikely to experience a hamstring injury in the gym because you are in a controlled environment and you do not exercise with as much speed. Hamstring strain means that one of the three hamstring muscles has been injured (semitendonosus, semimembranosus and biceps femoris), which will give you pain, and possibly swelling, at the back of the thigh. It is common for the front leg muscles (quadriceps) to create a more powerful contraction than the hamstrings at the back of the leg, which causes a muscular imbalance, leading to a hamstring injury. Stretch the injured hamstrings as soon as the pain has gone to make sure that the muscles do not shorten.

Keep your hamstrings strong with good training exercises and stretch them to maintain their optimum length.

Be careful not to overstretch your hamstrings – just get to the point where you feel the stretch. Making it painful will only activate the tendons at either end of the hamstrings muscle, which will prevent the stretch. Do not try to bounce in the stretch to make it go farther, as this could cause the hamstring to go into spasm and cause damage. To isolate the stretch to the hamstrings, tense your core muscles to prevent your lower back from moving.

To test your hamstring flexibility, lie on your back and push one leg into the floor. Keep it there while you raise the other leg, keeping it straight. For good hamstring flexibility, you should be able to get the leg you are raising to go past 90 degrees.

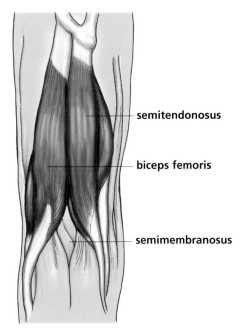

Above: This illustration shows the group of three hamstrings in the back of the thigh area that can be affected by injury.

— semitendonosus

— biceps femoris

— semimembranosus

Standing hamstrings stretch

This will stretch the lower hamstrings toward the back of the knee.

1 *Stand on one leg and place the other leg on a bench, keeping it straight. Lean forward until you feel the stretch in the hamstrings. Hold for 10 seconds before repeating, stretching slightly more.*

2 *For better effect, gently twist your upper body across the leg you are stretching, slowly pointing your foot toward you.*

Bent-forward hamstrings stretch

This is a simple stretch that can be done anywhere. Repeat three to five times.

Put your weight on to your back leg and bend it as you lean forward over your front leg. Pull the foot of your front leg up toward you until you feel the stretch in your hamstrings. Hold the position for 10 seconds before repeating.

Sitting hamstrings stretch

With stretches like this it is easy to overstretch. Just get to the point where you feel tightness. Repeat three to five times.

1 *Sit on the floor, pushing the back of your knees into the floor, and lean forward to touch your toes with both hands until you feel the stretch in the hamstrings. Hold the position for 10 seconds before repeating.*

2 *To make the stretch more effective, repeat the exercise as in step 1, but this time, as you reach to touch your toes, point your feet back toward you. This will stretch the lower hamstrings toward the back of your knees.*

Assisted hamstrings stretch

This is a good opportunity to try some isometric stretching. With an experienced trainer to help, you will achieve a full stretch. Repeat three to five times, both legs.

1 *Get your training partner to lift one leg up and push it back toward you until you feel the stretch. (Your partner should know when you feel the full stretch, because your other leg will automatically start to lift off the bench.) Hold the position for 10 seconds before repeating.*

2 *To bring the stretch lower down the back of your leg, assume the same position as in step 1 but get your partner to put pressure on your toes once you are in the stretch. As you feel the stretch, contract your hamstring muscles for 4 to 6 seconds, then relax before repeating.*

Thera band or towel stretch

You can do this stretch without a partner. Repeat three to five times, both legs.

Lie on your back on a mat on the floor, loop the thera band or towel around one foot and raise your leg straight into the air, keeping your other foot on the ground, until you feel the stretch in your hamstrings. Hold for 10 seconds before repeating. Then, repeat with the other foot.

Upper Leg: Stretches

The adductor muscles in the groin, the hip flexors and the gluteus muscles are all susceptible to strains and tears if they are overused repetitively, or are subject to powerful movements. Staying flexible can help you to recover from injuries.

Any sport or serious training places significant stress on the muscular regions that control movement at the centre of your body. As the intensity and speed increases, so too does the stress on the muscles around the area.

Your gluteus muscles, hip flexors and inner thigh muscles have to provide power as well as maintaining the stability that your other limb muscles rely on. These stretches should take priority and become part of a regular daily routine.

If the gluteus muscles get tight, they could cause your hamstrings and lower back to tighten also. The gluteus muscles are so big that they are often difficult to stretch once they are already too tight. The way to prevent this happening is to stay flexible.

Your hip flexors are susceptible to becoming very tight if you live a sedentary life. They should not stay in a seated position for long, or they will naturally shorten. But as soon as you need these muscles for walking, running

or any sporting activity, they will be too short. Make sure you stretch these muscles after long periods of sitting down, especially if you want to be able to run without injury. If they stay tight, they will eventually pull your pelvis down and forward, causing your lower back to arch more than it should, which could lead to lower back pain.

Your inner thigh muscles control fast powerful movements in your legs. They will tighten after exercise and shorten. Keep them long with regular stretching.

Common upper leg injuries

The following injuries are likely to occur due to lack of strength and flexibility, or a change in speed or stride strength.

Adductor tears
These are more commonly known as groin strains. They usually occur during explosive aggressive movements, such as sprinting, hurdling and changing direction in ball sports. A tear or rupture to any of the adductor muscles (brevis, longus, magnus, pectineus and gracilis) will cause a sudden pain in the groin area and loss of strength and control of inner thigh movements. You can expect

Below: The location of the adductor muscle tears and the hip flexor strains are shown in red.

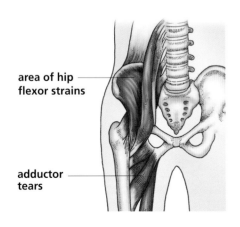

area of hip flexor strains

adductor tears

to see some swelling if it is a rupture. Often the top of the leg will need to be taped to the waist to restrict the outward movement of the leg. Have regular massage to restrict muscles in the surrounding area from tightening and causing more tension on the adductor muscles. Once the swelling has reduced and the pain has gone, you can begin a regular stretching routine with a groin stretch before (when you are warmed up) and after any sporting activity. Add adductor and abductor exercises, such as fit ball inner thigh squeezes.

Hip flexor strains
Overuse of the hip flexors, caused by excessive cycling or running (especially if you are doing hill intervals or speed sessions) will make you prone to this type of injury. You will feel pain in the hip flexors and you may find walking difficult as you will have lost strength and the ability to bring your leg forward. You will also feel the pain as you stretch your leg back behind you. Start stretching the hip flexors as soon as the pain has gone but don't start running until you have strengthened them. Swimming and cycling are good ways to regain fitness, as these forms of exercise involve a shorter stride pattern and no impact.

Hurdle stretch

This also stretches the hip flexors of the bent leg. Repeat three times.

Sit on the floor, with one leg bent behind you, stretch forward, reaching toward your straight leg until you feel a stretch in the hamstrings of the straight leg and the groin area of the bent leg. Hold for 10 seconds then repeat on the other side.

Effective stretching
For any lower body stretches, do the movements in a slow and controlled manner. If a muscle is already tight the weight of the upper body forcing the stretch on the lower body can cause injury if done quickly. After holding the stretch the same muscles won't get you out of the stretch. Use your arms to relieve the stretch. Using the same muscles that have just been stretched will defeat the object of the stretch.

Inner thigh stretch

Training that demands speed and change of direction leaves the inner thigh muscles prone to tightness. Repeat three to five times.

From a standing position, bend one leg, taking your body weight over to one side until you feel the stretch in the inner thigh of the opposite leg. Hold the position for 10 seconds before repeating.

Groin stretch

The groin is always under a lot of pressure to help stabilize the pelvis. Repeat three to five times.

Slowly push the outside of your knees down toward the floor until you feel the stretch in the groin and inner thighs. Hold the position for 10 seconds before repeating.

Gluteus split-feet stretch on all fours

The muscles in the buttocks are in constant tension so they need good flexibility. Repeat three to five times.

Get on all fours with your knees close together. Force your feet apart and hold this position as you push your hips back toward your feet. When you feel the stretch in the hamstrings and buttocks, hold the position for 10 seconds before repeating.

Kneeling hip flexor stretch

Sedentary lifestyles cause the hip flexor to shorten, causing back and pelvis pain, and injury. Repeat three to five times.

Kneeling on one knee, keep your body weight central and pull your pelvis forward until you feel the stretch in your hip flexor. Hold the position for 10 seconds before repeating.

Knee

The muscles attached to the knee in the front of the upper leg contract with a great deal of force and, therefore they tighten easily. To get the most out of these muscles, it is advisable to stretch them regularly using the range of exercises given here.

As there are many big muscles attached to the knee, it has to cope with a lot of stress, which can sometimes lead to injuries. Often knee injuries are caused by muscle imbalances elsewhere in your body. For example if your left buttock is weak, the muscles on the outside of the left leg will be tight. In time, they will pull at the knee to compensate for the weak buttocks. Use an expert sports physician to help you understand where the knee pain originates.

The force exerted by the muscles above and below the knee can cause injury to the tissues surrounding the knee through overuse or sudden aggressive movements. The knee joint relies on the muscles on both the inside and the outside of the thigh to keep the knee on the right track. The muscles located in the outside of the upper thigh are used in almost every leg movement. These muscles consist of a large mass that is unfortunately hard to stretch.

This part of the leg provides a lot of power and can often cause problems with the knee joint and even injury if it is not kept flexible. However, the muscle on the outside of the thigh is larger and more powerful than those on the inside of the knee, which can lead to the knee being dragged across to the outside, if the muscle on the outer area of the knee tightens through overuse. Consistent, repetitive exercise will inevitably make this happen, so make sure you do some of these stretches regularly to prevent injuries and poor performance.

Above: Cable leg extensions are a good exercise to strengthen the muscles above the knee.

Common knee injuries

The following injuries can occur as a result of repetitive movements, accidents and sudden, twisting movements.

Housemaid's knee
Also known as prepatella bursitis, it is often caused by direct impact to the knee or excessive kneeling. You may not experience pain at the front of the knee unless the bursa, a fluid-filled pouch at the front of the knee, enlarges and restricts movement. Stretch the quadriceps muscles to prevent them from tightening and pulling at the knee.

Dislocation of kneecap
This can be a recurring problem. It may happen at any time but most commonly occurs with sudden movement to change direction. You will instantly feel pain at the front of the knee and, in most cases, the kneecap will be out of its normal position. You may get further pain from other areas of the knee due to the change of position, and tendons and ligaments being stretched. Usually, the kneecap is pulled out of position by the quadriceps muscles, which contract due to weakness in the inside muscle of the quadriceps. The unequal force in the muscle will cause the kneecap to move sideways. Once the kneecap is back in place, keep stretching the quadriceps muscles, and get regular sports massages to balance the quadriceps muscles.

Cartilage pain
If the cartilage tissue – the knee's shock absorber – is torn, pain and swelling will occur immediately and it may feel as if your knee is locked. You will not be able to get much range of movement of the knee due to the swelling and the pain may continue to get worse. Once you have recovered, resume exercising with light stretches on the upper-leg muscles and exercises such as half squats and leg extensions using cables before moving on to free and machine weights.

Patella tendinitis
This injury is common in sports requiring repetitive movement, such as running and cycling. It is caused by overuse or overload of the tendon when bending the knee. You will feel pain just below or above the front of the knee and the pain will worsen as you squat. It is usually most painful in the morning, but improves as the day goes on.

Below: Several conditions can affect the knee, causing pain and discomfort.

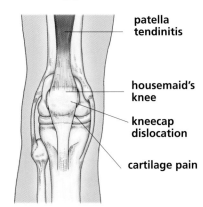

patella tendinitis

housemaid's knee

kneecap dislocation

cartilage pain

Standing quadriceps stretch

For a more effective movement, push your hips forward once you are in the stretch. Repeat three to five times, both legs.

Stand up, bend forward and hold the calf of your left leg with your left hand. Pull the leg up behind you until you feel the stretch in the front of your thigh. Hold the position for 10 seconds before repeating.

Seated quadriceps stretch

This stretch helps to stretch out your abdominal muscles and hip flexors. Repeat three to five times.

Kneeling on the floor, slowly lower your body weight back on to your heels, leaning your upper body backward as far as you can go. Once you feel the stretch in the front of your thighs, hold the position for 10 seconds before repeating.

Bench quadriceps stretch

If you suffer from back injuries, use this exercise to stretch your quadriceps. Repeat three to five times, both legs.

Hunker down in front of the bench, one foot flat on the floor and the other bent up behind you on the bench. Gently lean back to put more weight on the back leg and force the stretch in the quadriceps. Hold for 10 seconds before repeating.

Assisted quadriceps stretch

For a more effective stretch, use isometric stretching. Repeat three to five times, both legs.

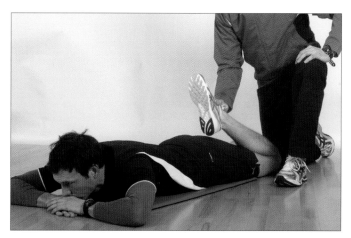

Lie on the floor, face down, and get your training partner to bend one leg up behind you until you feel the stretch in the front of your thigh. Contract your quadriceps for 4 to 6 seconds to resist the stretch before releasing and repeating.

Sports knee injuries

Medial ligament strain

The medial ligament supports the inside of the knee. Contact sports and swimming, particularly breaststroke, where the knee twists each time you kick, can cause damage to this ligament. If the injury is caused by sudden twisting, the symptoms will be acute pain and a swollen knee – the body's way of preventing further movement of, and injury to, the knee. An overuse injury will cause little pain to begin with, but it will gradually increase the more you use the knee. The kneecap may also feel a bit loose or off its normal line.

To avoid medial ligament strain, stretch the hamstrings and quadriceps muscles to prevent them from shortening and pulling at the knee. If you have injured this ligament, start exercising the knee with leg extensions and short squat type exercises as soon as the pain subsides.

Lateral ligament strain

The knee being forced outward causes pain in the lateral ligament. This happens in contact sports when people land on top of one another and legs are bent in awkward directions. You will experience pain in the outside of the knee and movement will be impaired, depending on the severity of the injury. Continue to stretch the quadriceps and wear a knee support to prevent too much lateral movement. Once the pain has gone, strengthen the ligament with quadriceps and abductor strength-training exercises.

Iliotibial syndrome

The large band of muscle that runs down the outside of the leg to connect the gluteus to the outside of the knee is the iliotibial tract. It can be damaged by overuse or changes in technique. If it gets tight, it will cause pain either in the underside of the muscle or farther down toward the knee. It may only be a dull ache at first, but can worsen. You are more likely to feel the pain when doing the activity that caused it in the first place. It may prevent you from striding out when walking and will limit your normal movements, for example, when squatting. Rest the leg and get sports massage to release the tension in the iliotibial tract. Start stretching the area as soon as possible.

Popliteal muscle problems

One of the smallest, not very strong muscles behind the knee, the popliteal muscle is nevertheless important for an athlete. The functions of this muscle are threefold: it helps to begin to bend the knee by unlocking the knee from full extension; when the knee is straight or in full extension, the upper leg rotates laterally on the lower leg if the foot is flat on the floor; and finally, it medially rotates the lower leg under the upper leg. This happens during running, when the foot of that leg is up in the air, ready for the next step. If the popliteal muscle is tight or shortened, the foot will not plant on the ground properly.

Cause of injury and treatment

Injury to the popliteal muscle is mainly caused by overuse, severe sprain or strain to the knee. The muscle can also be overstressed by running in old, worn shoes so that there is too much rotation on the lower leg. Wearing outworn shoes stresses the popliteal muscle and your body generally. If the muscle is tight, the foot will come downward on to its inner side (excess pronation).

Treatment is gentle manual trigger point therapy and ultrasound. Because the popliteal cavity contains many nerves and blood vessels, to be effective, the manual pressure should be light. After treatment, the muscle can be strengthened by using low resistance rotational exercises of the foot and lower leg at high repetition.

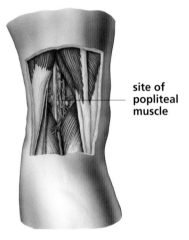

site of popliteal muscle

Above: The popliteal fossa is the hollow at the back of the knee that houses the popliteal muscle.

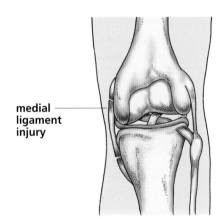

medial ligament injury

Above: The red shaded areas indicate the areas of likely injury on the inside of the knee.

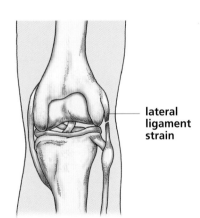

lateral ligament strain

Above: The ligament on the outside of the knee (in red) can be forced outward, causing pain.

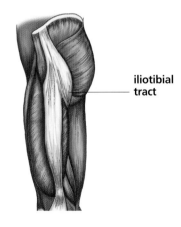

iliotibial tract

Above: The illustration shows the muscle in the leg that is often responsible for pain around the knee.

Outer thigh stretch

The knee joint is held in position by the muscles on the inside and outside of the thigh. You can use these stretches to prevent your outer thigh muscles getting tight and causing injury, especially overuse injuries and muscle imbalances. Massage helps to keep muscles supple. Repeat three to five times, both legs.

Cross your left leg over the right and use your right arm to pull the left leg across while you twist your upper body around to face to the left. When you feel the stretch in your lower back and down the outside of your leg, hold the position for 10 seconds before repeating.

Standing outer thigh stretch

This stretch will help to relax the outer thigh muscles and also your obliques. Repeat three to five times, both legs.

Push your right hip out to the side, leaning your upper body over to your left side until you feel the stretch in the outer thigh of your right leg. Hold the position for 10 seconds before repeating.

Kneeling outer thigh stretch

The outside of the thighs are connected to the front of the hips by the hip flexors. This exercise stretches both areas.

Kneeling on one knee, keep your body weight central between your legs and lean over to the other side. Once you feel the stretch down the outside of the thigh and ribs, hold the position for 10 seconds before repeating.

Ankle

Whatever training or sport you practise, you need to have good flexibility in the ankles, feet and surrounding muscles. Tight muscles will pull at the tendons in the ankles, causing a lack of flexibility and tightness in the soles of your feet.

There are more than 26 bones in your foot, and the sole of your foot has four layers of muscle and tendons. Treating feet with reflexology has taught us that tight feet and ankles can have an effect on the entire body. Regular stretching relieves muscle tension all over your body and will improve the function of your internal organs.

Farther up the leg, other muscles will have to work hard to compensate for poor flexibility in the ankles. For example, if your foot does not flex enough on impact while running, the muscles at the front and back of the lower leg will get overused, which will, in turn, cause injury. Because of poor blood flow to the

lower part of the leg, it can take longer to recover from injuries below the knee, so always make the time to maintain your ankle and foot flexibility. It is also important to ensure that the muscles in the rest of your body, especially the pelvis and lower back area, are relaxed in order to prevent them pulling at your foot and ankle.

Common foot, ankle and shin injuries

Foot, ankle and shin injuries are mainly caused by overuse or sudden changes in direction and balance. The following are some of the most common injuries.

Plantar fasciitis

This tendon runs from the heel to the front of the foot. It can become ruptured or inflamed, often due to overuse or a change in footwear with lower or higher arches than normal. The symptoms are pain in the heel that reaches the front of the foot. The arch of the foot tends to turn inward and collapse. To alleviate the symptoms, a doctor may tape the tendon to restrict its movement. You may need an arch support in your shoe to raise the arch of the foot and prevent it collapsing. Once you are free of pain, start stretching the bottom of the foot and the calf.

Below: This illustration shows the areas of the lower leg and foot that can be affected by injury.

Tenosynovitis

This occurs when the tendons on the top of the foot become painful as a result of inflammation of the sheath that surrounds the tendon. As well as pain, there may be swelling and there may be difficulty moving the inflamed joint. Tenosynovitis is caused by new footwear, wearing shoes that are too tight, laces rubbing on the tops of your feet, running fast downhill, running on uneven ground or excessive pointing of the toes. Don't do any activity or stretching until the pain has gone, then stretch with light toe raises and toe stretches.

Shin pain

The term given to a number of factors that cause pain in the shins is 'shin splints'. Symptoms of this condition may include swelling at the front of the shins, pain as you flex your foot and lumps on the front of the shin

bone. In most cases, pain is caused by inflammation of the periostium, a sheath that surrounds the bone.

To avoid shin splints, check your footwear to make sure that you have adequate support and cushioning for shock absorption, especially if you are running on hard or uneven surfaces.

Make sure also that your running technique is correct. Too much rotation of the hip can exacerbate the problem. If you do a lot of running, it may be worth seeing a professional who can assess your style and assist you with your running biomechanics.

Rest and ice the shin and the surrounding muscles to try to decrease the inflammation. Stretch your muscles at the front and back of the lower leg.

Ankle sprains

This common injury usually occurs when the ankle turns inward and the ligaments and soft tissues at the outside of the ankle are damaged. There are different levels of severity, depending on the amount of swelling and the range of movement you still have. Once the swelling is reduced and the pain has gone, start doing ankle stretches. Keep your ankle protected with a support at all times to restrict any sudden or big movements. Begin building strength in the ankle by balancing on one leg, then balance on a wobble board or BOSU (Both Sides Utilized) balance trainer.

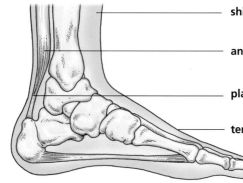

shin pain (swelling or lumps on shin)

ankle sprains (damage to ligaments)

plantar fasciitis (pain in a tendon)

tenosynovitus (painful tendons)

Ankle stretch

The tissues surrounding the ankle are likely to get tight during any exercise due to impact and change of direction. The ankles can suffer more tightness if you already have poor core stability. When the core muscles at the centre of the body are weak the ankles have to compensate farther down to keep stability. Repeat three to five times for each ankle.

Sitting on the mat, with your right leg out straight in front of you, grasp the middle of your left foot and twist it over to the right until the ankle is stretched. Hold the position for 10 seconds before repeating.

Ankle rotation

This stretch will move your ankle in all directions before exercise. Repeat three to five times for each ankle.

Standing upright, with your feet hip-width apart and arms by your sides, lift one foot off the floor and slowly rotate it in circles. Do ten circles in a clockwise direction and ten in an anticlockwise direction.

Foot stretch

Tightness around the ankle can cause injuries, so make time to do this stretch. Repeat three to five times for each foot.

Standing upright, lift one foot off the floor and point your toes until you feel the stretch in the front of the top of the foot. Be careful not to let your calf muscles cramp. Hold the position for 10 seconds before repeating.

Calf

Your calf muscles have to work hard throughout the day just to hold you upright when standing or doing exercise. The following exercises are suitable for maintaining flexibility in this crucial area and avoiding injury.

As calf muscles tire from long periods of standing and exercise, they start to tighten. When you are sitting, they shorten. If you do not spend time stretching them back to their optimum length, they will remain shortened. Tight calf muscles are one of the most common causes of Achilles' tendon problems. If the calf muscles are tight and you go to do exercise, the stress of the exercise will be put on the Achilles' tendon as a result of the calf muscles' poor elasticity.

Because of poor blood supply in the Achilles' tendon area, along with the constant use of your legs, it takes a long time for Achilles' tendons to recover from injury. Regular stretching to keep the calf muscles at their optimum length will prevent this happening in the first place. Tight calf muscles will also lead to tight hamstrings, making you prone to back injuries and tension in your feet.

As the calf muscle is made up of one part below the knee and another above, use a variety of stretches to maintain flexibility throughout the entire calf.

Common lower leg injuries

Strains are caused by pulling or twisting a tendon or a muscle. They occur as a result of overuse or training too much.

Achilles' strain and rupture
Ruptures are usually caused by a sudden acceleration forward while rising up on to your toes. This is a common injury among women who wear high heels and then play a game of tennis or squash or go running. The high heel shortens the calf and Achilles' tendon throughout the working day, then it has to lengthen for the sporting activity. Symptoms include a sudden sharp pain in the back of the lower leg followed by swelling; total lack of control of the back of the leg, and the calf muscles losing all strength and co-ordination; and being unable to walk even a few paces. A strain, or partial rupture, will result in the back of your leg being taped to restrict the movement of the Achilles'.

A complete tear will result in your leg being in plaster for six weeks or more. When the injury is starting to heal, do light calf stretches to get the range of movement back into the Achilles' and calf muscles. Wrap a thera band around your foot and pull it up toward you to get a stretch on the Achilles' and calf, then progress to standing calf stretches. As flexibility and strength improve, and you are able to walk, include some calf raises. You can put a heel lift in your shoe to relieve the pressure on the tendon.

Calf strains
Runners commonly experience calf strains, usually through overuse or a sudden increase in training load. Symptoms include pain in the calf muscles, which may go away when the muscles are warmed up, or get worse, depending on whether or not the muscle goes into spasm. If it does go into spasm, the blood supply to the muscles is restricted and the nutrients can't get to the muscles, causing them to tighten up. Have regular sports massages to loosen the calf muscles. Start stretching exercises soon after the injury to lengthen the calf muscle and prevent further tightening. To avoid calf strains, include calf exercises, such as calf raises, in your training plan.

Left: The areas that are white comprise the calf muscles and Achilles' tendon, which are both liable to injury.

Standing calf stretch

It is possible to stretch your calf muscles while you are in a standing position. Repeat the stretch three to five times for each calf.

Standing upright, slowly bend your back leg and push the back knee forward until you feel the stretch at the bottom of the calf muscles. Hold for 10 seconds before repeating.

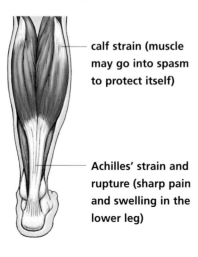

calf strain (muscle may go into spasm to protect itself)

Achilles' strain and rupture (sharp pain and swelling in the lower leg)

Assisted calf stretch

Although you can stretch your calf muscles using your body weight and by creating an angle to get a stretch, it can be more effective to have a partner stretch your calf. In cases of injury and possible rupture to the calf muscles or the Achilles' tendon, assisted stretches when lying on the floor, are recommended. Repeat three to five times, each calf.

Lie on an exercise mat on your back and get your training partner to stretch your calf by holding your heel and pushing your toes up toward you. When you can feel the stretch in the calf, hold the position for about 10 seconds before repeating.

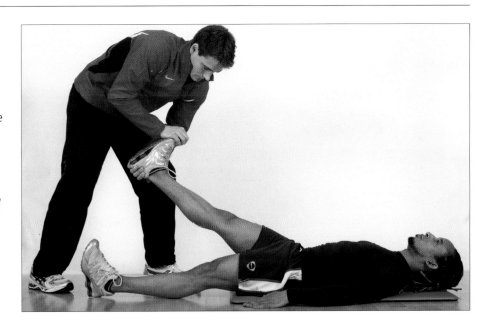

Step calf stretch

This stretch can be made more effective by doing it on one leg. Repeat three to five times for each calf.

Standing on a bench, with your heels just over the edge, and your arms hanging straight by your side, lower the heel of one foot down toward the floor until you feel the stretch in the calf. Hold the position for 10 seconds and repeat three to five times.

Calf stretch against a wall

For a more effective stretch, use isometric stretching. Repeat three to five times for each calf.

Lean face forward, palms flat against a wall, left leg back with heel on floor, and right leg forward. Slowly push against the wall to force the stretch on the calf. Once you feel the stretch, contract the calf muscles to resist it for 4 to 6 seconds. Hold the position for 10 seconds before repeating.

Arm

Upper-arm weight-training – particularly of the biceps – is a popular training exercise. To keep good flexibility in your upper arm, use the following stretches as a regular part of your training routine.

You use your arms in virtually every sporting activity and in everyday life. Most of us use our arms for small fine motor movements such as typing or texts and these smaller muscles in the arm can get overused. We are not designed to do constant small movements and the bigger muscles in the arms may suffer loss of tone and strength. On the sports field we expect our arms to provide strength to hit a ball, throw an object, punch or take our body weight. This can lead to muscle imbalances and susceptibility to injury. It is important to keep a balance. For example training biceps (at the front of the arms) will make the arms appear larger but this may create problems with the triceps (at the back of the arms). Weak arms may force other areas of the body to work too hard to keep up with the demands of the activity. An example would be using the neck muscles to lift a weight, rather than using the arms.

Common arm injuries

The upper arms are used in just about every training exercise, especially upper-body resistance training. They are susceptible to many different injuries. The following are just a few examples of the most common types.

Biceps and triceps strain
The usual causes of injury to the front and back of the upper arm are overstretching, an increase in workload and overuse. You will feel anything from a dull ache to a sharp pain, depending on the severity of the injury. Start stretching the affected muscle as soon as possible. When the pain has gone, begin strengthening exercises with light weights. Avoid sudden, loaded movements, such as hitting a tennis ball or throwing a javelin, until the muscle is strong again.

Tennis elbow – outside of elbow
Often the cause of tennis elbow is weakness in the biceps and forearms, poor technique or playing with a wet, heavy ball. The pain can be anywhere in the elbow, depending on which shot causes the pain. If you get pain when you play a forehand, it is medial tennis elbow, whereas pain on the backhand stroke is lateral tennis elbow. Avoid playing as aggressively as you did before until you are pain-free. Ask a tennis coach to check your technique – you are more likely to get tennis elbow if you play with your forearms and wrists as

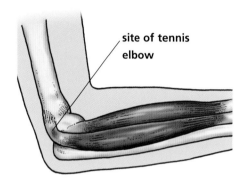

site of tennis elbow

Above: The part of the elbow coloured red represents the area of intense pain when suffering from tennis elbow.

opposed to putting your shoulder and body into the shot. Use simple forearm exercises to strengthen the forearms and elbow: tuck your elbow into your side, with your elbow bent at 90 degrees and your forearm out in front of you. Hold a light weight and rotate it, starting with your palms facing upward, and rotating until your palms are facing the floor. Then, using the same arm position, start with the palm facing inward and pull your thumb up toward your forearm. Do three sets of ten repetitions for each arm, gradually increasing the number of repetitions.

Golfer's elbow – inside of elbow
This is similar to tennis elbow, although the pain is most likely to be felt in the inside of the elbow of the leading arm. It can be the symptom of bad technique and poor strength in certain areas, such

as the wrist and forearms. This type of injury is also common in other sports such as baseball, in which the leading arm takes a lot of the impact when the club contacts the ball. Use forearm exercises such as this to strengthen your arm: tuck your elbow in next to your ribs. With your elbow bent at 90 degrees and your forearm out in front of you, hold a dumbbell or golf club in your hand and rotate the wrist with the palms facing upward to the palms facing downward. With the palms facing inward and the club held vertically, pull the top of your hand or thumb back toward you. Do three sets of ten repetitions for each arm, followed by stretching exercises to regain your full range of movement.

Forearm tenosynovitis
This injury involves the sheath of the tendon, where the forearm connects to the wrist, becoming inflamed and restricting the movement of the tendon within it. It can be caused by overuse of the forearm muscles, for example when gripping a racket or club too tightly. You will feel the pain whenever the tendon is stretched. Once the pain has subsided, do regular stretches on the forearms and biceps. To prevent forearm tenosynovitis happening again, make sure that the equipment you are using is right for you, and strengthen your forearms with biceps, triceps and wrist exercises.

Manual bicep stretch

To avoid your bicep muscles shortening, stretch between each set of exercises. Repeat three to five times, both arms.

Standing upright, hold one arm straight out in front of you, palm outward. Use the other hand to grasp your fingers and pull them toward the floor. When you feel the stretch in the biceps, hold the position for 10 seconds before repeating.

Assisted bicep stretch

For a more effective stretch, use isometric stretching. Repeat the stretch three to five times.

Sit on the bench, at a 60-degree angle, and get your training partner to grip your hands from behind, bending them backward until you feel the stretch in your biceps. Hold the position for 4 to 6 seconds before repeating.

Bicep wall stretch

When your arms are tired from training, use a wall to assist with a bicep stretch. Repeat three to five times.

Standing upright, facing a wall, place the palm of your hand, fingers pointing down, against the wall. Then pull your hand upward until you feel the stretch. Hold the position for 10 seconds before repeating.

Triceps overhead stretch

When training the chest and arms, stretch between exercises to keep flexible. Repeat three to five times for both arms.

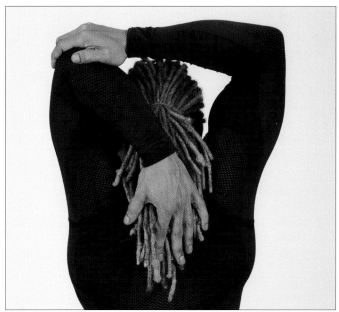

Take one arm over your head and bend it at the elbow to reach the back of your neck and upper back. Push down on the elbow with your other hand, forcing the hand farther down your back. Hold for 10 seconds before repeating.

Abdominals

Your abdominals are in constant use, not just during intensive exercise, but also for everyday tasks such as going to the toilet or even just breathing. To get the most out of them, keep them flexible with these stretches.

When taking a deep breath in, you can help your chest space to open wider by tensing your abdominal muscles and pulling them in. As you breathe out, you contract your abdominal muscles to release all the air and make room for a bigger intake of air. For this to happen, you need your abdominal muscles to remain at optimum length so that they are fully functional.

Your abdominals are hardworking; they are subject to constant tension, to help you move in any direction, and to enable your pelvis to tilt and rotate in any direction. Your abdominals act as a corset to hold your body together and provide a strong solid base that other limbs can rely on. Without good strength and flexibility in your abdominals, your spine and pelvis would be unsupported, making you much more prone to injury. Your abdominals never rest – they assist your every movement and even work when you are sitting or lying down. Therefore, the abdominal muscles should be stretched regularly to help them maintain their optimum length and to function as best they can.

There are a number of flexibility tests you can do to see if your abdominal muscles are at their proper length. As many of these involve leaning backward, which can be bad for your spine, simply use torso rotation. Sit on a chair with your back upright and your feet placed flat on the floor in front of you. Cross your arms, with your hands on opposite shoulders, and then rotate your upper body as far as possible before you start to feel uncomfortable. You should be able to rotate through 40 degrees for good flexibility.

Stretch your abdominal muscles regularly, especially after doing abdominal exercises that tighten the muscles even further. And always stretch before sporting activities that require lots of rotation, such as tennis or golf.

Common abdominal injuries

When a muscle is stretched beyond its limits, the tissue can tear; causing a strain. This type of injury is often sustained during stomach exercises.

A hernia can result when the muscles of the stomach wall are weakened and allow part of the intestines to bulge through, causing a lump under the skin.

Abdominal strain

This is the inflammation or rupture of the stomach muscles that usually affects the rectus abdominis muscles in the stomach. Throwing events and other activities that involve aggressive, big muscular movements are likely to cause this type of injury, which can occur gradually or suddenly. Repeated abdominal exercises such as crunches and serving balls for tennis can

Below: The site of abdominal strain or rupture after heavy activity is the red area shown here.

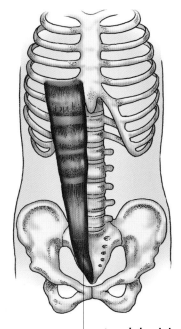

rectus abdominis muscle (often the site of inflammation or rupture)

overstrain the muscles and cause a gradual pain after the activity. If you get a sudden pain in your abdominals, it is likely to be a rupture of the muscle. This is more likely to happen during the actual activity. The amount of pain will depend on the severity of the damage to the muscle fibres. In severe cases, the tear could cause some internal bleeding. You should immediately bend forward after the injury to prevent your stomach muscles from being overstretched.

After two days, if your doctor advises it, stretch the muscle by doing abdominal stretches to prevent the muscle fibres from shortening and causing further problems. Once the pain has gone, start to add more abdominal strengthening exercises to your routine. Always warm up before sporting activities and cool down afterward.

Hernia

A sudden increase in abdominal pressure can cause part of an organ or other internal tissues to come through a weakened area of the abdominal wall, causing a hernia. While hernias are not usually initially caused by sporting activity (although lifting very heavy weights can cause hernias), exercises that force big contractions in the abdominal muscles may make an existing hernia worse. Coughing and undue straining can also cause hernias.

Avoid doing any exercise until you have consulted your doctor, and only resume light exercise or training once the gap of the hernia has been reduced. Build up your abdominal exercises slowly, doing half the repetitions you did before injury until you get back to full strength. Do abdominal stretches every day to make sure that the abdominals stay relaxed, and to prevent any massive increase in pressure.

Abdominal stretch

This stretch is also a great way to stretch your hip flexors and quadriceps. Repeat three to five times.

Kneel on both knees on the exercise mat and lean back so that your buttocks rest on your heels, with your hands behind you on the floor for support, taking your upper body as far back as possible. Once you feel the stretch in the abdominals and hip flexors, hold the position for 10 seconds before repeating.

Above: Whenever you are lifting a heavy weight, the abdominal muscles will come into play in an attempt to protect your spine from injury.

Side stretch

Your abdominal muscles don't just work back and forth to do sit up movements, they control sideways movement as well. Repeat three to five times on both sides.

Above: As you stretch sideways using a dumbbell, your abominal muscles will lengthen. On the way up, the muscles contract, to make them work harder.

Stand upright with your feet shoulder-width apart and lean over to one side to stretch the obliques. Hold the position for 10 seconds before repeating.

Common Muscle Injuries

Despite taking care when exercising and during sporting activities, backed up by regular stretching, muscle injuries do happen, and they can be painful and very debilitating. Here we look at some of the most common types of muscle injuries and their causes.

Repeated powerful muscle contractions can cause muscle cell damage, allowing calcium to flood into the cells, leading to cell death that peaks 48 hours after exercise. The body's inflammatory response stimulates the nerve endings in the damaged tissue, causing soreness that can last for a few days. This is known as Delayed Onset Muscle Soreness (DOMS).

A significant increase in training volume, participating in a new activity or heavy weight-training can all cause muscle soreness. Keeping your muscles hydrated will help the pain to subside; the discomfort is unlikely to last more than eight days.

Injuries
When working the muscles hard during training, there is always a risk of damage to muscles, such as pulling muscles or tearing them.

Acute muscle tears These tears can happen suddenly, causing severe pain, immediate loss of function and swelling. They can be caused by imbalances between opposing muscles (such as quadriceps and hamstrings), inflexibility, inadequate warm-up and muscle fatigue. The best treatment for acute muscle tears is the RICES method: rest, ice, compress, elevate and stabilize. Make sure that the tear has fully healed before attempting strenuous exercise.

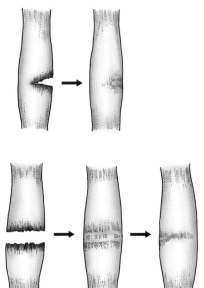

Above: Muscle tears can be partial or complete. Whichever type they are, a total break from exercise is necessary to allow them to heal.

Chronic muscle tears These types of injuries are common among endurance athletes. The first warning sign is pain that builds up gradually after exercise. It may be possible to start another training session the next day but the pain will continue to get worse until it is impossible to train. The muscle may spasm to protect it from further use, causing more pain. You can tell what type of tear it is by pushing into the area with two fingers – if it is a chronic tear, this will be very painful. Stretching and strengthening your muscles before and after exercise will help to prevent this type of injury.

If you do suffer a torn muscle, apply an ice pack immediately to try to reduce swelling, and if possible, elevate the injured area. To prevent muscle tears during exercise, always warm up beforehand and every day.

Left: Using weights which are much too heavy for you will be likely to cause muscle injuries.

Above: Muscle cramps will play havoc with your training, so ensure you eat sensibly to combat the problem.

Above: Having a good warm-up before you start exercising can loosen your muscles and help you to avoid cramp.

Above: Understanding why you get stitches can help to prevent getting them again.

Cramps

There are a number of reasons for muscle cramps, which are involuntary contractions of the muscle. Dehydration, lack of essential minerals and low carbohydrate levels are among the most common causes of cramps, especially when someone is exercising or training hard.

Dehydration is a common cause of cramps, especially in hot climates. Try drinking 350–450ml/12–15fl oz of water every hour to avoid it. In very hot conditions, you will need at least 450ml/15fl oz of water per hour. Muscles work harder in hot conditions because your heart rate increases by roughly five beats for every 1 degree rise (1°C/1.8°F) in core body temperature, therefore muscles will be working that much closer to their maximum workload and will dehydrate faster, making them prone to cramp.

Essential minerals such as potassium and sodium are needed by the muscles to function properly. Low levels will result in cramp. Sports drinks that have a high potassium and sodium content replace the minerals lost through sweat, especially in hot, humid conditions.

Low carbohydrate levels can cause your muscles to fatigue faster. This in turn, can lead to cramp. Make sure that your nutrition before, during and after training is adequate to cope with the demands that you are putting on your body. Leave enough time after eating before you exercise to allow blood to return from the gut – where it is helping to digest the food – to the muscles. You may have to experiment with this – some people can exercise just 30 minutes after eating, while others need to wait a few hours. Try not to eat a really heavy meal if you know you are going to be training soon afterward.

Stretching

A warm-up that includes a variety of stretches should play a significant role in your weekly training plan. While stretching does not prevent injury, if you have limited mobility, you are more likely to get injured. If your muscles are already tight before you start to exercise, then they are more likely to cramp. There is no substitute for hard work – the more training you do, the better your muscles will be able to cope.

Stitches

There are two common types of pain that you may experience in the torso, commonly known as a stitch. If you eat shortly before exercising, your body will have to transfer blood to the working muscles rather than to the digestive organs, leaving the stomach full of undigested food. By waiting at least 90 minutes after a meal before exercising, you will reduce the chance of getting a stitch. If you are intending to eat during long-distance training, use energy drinks and bars that have been specifically made to aid digestion and release energy fast.

If, however, the pain in your stomach is not caused by food, it is probably a side stitch. This type of stitch occurs when you are exercising at a high intensity. The diaphragm muscles contract to a shortened position and are not able to lengthen fully. If you exhale completely, the diaphragm muscles will be able to lengthen and the stitch will start to reduce in intensity. To recover completely, you must breathe out forcefully and try to empty your lungs completely before you take in your next breath.

Fatigue and Illness

Sometimes, you may not be able to train. For elite athletes, rest is as important as training and plays an important role in avoiding injury. Here are some essential pointers that you can use to decide whether or not you really are fit enough to train.

When it comes to training and, specifically, avoiding overtraining, the simple rule to follow is: listen to your body. It is hard to tell yourself to rest when you want to get stuck into the next training session. The symptoms of overtraining that you should watch out for are: a dip in enthusiasm to train; heavy legs; breathlessness during low-intensity exercise; progressive weight loss; reduced appetite; and a resting heart rate that is five to ten beats higher than normal first thing in the morning and during steady exercise. Increased fluid intake and cravings for

sugary foods can be another sign, as well as reduced sleep and bad moods. If you experience any or all of these symptoms, seek advice from your doctor.

Set your goals

To avoid overtraining syndrome, use a coach to help you set realistic short- and long-term goals. Keep in contact with your coach and keep a training diary so that you can monitor your training and recognize signs of overtraining. When your enthusiasm is running high, it is often hard to stop and assess how you feel and what you have done to make

your body feel tired. It is likely that you will carry on regardless, taking no notice of the signs of fatigue. You may just assume that you are feeling tired because you are not fit enough, and then struggle on without realizing what's actually happening. This is a massive mistake. Your coach should be able to analyse your performance using measurements such as heart rate and tell you when you need to take a break.

Below: However fit you may feel, you are not invincible and should not train all day. Be realistic and take rests.

Above: Listen to your body and do not overtrain; it can cause unpleasant symptoms and even illness.

Above: If you are too ill to get out of bed, training will only make you feel much worse.

Above: Take the right medication to recover from illness faster, and take adequate rest, too.

A good coach, taking an overview of the entire picture, will be able to stop you overtraining before it really gets a grip.

Training when unwell

If you are suffering from a cold, and have a runny nose and a small cough, the chances are that your immune system is not badly damaged. You can continue light training, so long as you stop before you reach maximum intensity or failure. If you are weight-training, reduce the weights you usually use by 25 per cent to avoid any further breakdown of your immune system. If you are doing cardiovascular training, you may experience a drop in heart rate during interval training. Your body will not want to reach its normal level of intensity and its natural defence mechanism will prevent your heart rate from going above 90 per cent of its normal maximum. Your body needs to be able to fight the infection rather than use its energy to repair and rebuild muscle after heavy weight-training.

If the symptoms have worked their way into other parts of your body, causing you to feel run-down and achy, with a sore throat and headache, stop exercise altogether until you feel better. To get better fast, eat healthy foods, maintain your weight and get plenty of sleep. When you do resume training, exercise at a lower intensity and give yourself more rest days in the first few weeks, as well as more rest time

between exercises and sets in the gym. Don't expect to resume your normal pace for cardiovascular exercise for at least two weeks.

Going forward

Ask yourself why you are suffering from overtraining or illness. Use your training diary to look back at what you have been doing so that you can avoid making the same mistakes. You may have increased your training too much over a short space of time, or the stresses of work or family life may have been making you particularly tired. Keep a record of your sleeping pattern, noting the time that you go to sleep, how well you sleep, and for how long. You can then check this record for irregularities.

Consult your food diary to see if you really are getting the nutrition you need for your body to cope with the demands of your training. Don't be afraid to be critical of yourself or ask for advice from a training partner, coach or nutritionalist.

When resuming exercise, take time to think about how you feel each day and listen to your body. Only change one thing at a time. For example, altering your diet, at the same time as including more intervals in training, can be too much for your body in one go, and it won't help you to pinpoint what it was that made you so unwell initially.

Below: Learn from your mistakes in training and resolve to take time to work on your weaknesses.

CORE STABILITY

Core stability is the strength of the muscles that hold the spine and pelvis in place. Without core strength, you will be prone to injury and poor performance. And the fitter, faster and more powerful you get, the more core strength you need to cope with the demands placed on your body.

Above: Maintaining a firm position to catch a medicine ball requires good core strength.
Left: Kneeling on a fit ball while holding weights demonstrates balance and stability, owing to core strength.

Importance of Core Stability

The term 'core stability' is used to describe the muscles of the trunk that hold and control the position and movement of the lumbar spine and pelvis. Because these muscles are rarely used in everyday life, they require special attention.

Thousands of years ago people had to be physically active to survive; our ancestors were hunters and gatherers who were constantly on the move, lifting materials to build shelters, tracking down animals for food and felling trees for fires. Today, we miss out on these everyday activities. In the past, we would regularly have used all the muscles that control the position and dynamic movements of the lumbar spine and pelvis. Now, many people live a sedentary lifestyle and have little or no core stability.

You need your core muscles to be strong and active all the time for everyday movements. For example, if you are about to lift something heavy from the floor, your core muscles will have to tense before the rest of your body exerts itself to pick the item up in order to keep a brace-like position to hold your spine and pelvis in place to assist the lifting movement. If your core muscles are not tensed, your spine and pelvis will not have the strength to maintain their correct position, leaving you prone to injury. Common problems related to poor core stability include lower back pain, rounded shoulders and back, and poor posture. With the appropriate core stability exercises, you will be able to recruit the correct core muscles to support your body effectively; the pressure on your back will dramatically reduce and your posture will improve.

Core stability is also important for optimum performance in many sports. You may have strong legs and shoulders but if your core stability is poor, the middle of your body may twist under pressure in a rugby scrum or tackle, for

> **Working together**
> It's not just a case of getting your core muscles to work; they need to work in conjunction with your other muscles and recruit in the correct order to help all your muscles to be effective in establishing core stability in your body.

The core stability muscles

The major muscles in the trunk that provide you with good core stability are:

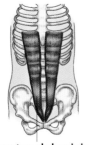

rectus abdominis

Above: This muscle helps you to sit up.

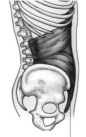

transversus abdominis

Above: This muscle pulls you in and helps you exhale.

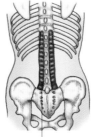

multifidus

Above: Controls movement of the spine in any direction.

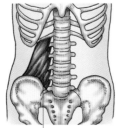

quadratus lumborum

Above: *Controls lateral movement of spine.*

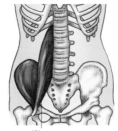

iliopsoas

Above: *Flexes the tops of the legs and hips.*

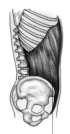

external oblique

Above: Controls lateral and rotational movements.

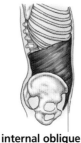

internal oblique

Above: This muscle controls lateral movement of the trunk.

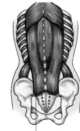

erector spinae

Above: This muscle supports you bending forward.

Below: Sitting at a desk all day may result in your core muscles becoming even weaker.

use in giving you good core stability, and, most people use poor technique when they do sit ups and crunches.

Avoiding injury
If you are looking to build strength in your upper and lower body using weights, it is important to have strong core stability to avoid injury. Adding core exercises twice a week to your training programme will give you greater stability and power, and help you to avoid injury. Once your core muscles are switched on and recruiting properly you will feel them working. When you do a chest press tense the core muscles also. The muscles you are targeting in the legs or arms work harder and feel more isolated. Using the core muscles during other exercises will make them stronger and more effective.

Below: In combat sports such as rugby, strong core muscles are essential to avoid sustaining injuries.

Above: An effective golf swing requires a good level of core stability to control the movement.

example. Likewise, if your torso muscles are weak, your golf swing will suffer: you will not be able to transfer as much power from your body to the ball, and your lack of control in your back swing and follow-through will leave you off balance and at risk of injury.

People often make the mistake of thinking that simply doing lots of sit-ups and crunches will provide them with good core stability – and it's not true. It doesn't matter how many sit-ups and crunches you do, they will only help you to firm up your muscles to make it look like you have a toned, flat stomach. These exercises are, in fact, of very little

Measuring Core Stability

It is difficult to measure core stability and muscle recruitment outside a laboratory environment. However, there are some basic tests that will reveal whether your core stability is working efficiently enough to support you.

Core strength is so important that if the results of the tests below show that there is any weakness in your core stability, you should take time to work on all aspects of it. The tests not only reveal how much strength you have in your muscles, but also the recruitment pattern of the muscles connected to the core. If your core is weak, these muscles may not be recruiting effectively in the right order.

It is important to consider which core muscles are most important for your sport, and in some cases this means designing a test that is relevant to you. A good physiotherapist or expert in biomechanics should be able to tell you which parts of your body are the most important and which movements

Ignore at your peril

Many people, including elite athletes, don't bother with core stability exercises, as it is difficult to measure the results. But core stability and correct muscular recruitment will relate directly to all sporting and exercise activities, so measure it, train it and monitor it.

Poor core strength

You may find you get cramp in your feet during these exercises – this is a sign of poor core strength, as your body has to compensate by using other muscles to keep your balance. If this happens to you, stop for a few minutes and try to relax your other muscles.

require help from your core-stability muscles. For example, in your golf swing, you need to have strong core muscles to prevent lateral movement at the hips. Doing a single-leg squat or lunge and watching the lateral movement at the hip closely will help you to see how strong your core is at maintaining the solid position required.

Film yourself from all angles doing the tests so that you can see for yourself where your core stability weaknesses are. Repeat these tests every six weeks to monitor your progress.

Below: You will be more prone to injury if you do not maintain core stability while you are training. A strong core is vital for effective exercising.

Single-leg stand

Check your core stability with this simple test: Stand still for at least 30 seconds, without putting your arms out for balance. If you can't do this, your core muscles are not working well. In this exercise, all the core muscles are used.

Stand on one leg with your arms by your sides. Shut your eyes and stand still for as long as possible. As soon as you shut your eyes, you should feel your core muscles tightening – they help to hold you still, just like the guy ropes of a tent. Keep your feet as relaxed as possible to put more emphasis on the core stability muscles, thus making them work harder. Restrict movement in the hips when changing from one leg to the other.

Single-leg squat

Do this exercise in front of a mirror to assess which parts of your body are weak. All of the core stability muscles are used in this exercise.

1 *Stand up straight on both legs with your arms out in front of you. Balance well so the head is still (a sign of weak core stablility is the head moving from side to side).*

The lunge

In this exercise, the signs of a weak core are the same as those for the single-leg squat. Include lunges with leans and lunges with rotation in your exercise plan to make your core muscles strong enough to support your body in your chosen sporting activity. The lunge uses all the core stability muscles.

1 *Stand up straight on both legs, with your feet hip-width apart and your arms hanging straight by your side. Try to keep the head and neck totally relaxed before you start the lunge.*

2 *Take a forward stride and lower your body weight by bending both legs, keeping your back as upright as possible. Try to avoid any lateral forward or backward movement during the lunge.*

Plank hand changes

Keep your core muscles switched on through this exercise. All of the core muscles are recruited for this exercise.

1 *Adopt the standard press-up position, with your legs wide apart and hands with palms flat on the floor, so that you can keep your hips still and progressively move your feet closer together to assess how much your core stability is improving. Focus on the hips and don't move them sideways or rotate them.*

2 *Squat until the thigh of your squatting leg is almost parallel to the ground. Pause for 2 seconds, then slowly stand up.*

Check your core stability

Look out for the signs of weak core stability: head moving from side to side; hips dropping down and not staying level (also indicative of weak gluteus muscles); leg crossing behind your squatting leg during the squat (also indicative of weak buttock muscles); knee wobbling from side to side (indicative of weakness higher up in core muscles); and trunk constantly moving.

2 *Slowly raise one hand off the floor and place it on top of your other hand. Feel and watch out for any lateral, upward and downward movement of the hips. Your core is working well when there is little trunk movement during the exercise. Lateral movement and/or rotation in the centre of the body will make you prone to injury.*

Basic Core Exercises

It is vital to begin with these basic core exercises in order for your core muscles to recruit correctly. If you jump to more advanced exercises, your core muscles will not benefit, and you will be prone to injury.

In addition to beginning with these exercises so that you can get your muscles recruiting correctly, you should also regularly revert back to using them to check whether you are doing the basics correctly.

If possible, you should also work with a training partner who can observe your exercising and give you some guidance on whether your core muscles are working properly. Where possible, try placing your hands on the core muscles you are supposed to be working during the exercise to see if they are held in tension or not.

For each exercise, take 2 to 3 seconds for each direction of the movement. Breathe out at the beginning of the movement, continue breathing through the hold, and breathe in as you return to the start position.

Think before you tense

It is easy to do core stability exercises without knowing which muscles you are trying to engage. Take your time to think clearly about which parts of the body are giving you the stability for each exercise, and be patient, focusing intently on that part of the body. If you are in a position that requires you to hold the core muscles tight, then keep your body as still as possible.

Many people think they have mastered an exercise and quickly move on to more advanced core work when, in fact, they only keep their balance by wobbling from side to side, waving their arms around or holding on to a wall. If you are really struggling to feel your core muscles, especially your abdominal muscles, then try feeling them when you are coughing. The tension that you feel around your abdominal area as you are coughing is caused by the core muscles tensing.

Plank (prone bridging)

Muscles used Rectus abdominis; transversus abdominis; internal obliques

1 Lie on your front with your legs out straight behind you and your hands clasped together in front of you, with your forearms flat on the floor. Keep your spine in neutral all the time and don't let your back arch.

2 Raise your hips so that only your forearms and toes are resting on the floor. Hold this position for as long as possible by tensing your core muscles. Push your chest out and keep your shoulders back to make the exercise harder. You should aim to hold the plank for as long as you possibly can. Begin by holding the position for 20 seconds, adding 5 seconds each time, until you can stay in this position for at least 1 minute.

Plank to single-leg raise

Muscles used Rectus abdominis; transversus abdominis; internal obliques

1 *Lie on your front with your legs out straight behind you and your hands clasped together in front of you, with your forearms flat on the floor. Keep your spine in neutral and tense your core muscles.*

2 *Raise your hips, keeping your forearms and toes on the floor, then lift one leg off the ground, keeping it straight out behind you. Hold for up to 30 seconds. Repeat the exercise with the other leg.*

Side plank raises (lateral bridging)

Muscles used Obliques – internal and external; transversus abdominis

1 *Lie on your side, with the legs out straight, a forearm flat on the floor, with the hand in a loose fist position, the other hand palm down on the floor, and one foot resting on top of the other.*

2 *Raise your hips, keeping one forearm on the floor and your feet together. Raise the other arm straight up in the air. Hold so your body is in a straight line.*

Gluteal bridge

Muscles used Rectus abdominis; gluteus maximus; erector spinae

Lie on your back on a mat, with the legs bent at 90 degrees. Tense your core muscles, especially the gluteus muscles, and raise your hips until your body is level in one line, from your knees to your shoulders. Begin by holding the position for 10–20 seconds, gradually building up to a 1-minute hold.

Tips for core exercises

Start by keeping your body as still as possible, then begin tensing your core muscles. Try pushing through your heels to put more emphasis on the gluteus and less stress on your knees. Focus on tensing your buttocks. Keep your hands and elbows off the ground to make your core muscles work harder. Breathe out to begin and in when you return to the start.

Single-leg stand

Muscles used All the core muscles are used for this exercise.

Stand on one leg, with your eyes closed and both arms hanging by your sides. Try to keep your body still and as relaxed as possible, then tense your core muscles to maintain your balance. Hold your position for 10–20 seconds, gradually building up to a 1-minute hold. Keep your spine in neutral throughout the movement and focus on working the obliques. After you have completed a 1-minute hold, try holding the position for as long as possible, tensing your core muscles all the time.

Intermediate Core Exercises

As your core stability muscles get stronger, you can start to introduce exercises – of the kind given here – that involve making a strong connection between your core muscles and the muscles of your limbs.

When you start using your limbs to press and pull weights, it is important to be able to keep your spine and pelvis in their natural positions in order to make your core-stability muscles stronger for everyday activities and sporting movements.

Remember that you are only as strong as your core-stability muscles. Without strengthening the core, you will not increase your physical power and will always be more prone to injury.

Taking your limbs away from the centre of your body will act as a lever to make your core muscles work even harder. Exercises that involve rotation will force some core muscles to keep your body still, with other core muscles working to allow parts of your body to rotate, but in a controlled way. If you don't take time to get this correct, other muscles – mainly in the lower back – will be forced to do the work, which will not give you the core strength that you are looking for.

For each exercise, take 2 to 3 seconds for each direction of the movement. Breathe out at the beginning of the movement, and breathe in as you return to the start position.

For the following intermediate core exercises, start with three sets of five repetitions and build up gradually over the weeks until you are doing five sets of ten repetitions.

Rest-day exercise

For you to get the maximum benefit from your core exercises, they need to be given your full attention and energy. At the intermediate stage you should try to plan two core-stability workouts a week. You need to do these sessions separately from your normal cardiovascular or strength-training sessions. Try fitting them in on the days that you would normally rest.

Plank leg kick

Muscles used Rectus abdominis; transversus abdominis; internal obliques; gluteus maximus; tensor fascia lata

1 *Lie on your front, legs out straight, hips raised, with forearms and toes on the floor.*

2 *Raise one foot, bend your knee and bring it in toward your chest until your thigh is perpendicular to the ground.*

3 *Kick the leg back out, slowly but forcefully, until it is straight out behind you. Hold for 5 seconds, then bring the knee in. Repeat with the other leg.*

Hip-raise, single-leg changeovers

Muscles used Rectus abdominis; gluteus maximus; erector spinae

1 *Adopt the gluteal bridge position. Tense your core muscles, especially the gluteus muscles. Raise your hips until your body is in one line from your shoulders to the knees.*

2 *Slowly raise one leg until it is in line with the rest of your body. Hold this position for 5 seconds then change legs, keeping your hips off the floor and your body in line.*

Superman

Muscles used Erector spinae; gluteus maximus; rectus abdominis

1 *Start with your hands and knees on the floor, and your belly button pulled in toward your spine to keep your core muscles tense.*

2 *Raise your right leg off the floor, straighten it behind you, lift and straighten your left arm in front of you. Hold for 5 seconds, return to the start position and repeat with the opposite limbs.*

Cable wood chops, high to low

Muscles used Rectus abdominis; obliques – internal and external

Work the core muscles

Try to visualize a poker going through the top of your head and down the length of your spine. If you imagine turning on this 'axis', you will find that the exercise is more effective.

Use a weight that is lighter than you think you need to start with. Use a mirror to check your technique, to help you eliminate any lateral hip movement.

With rotational exercises, your hips will try to move. To create a strong core, keep the hips still; get the core muscles to work.

This is a great exercise for golfers as it involves the same muscles used for the golf swing.

1 *Stand side-on to the cable machine, with your feet just over hip-width apart. Turn toward the machine by twisting upward from just above the hips, and grip the rope in both hands.*

2 *Slowly rotate your upper body, keeping your arms straight out in front, until the handle is level with your opposite knee. Pause for a second, then slowly rotate back to the start position.*

Advanced Core Exercises

When you get to an advanced stage of your core stability training, you can start to involve dynamic exercises that will simulate the movements you might use in your sport. These exercises make it hard to balance, so that your core muscles have to work hard.

Most people believe that you are either naturally blessed with having good balance or not, when in fact it really comes down to your core muscles giving you enough stability to achieve really good balance.

Most sporting movements call for good balance to cope with changes in direction and transferring weight and stress from one limb to another. Some of the following exercises use weights to make the exercise harder and to help build core muscles. If you want to move your limbs with strong, rapid movements, you will need to have very strong core stability with great balance.

For each exercise, take 2 to 3 seconds for each direction of the movement. Breathe out at the beginning of the movement, continue breathing through the hold, and breathe in as you return to the start position.

For all of these exercises, begin with three sets of repetitions each side of the body, gradually building up to five sets of ten repetitions each side.

> **Exercise to stay injury-free**
> When you have reached the advanced stage, just build the exercises into your normal training programme. Do them between cardiovascular exercises and resistance exercises to help keep your core muscles switched on through all of your movements. It will also help you avoid injuries in training and make the core muscles focus and become recruited to support your limbs as they start to fatigue.

Two-point superman

Muscles used Erector spinae; gluteus maximus; rectus abdominis

1 *Start on all fours on a mat, with both hands and knees on the floor, hands palm down. Try to prevent your lower back from arching.*

2 *Raise and straighten your right leg out behind you. At the same time, raise and straighten your left arm in front of you. Pull your belly button in toward your spine.*

3 *To make this a two-point superman, lift the foot of your supporting leg off the floor to work your core muscles harder.*

4 *Hold for 5 seconds, then bring your right leg and left arm in until the knee and elbow touch. Repeat on the other side.*

Press-up plank to side waves

Muscles used Rectus abdominis; obliques – internal and external; pectoralis major

1 *Start in a standard press-up position.*

2 *Lower your body toward the floor by bending your elbows out to the sides.*

3 *With elbows bent at 90 degrees, hold for 2 seconds then push back up.*

4 *Take one arm out to the side and twist your body until you are side-on to the floor in a side plank position. Think of your trunk as a brace and don't let your hips drop in the rotation. Let your feet rotate over on to their sides.*

Single-leg cable wood chops, high to low

Muscles used Erector spinae; gluteus – maximus, medius; rectus abdominis

1 *Stand on one leg, with the other foot raised just slightly off the floor, side-on to the cable machine. Turn your upper torso slowly toward the machine and grip the rope with both hands. Try doing this exercise sitting on a fit ball, with only one foot on the floor.*

2 *Slowly rotate your upper body, keeping your arms straight out in front of you until the handle is level with your opposite knee. Pause for a second, then slowly rotate back to the start position. Keep your hips facing forward to put greater emphasis on the core muscles.*

Superman row

Muscles used Erector spinae; rectus abdominis; obliques; latissimus dorsi

1 *Stand on one leg and hold your other leg straight out behind you, and your opposite arm straight out in front of you. Hold a dumbbell in the other hand at knee height. Keep your back parallel to the floor.*

2 *Pull the dumbbell up to your ribs, taking your elbow past your ribs and back behind the line of your body. Avoid twisting your trunk as you pull the weight up. Pause for 1 second, then return to the start position.*

Fit Ball Core Exercises

The fit ball is an effective piece of equipment for improving core stability, because it forces your body to stimulate more neuromuscular pathways, which in turn activate a larger number of muscle fibres in the core.

The fit ball was first introduced in the 1980s as a way of improving posture and rehabilitation for injuries. But because the fit ball helped to achieve great results in increased core stability among top athletes, it has become a great tool for people of all abilities.

Being round, a fit ball is an unstable surface to work on, unlike a conventional flat bench in the gym. As a result, core-stability muscles have to stay switched on throughout any movement when you are on the fit ball if you want to stay on the ball. Just sitting on a ball holding your body upright requires the majority of your core-stability muscles to work. The ball also allows you to get a greater range of movement for exercises that you would usually do on the floor. For example, with gluteal bridges, you can lower your hips to the ground before tensing them to come back up.

By using a fit ball, your body awareness and balance will improve, which is a bonus for any sporting activity. Do not try using these exercises until you have completed the intermediate stage of your core stability training.

Building connections

Replace some of your regular gym exercises with fit ball exercises to build the connection between your core and limbs. For example, when training your legs, include some single-leg fit ball squats; for a chest session, include fit ball press-ups; and for a shoulder workout, include some fit ball shoulder presses. Many of the exercises used in the gym can be replicated using the fit ball; this will make them significantly harder and ensure that you are using your core muscles correctly. Many world-class athletes have stated that using a fit ball made a big difference to their performance.

Fit ball hip raises, feet on ball

Muscles used Gluteus maximus and medius; rectus abdominis; obliques – internal and external; biceps femoris

1 *Lie on your back on a gym mat on the floor, with your feet on the top of the fit ball and your hands flat on the floor, palms down. Tense your core muscles, especially your buttocks. Keep the ball as still as possible.*

2 *Raise your hips until your body is in one line from your shoulders to your knees. Try to maintain your balance throughout. Hold this position for 5 seconds, then slowly return to the start position.*

Single-leg fit ball squat

Muscles used Rectus abdominis; gluteus medius; quadriceps

1 *With the fit ball between your lower back and a wall, slowly squat in front of a mirror, pushing your weight through your heels, until your heel is almost parallel to the floor.*

2 *Pause for 2 seconds, check that your hips are staying in line, then gradually extend your legs until you are standing fully upright. Tense your buttocks as your legs straighten.*

Fit ball plank

Muscles used Rectus abdominis; transversus abdominis; internal obliques

Adopt a plank position with your elbows and forearms resting on the ball and your feet out behind you, resting on your toes. Hold this position for as long as possible by tensing your core muscles. Keep your spine in neutral all the time and don't let your back arch. If your back does start to arch, stop the exercise immediately; it will have a negative effect by teaching your body to do the exercise using the wrong muscles. Aim to hold the plank for as long as possible. Begin by holding the position for 20 seconds, building up to a 1-minute hold for three sets.

Fit ball side roll

Muscles used Obliques; gluteus medius; rectus abdominis; tensor fascia lata

1 Rest the fit ball under your shoulders and neck. Keep your knees bent at 90 degrees and your feet flat on the floor. Tense your core muscles to keep your hips up in line with your knees and shoulders. Look down toward your feet to help you balance at first. Focus on working your obliques and gluteus medius.

2 Roll your upper body over to one side of the fit ball until you reach the point where you start to lose your balance. Pause for 2 seconds, then slowly return to the start position. Start with your feet wide apart and gradually bring them closer together as you get better at the exercise. Start with three sets of five repetitions to each side.

Fit ball shoulder press

Begin with three sets of five repetitions, then build up to five sets of ten repetitions.

Muscles used Rectus abdominis; gluteus – maximus and medius; deltoid

1 Holding dumbells in each hand, sit on the fit ball, raise one foot off the floor and lift the dumbbells up to ear level. Have a training partner close to you throughout this exercise to help you get used to balancing on the ball.

2 Keeping your core tensed, raise the dumbbells up above your head, pause for 2 seconds, then slowly return to the start position.

BOSU Core Exercises

The BOSU, an acronym for Both Sides Utilized, is an excellent tool for recruiting and strengthening your core muscles. Every time you move on a BOSU you have no choice but to switch on your core muscles in order to maintain balance and co-ordination.

When using either side of the BOSU (one side has a flat base and the other is similar to a rounded jelly), the slightest movement will force your core muscles to work, thereby strengthening the connection between your limbs and core muscles. For each exercise, take 2 to 3 seconds for each direction of the movement. Breathe out at the beginning of the movement, throughout the hold, and in as you return to the start position.

BOSU plank knee tuck with rotations

Muscles used Rectus abdominis; transverse abdominis; gluteus – maximus and medius

1 *Adopt the standard plank position, firmly gripping the sides of the BOSU with your hands and keeping your core muscles tense, so that you can raise your body upward on to your toes. Keep the shoulders level so the core works harder.*

2 *Raise one leg until the knee touches the opposite elbow, your trunk rotating slightly to get the full range of movement. Pause for 2 seconds, then return to the start. Begin with three sets of five repetitions. Build up to three sets of 15 on each side.*

BOSU superman

Muscles used Rectus abdominis; transverse abdominis; and gluteus – maximus and medius

1 *Position yourself carefully on all fours on the BOSU so that you can maintain your balance. Pull your belly button in to maintain a flat back and keep your head in line with your spine. Keep your core muscles tense all the time to keep your spine in neutral.*

2 *Raise your left leg and straighten it out behind you. At the same time, extend your right arm in front of you. Hold this position for 5 seconds, then return to the start position. Keep breathing during the exercise. Start with five repetitions, change limbs and build up to twenty repetitions on each side.*

BOSU squat

Muscles used Rectus abdominis; transversus abdominis; gluteus – maximus and medius; quadriceps

1 Start by placing one foot on the BOSU, allowing it to rock to one side, then slowly add your other foot and attempt to find your balance. Get your training partner to help you to balance if it's the first time you have tried using the BOSU.

2 Squat down slowly until your thighs are parallel with the floor. Pause for 2 seconds, then slowly extend your legs and stand upright. When you can keep your balance and there is no visible wobble, try squatting on one leg to place greater emphasis on your gluteus medius. Begin with three sets of five repetitions, building up to three sets of twenty repetitions.

Cable wood chop on BOSU, high to low

Muscles used Gluteus medius; obliques

1 Begin with a light weight and practise keeping the top of the BOSU as flat as possible as you rotate, before progressing to heavy weights. Stand on both feet, facing forward on the BOSU, then twist your upper torso toward the cable machine. Grip the rope in both hands.

2 Slowly rotate using core muscles, taking the cable across your body until it is level with your opposite knee. Pause for 1 second, then slowly rotate back to the start position. This exercise is a great one for golfers, as the rocking motion of the BOSU is similar to the lateral movement needed when swinging a golf club.

BOSU lat pull-down

Muscles used Latissimus dorsi; transversus abdominis

1 Stand on the BOSU and grip the rope with both hands.

2 Pull the rope in toward the bottom of your chest, taking your elbows out to the side.

Combination exercises

You can introduce these BOSU core exercises on their own or use them in conjunction with and to advance your normal resistance exercises. The BOSU can be used in conjunction with other core-stability exercises to make them harder. For example, doing fit ball press-ups with your feet resting on the flat side of the BOSU.

Medicine Ball Core Exercises

Medicine ball exercises are an effective and fun way to work your core muscles. The exercises given here will also help you to develop power, co-ordination and balance, all of which are important in most sporting activities.

If you are trying to catch or throw a medicine ball, you are forced to tense your core muscles in order to take the impact of the throw when catching it. You are also compelled to tense your core muscles to brace your body to hold it still while releasing it in the throw. Having a stable base for most sports is essential. If you use the ball in exercises that involve big movements, your core muscles will have to work against the inertia of the ball when moving it. Medicine ball exercises can also teach your core-stability muscles to

contract rapidly, just as they would in the movements involved in a boxing punch or a tennis serve.

Medicine balls come in different sizes, typically 1–10kg/2.2lb–22lb. Use the ball that matches your size and strength. Start with a lightweight ball and gradually progress to heavier ones when you feel ready.

For each exercise, take 2 to 3 seconds for each direction of the movement. Breathe out at the beginning of the movement, throughout the hold; breathe in as you return to the start position.

> **Slowly does it**
>
> It is important not to try to progress too fast with these exercises. First, master the basic and intermediate core exercises to take full advantage of what these medicine ball exercises have to offer, which will increase your heart rate by working many muscles simultaneously. Introduce the medicine ball gradually: try occasionally replacing one of your weekly cardiovascular sessions with a medicine ball core workout.

Medicine ball press-up

Muscles used Pectoralis major; rectus abdominis

Get into a press-up position, with one hand resting on the ball. Slowly lower your body, taking your elbows out to the side until they are at 90 degrees. Pause for a second, then return to the start position. As you get stronger, transfer more weight to the medicine ball side to make your stabilizing muscles work harder. Try taking one leg off the ground to make the exercise harder still. Begin with three sets of five repetitions, building up to five sets of twenty

Single-leg squat to medicine ball shoulder press

Muscles used Gluteus medius; quadriceps; rectus abdominis

1 *Start by standing on one leg until your are balanced, with the other leg slightly bent, arms straight, holding the medicine ball above your head. Hold the ball still for a few seconds; this action will force the core muscles to tense involuntarily.*

2 *Bring the ball to chest height when you start squatting, to avoid putting pressure on the lower back. When the thigh of your squatting leg is parallel to the floor, pause, extend the leg and press the medicine ball above your head. Repeat with other leg. Do three sets of ten repetitions for each leg.*

Lunge with medicine ball; wood chop, high to low

Muscles used Obliques; gluteus – maximus and medius; quadriceps

1 *Stand with one foot in front of the other, about 60cm/2ft apart. Hold the medicine ball above your head with straight arms.*

2 *Lunge and rotate your upper body across your front leg, lowering the ball until it is level with the hip. Pause for 1 second, then slowly return to the start position. Begin with three sets of five repetitions, then build up to three sets of ten repetitions.*

Medicine ball lunge with rotation

Muscles used Quadriceps; obliques – internal and external; gluteus medius

1 *Catch the medicine ball with your arms out in front of you. Keep yourself as stable as possible by tensing your core muscles to take the impact.*

3 *Turn back past the centre point and rotate your upper body out to the left. Focus on keeping your hips in line and stop the hips from rotating in the movement. Throughout the exercise, remember that it is the core muscles you are trying to work, so when they get tired, rest before your arms and back take over.*

2 *At the bottom of the lunge, turn your upper body to your right. Keep your arms straight throughout the rotation and maintain good shoulder posture.*

4 *When you come back up from the lunge, throw the ball back to your partner from chest height, keeping your core tense to give you a balanced base. To make this exercise harder, you can create more instability by placing your front foot on the flat surface of a BOSU. Begin with three sets of five repetitions, then build up to three sets of ten.*

Plyometrics Core Training

Plyometric exercises involve preloading a muscle and then aggressively leaping and bounding. They cause the neuromuscular system to respond faster and more powerfully than any other resistance or cardiovascular exercises.

Good core muscles are essential for plyometric exercises, which in turn are an advanced method of improving the strength of the core muscles. You need advanced core stability before you try plyometric exercises. If your core muscles are not strong, you will be prone to injury, and the power you generate with the leg muscles will be less effective.

Rapid response

Plyometrics refers to human movements that involve an eccentric (lengthening) muscle contraction followed immediately by a rapid concentric (shortening) muscle contraction. These type of training exercises are essential for fast sporting performance such as running, jumping and throwing. For example, a sprinter has their feet on the ground for less than 0.01 of a second so their muscles must respond to the rapid change in direction from when their foot strikes the ground to taking off again. A massive amount of force is required in a very short space of time. Plyometric exercises will not necessarily make you faster by enhancing your speed, but they will help to speed up the change in the period between a muscle lengthening and shortening. The phase between the muscle lengthening and shortening is called the amortization phase.

Preparation for plyometrics

You need to have a good base of strength training before you can do plyometrics. It would be advisable to be able to squat at least your body weight before you start plyometrics training. If your muscles are not strong enough you will be susceptible to injury. Plyometrics workouts should be classed in the same bracket as strength training workouts, in terms of the afterburn of calories. Endurance athletes will get little advantage from doing plyometrics. Your muscles will be broken down and therefore your body will take time to recover with an increase in calories used to make this recovery happen.

You should always have someone watching you in your first few weeks of plyometric workouts. It is easy to get the techniques wrong and this will seriously impinge on the effectiveness of the workouts. Neuromuscular pathways will be enhanced with plyometrics training if it is done correctly. Your neuromuscular system must be continually stimulated in anaerobic activities to make improvements in your sporting activity.

Lunge jump

Muscles used Quadriceps; gluteus medius

1 *Lunge down, with your left foot forward, and your arms hanging down by your sides. Keep your left knee just over the foot.*

2 *Spring up into the air, at the same time changing over your legs so that you can land with your right foot in front.*

3 *Land on both feet, and soften the impact by bending your knees, arms still at your sides. Begin with three sets of four repetitions for each leg.*

THE HENLEY COLLEGE LIBRARY

Single-leg squat jump

This uses the same technique as the squat jump, but using one leg only. Your stabilizers have to work hard to prevent lateral movement and your leg takes double the normal force. Begin with three sets of five repetitions, and build up to three sets of ten repetitions.

Muscles used Quadriceps; gluteus medius

1 *Stand on one leg with the other leg trailing behind you and squat down. Move left arm forward for balance.*

2 *Straighten your leg as forcefully as possible to take off the ground using your arms to help to drive you upward.*

3 *Land softly on the same leg; bend at the knee on impact with the floor and push your hips back behind you.*

Lateral jump

Muscles used Quadriceps; gluteus medius

1 *From a squatting position, straighten up to extend your legs as fast as possible.*

2 *Jump up with a sideways movement over a box, with your arms held out at the sides.*

3 *Land on both feet, softening the impact by bending your knees. Begin with three sets of five repetitions.*

Getting it right

Teaching your body to use muscles in the wrong way will lead to poor muscle recruitment and a need to start all over again because neuromuscular pathways will not be working correctly. Therefore it is crucial to get these exercises right first time. To get the most out of this type of training leave at least two days between sessions and avoid any strength training in between. Make sure you are wearing the correct footwear for your plyometric workouts to give you adequate stability. Good quality running shoes will give you the support and cushioning you need.

Sport and weight loss

If you take time to do exercises in your training to advance your core stability, your body will become better equipped to cope with your chosen sporting activity. If you are trying to lose weight, plyometrics core training will challenge your body to work in a different way, making you burn more calories and increasing your lean muscle mass – just 20 minutes a week will be enough to reap the benefits and feel the difference. You should have at least two days' rest between plyometric exercise routines to allow your muscles and joints to recover fully.

Warm up well

Because a large amount of force is generated very quickly, for example when doing a jump, there is a lot of stress on joints and a possibility of injury to muscles and joints so any training session which includes plyometric exercises should include a good dynamic warm-up, designed if possible to suit your sport. Go through some of the plyometric exercises in slow motion to prepare your muscles for the movements. Your muscles will come under huge stress, so they need to feel warm and high in energy. Avoid doing this after strength or cardiovascular training.

Squat jump

Muscles used Quadriceps; gluteus maximus

1 *With your feet slightly apart and flat on the floor, bend your knees and squat down so that you feel stable and balanced, then push your hips backward. Straighten the arms and stretch them out behind you so that they are straight and parallel to the ground.*

2 *Quickly move your arms forward and stretch them out in front, so they are raised just above head height. Extend your legs as fast as you possibly can, then jump high into the air. For the maximum effect, you need to make the movement as quickly and as smoothly as possible.*

3 *Land on both feet, softening the impact by bending the knees until you are in the starting position. Pause for 1 second, then repeat. Try jumping forward across the room and see how far you are able to jump. Begin with three sets of five repetitions, building up to three sets of twenty repetitions.*

Squat throw

Muscles used Quadriceps; rectus abdominis

1 *Catch a medicine ball in front of your chest and squat down at the same time, pushing your hips back behind you. Focus on tensing your abdominals to keep a solid base.*

2 *As you extend your legs to stand back up, throw the medicine ball back to your training partner. Do the movement as fast as possible to make it more effective. Begin with three sets of five repetitions, building up to three sets of ten repetitions.*

Overhead slam

Muscles used Rectus abdominis; pectoralis major; latissimus dorsi; seratus anterior; triceps

1 *Stand with feet hip-width apart and hold the medicine ball above your head, tensing your core muscles.*

2 *Keeping your core tense, throw the medicine ball down in front of your feet as hard as possible and catch it on the rebound. Rest for 2 to 3 seconds after the first set, then repeat for three sets of five repetitions, building up to five sets of ten repetitions.*

Combining Core and Resistance Exercises

Once you have built up your core muscles, and you have confidence in your ability to recruit them for balance and stability, you can use them to help you perform a range of bigger exercises for increased muscle mass and greater strength.

Combining core and resistance exercises is the most advanced form of core-stability training. It is crucial that these exercises are not attempted until you have been through the process of beginner, intermediate and advanced core training. Once you have reached this stage, you will really begin to appreciate the benefits of your core strength when you are taking part in any of your sporting activities. Your body will subconsciously switch on the correct core muscles to help you to perform appropriately in any movement or exercise.

Squat to cable shoulder press

Muscles used Quadriceps; deltoids; gluteus maximus; rectus abdominis

1 *This exercise is an efficient way of building power from your feet up toward your hands. Stand comfortably, with your feet hip-width apart. Holding the cables in both hands, squat down and pause for 1 second when your thighs are almost parallel with the floor.*

2 *Press the cables above your head, keeping your core tense. Try doing this exercise on one leg and using just one hand to make your core muscles work harder. Begin with three sets of five repetitions; build up to three sets of 15 to 20 repetitions.*

Press-up to single-arm dumbbell row

Muscles used Gluteus medius; latissimus dorsi; obliques – internal and external

1 *Adopt a press-up position, gripping one dumbbell in each hand. Lower your body toward the floor.*

2 *With the elbows at 90 degrees, pause for a second, then return to the start position, taking one dumbbell into the side of your ribs, your elbow brushing past your ribs and back behind you. Begin with three sets of three repetitions, building up to three sets of ten repetitions.*

Single-leg squat to single-arm dumbbell row and frontal raise

Muscles used Quadriceps; gluteus maximus; deltoids; rectus abdominis

1 *Gripping a dumbbell in one hand, balance and squat down on one leg, then lift the other leg off the floor, and at the same time, pull the dumbbell in toward your ribs. Throughout the exercise, maintain a neutral spine to prevent your back muscles overworking.*

2 *Pause for a second, then, with a straight arm, raise your hand out in front of you to just above eye height. At the same time, straighten your leg. Make sure your belly button is sucked in all the time. Begin with three sets of three repetitions for each side of the body, building up to three sets of ten.*

> **Daily benefit**
>
> After doing these exercises, and you find that you are able to do the maximum set of repetitions with ease, you will notice that your core muscles start to respond naturally to everyday actions such as bending down and twisting to pick something up from the floor.
>
> The exercises will also provide you with the stability and focused training that you need for your chosen sport. You will find that actions such as hitting a golf ball, tackling your opposition to the ground in a rugby game or hitting a tennis serve, will become easier.
>
> To benefit from these exercises, they do not have to take up an entire exercise session – you could simply include one or two advanced core exercises in each of your weekly training routines. This way, you won't get bored with your routines, and your core muscles will remain switched on throughout the rest of your cardiovascular or weight-training session.

Squat to cable rotation

Muscles used Quadriceps; gluteus medius; obliques – internal and external

1 *With the feet shoulder-width apart, grip the cable in both hands, squat down and rotate toward the machine, keeping your arms as straight as possible. Keep your legs bent in the squat.*

2 *Rotate across your body away from the machine. Pause, then return to a straight position. Keep your hips pushed back behind you to take the strain from your knees. Begin with three sets of four repetitions, build up to three sets of ten.*

NUTRITION

To get the most from your fitness training, you need to focus on nutrition as much as exercise. No matter how hard you train, if you eat the wrong food at the wrong time, you will hinder your progress and may also experience fatigue, illness and injury. This chapter reveals the reality behind quick-fix diets and explains why you should simply eat healthily. The key is to know which foods are good for you, when to eat them and their effect on your performance. Equipped with this knowledge you can adopt a healthy eating plan to suit your lifestyle and help achieve your exercise goals.

Above: The tape measure will reveal whether you are eating an appropriate diet.
Left: Enjoy getting fit and healthy with exercise and nutritious food.

Eating Healthily

With so much conflicting advice on how to eat healthily, it can be difficult knowing which foods are best and the correct time to eat them, especially when you are exercising hard. But it doesn't have to be such a problem.

A regular exercise routine throws up many questions about diet. Should you eat a diet rich in carbohydrates or go for the high protein option? Should you have separate protein days and carbohydrate days? Should you focus on eating foods labelled low fat? Is it best to have three meals a day or several smaller meals? If you are exercising hard, what and when should you eat? Which diet will work for you?

Diet confusion

Before changing your eating habits, consider what our ancestors ate 10,000 years ago. After all, the human body has not changed in all that time, and neither have our dietary requirements. We are designed to be hunter-gatherers, not to live sedentary lifestyles, consuming convenience foods rich in sugar, saturated fats and salt. Despite the lack of healthcare, our ancestors had relatively good health – chronic diseases, such as obesity, diabetes, liver disease and heart disease were far less prevalent than they are today. There are still areas of the world where people live as our ancestors did 10,000 years ago.

Below: Apples and carrots make a great, low-calorie snack when you are hungry. And they are full of vitamins and fibre.

Above: Fruits tend to be low in calories and fat and provide fibre and vitamins as well as natural sugars.

These people do not suffer from high cholesterol, high blood pressure and insulin problems. Instead, they have a low percentage of body fat and very efficient cardiovascular systems.

A natural diet

Hunter-gatherers had to think of food as fuel. They ate what they were naturally meant to eat. In the modern developed

Below: Don't rely on fast food; take your own healthy lunch of nuts, seeds, dried fruit and canned fish.

Above: Fish, such as smoked salmon with scrambled eggs, makes a tasty and delicious start to the day.

world, people choose foods that satisfy their tastebuds without considering how it will affect their daily performance, whether it's running for the bus or concentrating in the office. Far too many modern-day city dwellers do not eat a natural diet, as dictated by our genes. Instead, the supermarkets tell us what we should eat, even though 75 per cent of the food available in those packed aisles would not have been available 200 years ago. For example, adverts extol the virtues of cereal as a breakfast food, but cereals were only introduced at the time of the agricultural revolution.

Slowly does it

Don't alter your eating habits all at once; it is important to remember that you should make any changes to your diet gradually so that your body can adjust and get used to the healthier foods. Don't expect to see spectacular results such as weight loss overnight. The first thing you should notice, though, if you are making the right changes to your diet is an increase in your energy levels.

Above: Fresh vegetables supply vitamins and minerals. It is important to eat a good variety to get vitamins A and C.

Many types of cereals are of little nutritional value. Eating fresh fish and fruit for the first meal of the day is a much healthier option than a bowl of cornflakes.

What's on your plate?

Because we are not eating a diet to which we are naturally suited, we are suffering from a wide range of health problems. Just as you need to use the correct fuel in your car, your body needs the correct food to function properly, and to avoid being damaged. So, take time to study foods and find out where the food you eat comes from. Are the meats, fruit and vegetables on your plate organically or agrochemically produced? Wherever possible, it is better to eat organic food for a number of reasons:
• Organic foods contain higher levels of essential vitamins and minerals.
• It tastes better, especially fruit and vegetables, which take a longer

time to grow and contain a lower proportion of water than the equivalent agrochemical produce.
• Only 32 of the 290 food additives used in food production are used in organic food. Many food additives have been linked with health problems.
• Organic foods have not been genetically modified.
• There are no drugs in organic foods.
• Organic foods contain none of the many chemicals used to make agrochemical foods grow faster.
• Producers of organic foods undergo regular inspection to ensure high standards are maintained.
• Organic food production does not contribute to the pollution and degradation of the environment.
• Animal welfare is a priority for organic producers. Animals reared humanely and fed the appropriate diet in free-range environments means better, more nutritious food – which, in turn, means a healthier you.

The bonfire theory

Your body's metabolism works in exactly the same way as a bonfire. But which type? Essentially, there are two types to choose from:

The log bonfire is fed with logs every two to three hours. It takes time to light this fire, but once lit, it burns with intense heat for a long time.

The twig bonfire is easy to light, but soon goes out and emits very little heat.

If you fuel your body with foods high in sugar, your metabolism will be very sluggish and your body will only be able to perform when you keep taking more sugar. In this scenario, your metabolism is just like the twig bonfire. Your body never burns fat because it is constantly being provided with top-ups of sugar to keep it going.

However, fuelling your body with the correct fats, proteins and natural, slow-releasing carbohydrates will keep your metabolism high and enable your body to use fat as a good energy source – just like the log bonfire. If you can follow this theory for most of your everyday meals, you will be on the way to becoming a healthier person, and you will soon experience an increase in energy levels and improved body shape.

Below: The bonfire analogy is that, fed with nourishing food every few hours, the body will keep going for a long time.

Carbohydrates, Proteins and Fats

These are the three pillars of diet that keep the human body fit, functioning and healthy – as long as they are in correct proportion and balance. All too often, unfortunately, that's not the case. It's time to redress the balance.

A balanced diet consists of three main essential food groups: carbohydrates, protein and fats.

Carbohydrates

There are two types of carbohydrates: simple carbohydrates and complex carbohydrates, also known as sugars and starches. Simple carbohydrates are higher in refined sugars, contain empty calories (non-nutritious) and can cause food cravings and upset your energy levels. Complex carbohydrates are also high in sugars but take longer to digest and absorb and keep blood sugar levels stable.

Good carbs, bad carbs For athletes, a carbohydrate-rich diet is essential for constant energy. For those living a sedentary lifestyle, carbohydrates are less essential. Common foods high in carbohydrate are pasta, bread, potatoes, rice, fruit, vegetables, jams and honey. Carbohydrates account for more than 50 per cent of our daily food intake in

> **Cholesterol and heart disease**
> Found in every cell in the body, cholesterol is an essential lipid for good health. However it is present as two different types of lipoproteins: low-density lipoproteins and high-density lipoproteins. Low-density lipoproteins are the bad guys. They cause surplus fat to build up on the walls of the arteries that supply the heart and brain. High-density lipoproteins are good cholesterols – they are essential for a healthy immune system and for controlling weight.

the developed world, while for our ancestors, they made up less than 35 per cent. We simply eat too much carbohydrate. You can be forgiven for assuming that all carbohydrates are good for you – because some of them are. But take time to work out which ones are, and which are not. For example, most breakfast cereals contain around

Above: When it is made from whole grains, bread supplies us with fibre, essential fatty acids and some protein.

70g/2.5oz carbohydrate per 100g/3.5oz. Cereal, however, has little nutritional value and will affect your metabolism because the rate of sugar release is too rapid. It can also contain anti-nutrients, which actually stop you absorbing proper nutrients that are vital for digestion and the immune system. Oats, however, are a good source of protein and help to reduce low-density lipid (LDL) cholesterol; the so-called 'bad' cholesterol.

Fruit and vegetables are sources of good carbohydrates. They have a slower rate of energy release and also provide more fibre in your diet. Ultimately, it is not a matter of how much you eat, but what you eat. If you are unsure which carbohydrates are good for you, then choose fruit and vegetables, preferably those that have been grown organically, as they are much more nutritious and tasty.

Proteins

Essential amino acids from proteins help to repair muscle. Fish, poultry, meat, eggs, milk and cheese are examples of protein-rich foods. In the US and most western countries, protein provides only

Food pyramid

The food pyramid suggests how our daily diet should be divided, for optimum nutrition, depending on your age, sex and physical activity.

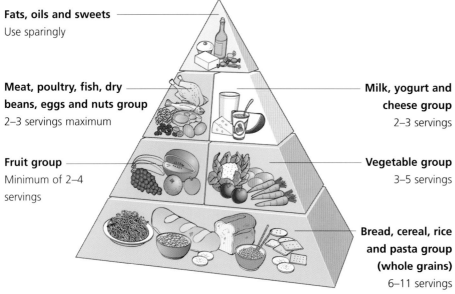

Fats, oils and sweets
Use sparingly

Meat, poultry, fish, dry beans, eggs and nuts group
2–3 servings maximum

Fruit group
Minimum of 2–4 servings

Milk, yogurt and cheese group
2–3 servings

Vegetable group
3–5 servings

Bread, cereal, rice and pasta group (whole grains)
6–11 servings

Above: Chicken, cheese, lentils, couscous and oats contain protein, which provides energy and nutrients.

15 per cent of daily food intake. We should be consuming closer to 30–40 per cent. Protein provides useful energy that helps to burn calories and promote weight loss. Without protein, your muscles cannot be fed with the correct nutrients for repair and growth. Some foods contain more protein than others, and those with a higher protein content often contain less fat. For example, the calorie content of two slices of skinless turkey breast contains 3g/0.1oz fat, 0g/0oz carbohydrate, 11g/0.4oz protein, 75 calories, 32 milligrams cholesterol and 1g/0.04oz saturated fat. By comparison, a fried egg contains 7g/0.3oz fat, 1g/0.04oz carbohydrate, 6g/0.2oz protein, 90 calories, 211 milligrams cholesterol and 1.9g/0.07oz saturated fat.

Whereas, today, we mainly get our protein from animals, 10,000 years ago, we obtained it from pulses, nuts and seeds, and animals. Our current over-reliance on animal protein is responsible for the high LDL (bad) cholesterol levels in developed countries. So, take time to compare the labels on the foods that you buy to make sure that the meat and fish you eat is high in protein, and not high in saturated fats.

Fats

The majority of people, particularly overweight people, eat too much fat. Though essential for energy, fat takes a lot longer to break down than carbohydrate. Fat provides energy for long periods of exercise but the exercise intensity has to be lower so that there is a good supply of oxygen available for the fat to burn. Examples of foods high in fats are cheese, butter, oil and some meat. Per gram or ounce, fat provides twice as many calories as carbohydrates and proteins. The World Health Organization recommends that 25–30 per cent of daily calories should come from fat, but most of the population in the developed world get 40–50 per cent of their daily energy from fat.

Saturated and unsaturated fats The problem is not necessarily the amount of fat that you eat but the type of fat. Saturated fats clog arteries and cause poor health, such as heart disease, obesity and cancer. Foods containing saturated fats include meat, eggs, dairy products and foodstuffs containing these ingredients, such as cakes and chocolate, pastries and pies.

Regulating fat intake

• Eat lean meat and cut off visible fat. Choose poultry, where the fat is in the skin and is easy to remove, over red meat.
• Eat oily fish containing polyunsaturated fats (see below)
• Choose low-fat varieties of dairy products and limit the use of butter and spreads.
• For cooking, only use oils that contain lower levels of saturated fat and which also contain monounsaturated and polyunsaturated fats, which help reduce your LDL (bad) cholesterol.
• Eat chocolate, cake and biscuits only on rare occasions.

Unsaturated fats are better for you. They promote high-density lipid (HDL) or good cholesterol and reduce the risk of illness. Oily fish – for example salmon, herring, mackerel, fresh tuna (not canned), anchovies, sardines, kippers and whitebait, among others – are rich in beneficial omega 3 polyunsaturated fat, which can help protect against heart disease. Vegetables oils like sesame, olive, sunflower, corn, soya bean, walnut and canola are sources of monounsaturated and polyunsaturated fats.

Below: Oily fish, such as sardines, mackerel and anchovies are a good source of essential oils. Two to four portions a week are recommended.

Oily fish – recommended weekly portions

The Food Standards Agency (UK) recommends the following portions, according to age and gender:

Age group/gender	Weekly portion
Girls under 16	Up to 2 portions (280g/10oz)
Boys under 16	Up to 4 portions (560g/20oz)
Women over 16	Up to 4 portions (560g/20oz)
Women who are pregnant, who might be pregnant or breastfeeding	Up to 4 portions (560g/20oz)
Men over 16	Up to 4 portions (560g/20oz)

Healthy Eating for Vegetarians

A vegetarian diet can be healthier than a meat-based diet, but it's not just a question of cutting out meat. It takes knowledge and adequate preparation for a meat-free diet to include enough protein, vitamins and minerals for you to stay fit and healthy.

Many people believe that eating a vegetarian diet will help them to lose weight and this can be true, but zero animal fat does not necessarily equate to a low-fat diet. In fact, since vegetarians rely on foods such as eggs, cheese and other dairy products for protein, they can easily consume as much fat as a meat-eater.

A healthy vegetarian diet calls for a finely balanced, closely monitored diet. Adequate protein must be consumed for growth and maintenance of the muscles and for wound healing – otherwise the metabolism will decline, which can result in weight increase. Proteins are also a source of energy.

Below: Vegetarians can select foods such as nuts, grains and seeds to ensure they get sufficient essential nutrients, such as protein.

Protein intake

A vegetarian diet can be deficient in protein. To combat this, make sure that you include eggs and dairy products in your diet. This will also increase the availability of minerals such as calcium, phosphorous and especially vitamin B12, which is otherwise difficult to obtain.

However, dairy intake must also be regulated to prevent weight gain. If you are exercising hard, careful planning is vital to make sure that you can keep up with the demands of your training plan.

What to eat

To achieve a good balance of nutrients and amino acids from a vegetarian diet, you should include a wide variety of foods in your diet. A combination of

RDAs of protein

The following table shows recommended daily amounts (RDAs) of protein. The UK's Department of Health advises vegetarians and vegans to multiply the figure for their age group and gender by a factor of 1.1, because protein from plant sources is harder to digest than other sources.

Boys/girls	RDA
0–12 months	12.5g/0.4oz
1–3 years	14.5g/0.5oz
4–10 years	19.7g/0.7oz
Girls	
11–14 years	41.2g/1.5oz
15–18 years	45g/1.6oz
Boys	
11–14 years	42.1g/1.5oz
15–18 years	55.2g/1.9oz
Women	
19–50	45g/1.58oz
50 +	46.5g/1.6oz
In pregnancy	extra 6g/day
Breastfeeding	extra 11g/day
0–6 month	
6 months +	extra 8g/day
Men	
19–50	55.5g/1.9oz
50 +	46.5g/1.6oz

Below: Bread is a carbohydrate, and while it is beneficial, it is not enough to sustain a healthy diet.

Above: You can't look and feel fit and healthy unless you plan a nutritious diet that includes vegetables and fruits.

foods is vital, as different foods contain different nutrients: grains are rich in sulphur but lack lysine, an essential amino acid, whereas beans, peas and lentils are high in lysine but lack sulphur.

Pros and cons of a veggie diet

Most vegetarian diets are high in carbohydrates, fibre, fruit and vegetables. Health problems such as heart disease, increased blood pressure

Below: Some fats are needed in the diet, but saturated fats such as butter, cheese and ice cream should be eaten sparingly.

Foods for vegetarians and vegans

Commonly available foods that provide the most protein in a vegan diet are:

Pulses – peas, beans, lentils and soya products
Grains – wheat, oats, rice, barley, buckwheat, millet, pasta and bread
Nuts – brazil nuts, hazelnuts, almonds and cashew nuts
Seeds – sunflower, pumpkin and sesame
Eggs – hen's eggs
Dairy foods – milk, cheese and yogurt

Foods that provide 10g/0.4oz of protein, eaten in the following amounts:

Eggs	1 whole egg
Low-fat cheese	30g/1.1oz
Low-fat milk	300ml/½ pint/1¼ cups
Low-fat yogurt	300ml/½ pint/1¼ cups
Soya flour	24g/0.8oz
Peanuts	39g/1.4oz
Pumpkin seeds	41g/1.5oz
Almonds	47g/1.7oz
Brazil nuts	50g/1.8oz
Sesame seeds	55g/1.9oz
Hazelnuts	71g/2.5oz
Wholemeal (whole-wheat) bread	95g/3.4oz
Lentils	114g/4oz
Chickpeas	119g/4.2oz
Kidney beans	119g/4.2oz
Wholemeal (whole-wheat) spaghetti	213g/7.5oz
Brown rice	385g/13.6oz

and obesity may be reduced due to the low cholesterol and high antioxidant content of a vegetarian diet. However, the lack of low-fat protein can lead to a deficiency in vitamins B6 and B12, and calcium so vegetarians must include quantities of low-fat dairy products,

cereals, nuts and seeds, particularly in the winter months, to ensure that they receive all the necessary nutrients.

Below: Beans and lentils are a source of protein for vegetarians; nuts and rice also contain small amounts of protein.

Fluid Intake

Your body is 70 per cent water and you should do your best to keep it that way during exercise, so fluid intake is vital. Fluid loss will depend on the intensity of your exercise, the duration, temperature, humidity and your fitness level.

Muscles produce heat, which makes you sweat. This, in turn, provides a layer of moisture on the skin that helps to keep the core temperature down. Your body's temperature has to remain between 37°C/98.6°F and 38°C/100.4°F for it to function properly. For every 1 litre/ 2 pints of sweat that evaporates, you lose 600kcal of heat energy. A depletion of body fluids is called dehydration.

Below: Dehydration is one of the main causes for poor sporting performance. Your body is 70 per cent water and needs hydration during sporting activities.

It is important to know how to avoid becoming dehydrated, and to recognize the symptoms if you become dehydrated. One simple test is to weigh yourself before and after exercise. Typically, you will lose 1 litre/2 pints of fluid per hour and around 2 litres/4 pints per hour when the temperature and humidity are high.

A 2 per cent weight loss will mean a 20 per cent decrease in performance; lose 4 per cent and you may have nausea, vomiting and diarrhoea; 5 per cent and your brain will start to shut down; 7 per cent and you hallucinate; 10 per cent and heatstroke sets in.

Above: Always carry water with you so you can keep well hydrated at all times in training at the gym.

Exercise and hydration

To avoid dehydration, drink plenty of fluids before, during and after exercise. Drink 400–600ml/ 13–20fl oz of fluid in the two hours before exercise. It may be fairly easy to drink on a bike, but it is much harder to drink during activities such as running, so make sure that you have plenty of fluid in your system before you start exercising. It is not possible to take in extra fluid and store it. Above a certain level, your body will pass it as urine. Include some carbohydrates in a drink, such as simple sugars: 1g/0.04oz of carbohydrate for every 1kg/2.2lb of body weight, or 14g/0.5oz per 18kg/ 40lb will help to sustain energy levels.

To maintain the exercise intensity level during exercise, you must replace 80 per cent of your fluid loss during exercise.

> **Dehydration test**
> Check the colour of your urine – the darker the urine, the more dehydrated you have become.

Above: Staying hydrated means you will need to calculate how much fluid to drink, how often and what your fluids should contain.

Try to drink before you feel thirsty. Aim to drink 400–1,000ml/13–34fl oz per hour. If you leave it too long, you may end up feeling sick and bloated. Drink plain water if exercise lasts up to 1 hour. For longer exercise sessions, use sports drinks that contain hypotonic or isotonic solutions, which will help with water absorption; and glucose polymers, which will allow you to absorb a greater quantity of carbohydrate to keep your energy levels high.

The following is a guide to which drinks are best according to the exercise you are doing:
• Isotonic: Use for middle- or long-distance running events and team sports. It provides glucose, the body's preferred source of energy. For a concentration of 6–10 per cent, for example, try Lucozade Sport, 515g/18oz, and High Five; or mix 200ml/6.7fl oz orange squash, 1 litre/2 pints water and 1g/0.04oz salt.
• Hypotonic: Use for car racing and horse-racing. It quickly replaces fluid loss but contains no carbohydrate; mix 100ml/3.4fl oz orange squash, 1 litre/2 pints water and 1g/0.04oz salt.
• Hypertonic: Use to top up carbohydrate during long-distance events. It is suitable when energy is required for long periods, can be taken on the move and is easy to digest; mix 400ml/13.5fl oz orange squash, 1 litre/2 pints water and 1g/0.04oz salt.

After exercise To enable a fast, efficient recovery, slowly drink 1.5 litres/3 pints of fluid for every 1kg/2.2lb of weight loss. Between exercise sessions, drink 1 litre/2 pints for every 1,000kcal of energy expenditure.

Overhydration

It is possible to overhydrate if you drink too much. This leads to circulatory problems and dizziness as the blood becomes too diluted, or even seizures or coma if overhydration occurs quickly. If you suspect that you are overhydrated, stop drinking and consume something salty, as your sodium levels will probably have become dangerously low.

Caffeine

Your performance can be improved by caffeine; it helps your body to use fatty acids instead of glycogen, which will enable you to exercise at a high intensity for longer. But more than 300mg of caffeine can be detrimental to your health, as it may cause dehydration (a cup of coffee typically contains 50–100mg of caffeine). Increase your water intake to counteract the dehydrating effect of caffeine.

Alcohol

There are very few benefits to drinking alcohol. It may be useful in social situations – even then, in moderation only – but beyond that, there's little to recommend it. It will affect your reaction time and co-ordination, and you will experience a decline in your speed, power and strength. It will hinder your body's ability to regulate temperature and can lead to blood-sugar level problems and dehydration. The empty calories in alcohol will also lead to weight gain. If you do choose to drink alcohol, make sure that you also drink plenty of water to dilute its effects and reduce the risk of dehydration.

Below: Drinking tea and coffee will make you even more dehydrated. It is best to stick to water or juice.

Below: Lack of fluid can make you prone to headaches, lower your energy levels and make you feel unwell.

Vitamins and Minerals

The importance of vitamins and minerals is well known, but where do they come from and what are they for? The information below highlights some of the most important vitamins and minerals, their uses and where to find them.

Vitamins are essential for your body to function properly. Vitamins fall into two categories: fat-soluble and water-soluble. Fat-soluble vitamins are found in animal fats and other fatty foods. These vitamins are stored in the body for long periods of time. They are available when you need them, so you do not have to eat fatty foods every day.

Water-soluble vitamins can be found in a wide variety of foods. Unlike fat-soluble vitamins, these are not stored in the body, so you need to make sure that you have an adequate amount of them in your daily diet. Don't take too many vitamins especially vitamins A, D, E and K as the body finds it harder to get rid of the excess in the urine. To get the most from your food, steam it or eat it raw. Baking, grilling and frying all lower the vitamin content of food. Be aware that as fruit and vegetables age they lose their vitamin content, so try to eat fruit and vegetables that are as fresh as possible. Frozen vegetables from the supermarket, in which the vitamin content has been preserved, are often better than fresh.

Trace elements

Compared with vitamins and minerals, far smaller amounts of trace elements are required for optimum health, proper growth and development. With today's modern diet and cooking methods, there is concern that the body is not getting an adequate supply of trace elements.

Above: Discover what vitamins are present in your vegetables so that you can design a balanced diet.

It is possible to take supplements but the correct dosage is difficult to work out because different foods and diets have varying concentrations of trace elements, and their rate of absorption also differs. It is better to consume trace elements as part of your daily diet.

Below: Citrus fruits such as oranges and lemons are rich in vitamin C, which is essential in the diet for healthy skin, joints, bones and the immune system.

Vitamins: their uses and sources

Vitamin	Use	Source
Vitamin A	Good eyesight; good night vision; moisturized skin	Green vegetables, eggs, dairy products and apricots
Vitamin D	Strength; healthy immune system; good calcium levels	Herring, mackerel, salmon and eggs
Vitamin E	Healthy nervous system; healthy circulation system	Nuts, fish, chicken, meat and oils
Vitamin K	Blood-clotting agent	Dairy products, fish and cereals
Vitamin B6	Helps in the breakdown of foods to make protein	Meat, cereals, green vegetables and fruit
Vitamin B12	Healthy nervous system; healthy blood	Meat and dairy products
Vitamin C	Antioxidant; healthy immune system; healthy bones	Fruit and vegetables (oranges, papaya, blackcurrants, mangoes and cherries)
Vitamin B3	Assists digestive system	Meat, fish, mushrooms and grains
Biotin	Assists metabolism of glucose and fatty acids	Dairy, peanuts and cauliflower florets
Vitamin B2	Release of energy to cells; healthy metabolism	Dairy, spinach and mushrooms
Folic acid	Red blood cell maintenance	Meat and green vegetables
Vitamin B1	Metabolism of carbohydrate	Wholegrains, seeds and meat
Vitamin B5	Aids chemical reactions; helps to convert food to energy; healthy nervous system	Cereals and meat

Essential minerals and trace elements

Daily consumption of the following minerals and trace elements is essential in order for your body to function efficiently. They help the body turn the food you eat into energy and maintain a healthy body. Deficiencies in vitamins and minerals lead to illness.

Mineral	Use	Source	Daily amounts
Sodium	Healthy water balance	Cereals, bread and dairy	6g/0.2oz
Magnesium	Structure of bone and tendons	Wholegrains, cereals, fruit, cocoa and seeds	Men 300mg; Women 270mg
Iron	Maintains red blood cells; oxygen in blood	Meat, raisins and kidney beans	Men 8.7mg; Women 14.8mg
Calcium	Strong bones and teeth; helps convert food to energy; healthy muscular nervous system	Dairy, sardines, broccoli and dark green vegetables	700mg
Potassium	Healthy muscular nervous system; maintains fluid balance	Nuts, fruit, broccoli, mushrooms and seeds	3,500mg
Phosphorus	Strong bones and teeth; helps convert food to energy; healthy muscular nervous system	Dairy, chicken, eggs and nuts	550mg

Trace element	Use	Source	Daily amounts
Selenium	Antioxidant; aids metabolism	Fish, eggs, meat and cereals	200mcg
Manganese	Bone structure; aids metabolism	Bread, nuts, cereals, vegetables, soya beans and chickpeas are good sources	5mg
Molybdenum	Metabolism of proteins	Nuts, wholegrains	500mcg
Zinc	Healthy skin; immune system	Meat, fish and dairy	15mg
Iodine	Healthy nervous system; cell maintenance	Fish (haddock, mackerel, herring, trout and salmon are good sources), salt and vegetables	75mcg
Chromium	Regulates blood-sugar levels	Dairy, wholegrains and meat	200mcg
Fluoride	Teeth and bones	Fish	3mg

Above: Steaming vegetables seals in the flavour and retains taste and food value.

Right: You will need a variety of vegetables to get all the essential minerals and vitamins you need.

Glycaemic Index

Using the GI system, carbohydrate foods are divided into three categories – low, medium and high – according to the speed with which they raise the body's blood-sugar levels compared with pure glucose.

Carbohydrates with a high glycaemic index (GI) release sugar fast, and are far more likely to cause you to put on weight and therefore slow your athletic performance. The reason for this is a complex glucose–insulin reaction that takes place in your body when you eat. Your body needs to produce glucose from food in order to survive. This production can be rapid or slow, depending on the GI of the food consumed. High GI foods lead to the rapid production of blood glucose, which in turn has a feedback response that can lead to the body releasing high levels of insulin in an attempt to deal with high glucose levels in the blood. This will then turn the glucose into fat, causing weight gain and, over time – if left unchecked – obesity and type II diabetes, which are currently reaching epidemic proportions in developed societies, among young children and adults. There is evidence, however, that some people who eat a lot of high GI

Above: Some foods affect your blood sugar more than others; using the GI system will help you choose carefully.

Below: People with type II diabetes need to test for blood sugar regularly. Understanding the glycaemic index will help you deal with diabetes.

High, medium and low GI foods

Breakfast
High GI: most refined cereals with added sugar
Medium GI: porridge and fruit muesli
Low GI: oat meal, rolled oats, natural muesli and rice bran

Breads
High GI: white, French bread, bagel and black rye bread
Medium GI: pitta bread, wholemeal (whole-wheat), wholemeal roll and fruit bread
Low GI: soy bread, sourdough rye, wholegrain and pumpernickel

Dairy
High GI: ice cream and cheesecake
Medium GI: fruit yogurts
Low GI: full-fat (whole) milk, semi-skimmed (low-fat) milk, skimmed milk and natural yogurt

Vegetables
High GI: parsnips, pumpkin, turnips, swedes (rutabagas), carrots, squashes and pumpkins
Medium GI: beetroots (beets), corn on the cob, kidney beans, pinto beans, dried green peas and carrots
Low GI: peas, corn, broccoli, cauliflower florets, onions, peppers, tomatoes, cabbages, mushrooms, lettuces, aubergines (eggplant), courgettes (zucchini), sprouts, cucumbers, green beans, rocket (arugula), spinach, asparagus, artichokes, kale, radishes and celery sticks

Fruit
High GI: watermelons, dates, bananas, raisins, dried apricots, dried peaches, dried apples, pineapples and cantaloupe melon, canned fruits in syrup
Medium GI: papayas, mangoes, blueberries, sultanas (golden raisins), figs, pears, grapes, orange juice, apple juice, grapefruit juice and fruit cocktail
Low GI: prunes, peaches, pears, grapefruits, apples, kiwi fruits, cherries, plums, apricots, raspberries, strawberries, blueberries, blackberries and avocados

Staples
High GI: white rice, mashed potato and French fries
Medium GI: gnocchi, basmati rice, cornmeal, couscous, baked potato, wild rice, buckwheat, barley, noodles and new potatoes
Low GI: wholemeal (whole-wheat) spaghetti, quinoa and egg noodles

Snacks
High GI: rice cakes, biscuits (cookies), doughnuts, cakes, pretzels, jelly babies and wine gums (fruit candy), jam, French fries, potato crisps (chips)
Medium GI: muffins, oatmeal cookies, muesli bars and chocolate bars
Low GI: cashew nuts, peanuts, mixed nuts and raisins, carrot cake, seeds, hummus and peanut butter

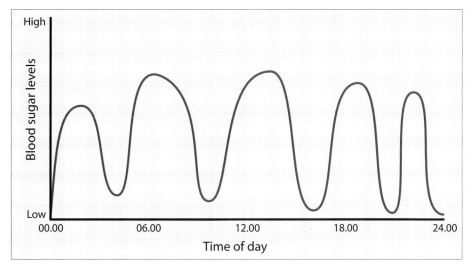

Above: High GI foods can cause sharp increases and falls in blood sugar through the day, as this chart shows.

foods – in Asia and Peru, for example – do not suffer high levels of obesity or diabetes. This is because they also eat a lot of fresh fruit and vegetables, which counteract the effect of the high GI foods. Mixing high and low GI foods produces moderate GI values.

Foods with a low GI have little effect on your body's blood-sugar level because it takes the body a long time to

Below: To keep sugar levels balanced, mix high GI foods with those which have a lower GI.

metabolize them. Foods with a high GI, however, cause an immediate increase in blood-sugar levels.

Advantages of a low GI diet

Eating low GI foods will help you to lose weight, reduce the risk of certain cancers, increase the amount of fibre in your diet, decrease the chances of developing type II diabetes and coronary heart disease, boost your immune system, and increase your stamina and energy levels. There are no disadvantages to eating low GI foods.

Below: Before a competition, eat the right mix of high and low GI foods for optimum performance.

Surprisingly high

You may be surprised to find that some of your favourite foods are high GI. To help balance your body's blood-sugar levels, and to give you energy for the whole day, you should avoid or cut down on these foods. Following the principles of the GI will help you to lose weight, improve your sporting performance and aid recovery after exercise.

Athletes

Ultra-marathon runners and Ironman triathletes who take part in events lasting more than two hours, have become increasingly aware of the importance of the GI value of foods taken before and after competition. In preparation for training or events, athletes need to consume low GI foods in order to release energy slowly. During their training or event, athletes should try to balance high and low GI foods to maintain their energy levels on an even keel.

> ### Mix high and low
> If you still feel the need to include some high GI foods in your diet, make sure you counteract the effect of the high GI food by also eating lots of foods that have a low GI.

Eating to Lose Weight

Fad diets are everywhere and promise miraculous results. In truth, however, beyond healthy book sales and magazine circulation figures, they do little good. Long-term weight loss involves a realistic plan that encompasses lifestyle, diet and exercise.

No single diet, whether it is low fat, reduced calorie or low carbohydrate, will help you to maintain your new size once you have lost the initial weight. One of the first things all of these diets do is lower your normal calorie intake. This will cause you to lose weight, but much of this weight loss will be muscle, which you need to retain, because it is living tissue that helps you to maintain a high metabolism and keep you trim. If you want to lose weight, and keep it off, you need to change your lifestyle and eating habits. Another important factor is to understand the relationship between what you eat and what you look like. Also regular exercise will help you in your goal.

Here are 16 steps that will help you to lose weight:

1 Portion control This is one of the fastest ways to lose weight. If you use a smaller plate, and don't pile food up, you will soon find that your stomach starts to shrink and that you feel full

Below: When you are trying to lose weight, choose ingredients for your meal that are fresh and healthy.

after eating less food. Aim to eat 80 per cent of what you think you need at each meal.

2 Eat slowly Chew each mouthful at least 20 times before you swallow it. Taking longer to eat your food will send a signal to your brain to register that your stomach is full. While you are chewing, put your knife and fork down to create a slight pause between mouthfuls. Again, this will enable you to feel full before you have time to have a second plateful.

3 Leave leftovers Only eat the food on your plate if you really need it. There is no shame in not finishing a meal, especially if you are out in a restaurant and you have been presented with a larger portion than you wanted.

4 Less fat Eat less fatty food. In particular, avoid eating fat from foods that have been processed. Also, cook with less fat to avoid adding extra fat to your meal.

5 More fruit and vegetables A low-calorie way to feel full is to eat lots of fruit and vegetables. Eating more of these foods will also help to increase the fibre in your diet, which will help

Above: Don't feel you always have to finish everything on your plate – stop eating when you are satisfied.

to lower your cholesterol level. Aim for at least five portions of fruit and vegetables each day.

6 Read the label Be wary of foods that are labelled 'low fat'. They may be low in saturated fats but the likelihood is that they are high in sugar, which will

Below: Eat foods that are not processed and are as natural as possible so you know what is in them.

Above: Above: If you need to lose weight, select low-fat foods, such as fruits and vegetables, and control the portion size.

Above: If you are trying to lose weight, and you eat in a restaurant, ask about the ingredients and how the food is cooked so you can make the right choice.

have the effect of raising your blood sugar, then your insulin levels and make you deposit fat.

7 Low GI Eat low GI foods to prevent your body becoming insulin-resistant (a pre-diabetic state in which normal amounts of insulin are no longer sufficient to produce a normal insulin response from fat, muscle and liver cells). Eating low GI foods will keep your blood-sugar levels constant and enable you to feel good and crave healthy foods.

8 Be prepared When travelling, take with you food such as nuts and fruits, so that you don't have to rely on what is on offer at the service station or garage and be tempted to buy chocolate.

9 Little and often Eat small meals regularly to make sure that your metabolism is working all the time. Don't let yourself go hungry, because your body will then go into 'famine mode' and start to store all the calories, thinking it won't be fed again for a while.

10 Drink more water You might often think that you are hungry when, in fact, you are just thirsty. Avoid excessive calories from other beverages such as fizzy drinks and alcohol. Aim for eight 200ml/6.7-fl oz glasses per day.

11 Avoid sugary snacks You may think that just one sugary snack a day won't do much harm when you count the small number of calories in it. However, the knock-on effect on your energy levels, and the associated problems with insulin levels, should not be underestimated.

12 Ask about what you are eating If you are eating out, find out what the ingredients of a dish are, and don't be embarrassed to ask the chef to omit a sauce, dressing or gravy, if necessary.

13 Get active No matter how healthily you eat, if you don't do any activity, you will not be able to burn off calories. You need to be burning off more calories in a day than you consume in order to lose weight.

14 Slowly does it Don't rush it – aim to lose weight at a sensible speed. A loss of 0.5–1kg/1.1–2.2lb per week is sustainable, and will give your body a chance to adjust to the changes it is going through.

15 Obstacles Note down anything that gets in the way of losing weight, then work out ways that you can get around these obstacles.

16 Downfalls List the foods that made you put on weight in the first place. You need to understand which foods are bad for you in order to make yourself avoid them altogether by not buying them or, at least, cut down on the amount you eat.

Below: Sugary snacks such as chocolate will be detrimental to weight loss; instead, opt for fruit or nuts.

Eating to Gain Muscle

Some people think that hour after hour at the gym is all they need to build muscle. You can train all day long, but if you don't put the right fuel into your body, your muscles will fail to recover after exercising and simply will not grow.

To gain muscle, you need to adopt a diet that is rich in carbohydrate and protein, with some fat. Choose low GI foods over high GI ones and consider including a dietary supplement.

Small and frequent meals will help to increase metabolism, burn more fat and give you better muscle definition – great definition will make your muscles look bigger, even if they aren't. Eat little and often; every three to four hours to avoid going into a catabolic state, in which your body starts to eat muscle to get energy, resulting in more fat and less muscle.

A balanced diet

Each meal should consist of 40 per cent carbohydrate, 40 per cent protein and 20 per cent fat. You need protein to build muscle and carbohydrates to give you the energy to turn protein into muscle. Fats are also important, as every cell in the body has fat in it and hormones are made from fats. Choose unsaturated fats – good sources are fish oils, peanut butter and olive oil.

Testosterone is the most important hormone as far as muscle growth is concerned. A low-fat diet leads to low

Above: Putting in a sustained effort at each session in the gym will pay off over time as you get fitter.

Left: Protein, such as a lean steak, is an essential nutrient for repairing and building muscles.

Measure fat

You should aim to gain around 250g/0.5lb of muscle per week. If you gain any more than that, you will be in danger of putting on fat instead of muscle. In addition to using the scales, measure your body fat on a regular basis.

levels of testosterone, and therefore no muscle growth. Every tissue in the body is made from protein, so it is very important to maintain a high-protein diet, especially if you need to repair damaged tissue after exercise.

Protein levels

For basic training of up to an hour a day, you need to consume 2.5g/0.08oz of protein per 1kg/2.2lb of body weight. If you aim to train hard and gain muscle, you will need to increase this to 3–4g/0.10– 0.14oz of protein per 1kg/2lb of body weight, or approximately 57–85g/2–3oz per 18kg/40lb.

There is no point in eating more than 4g/0.14oz of protein per 1kg/2.2lb of body weight, or approximately 3oz per 40lb, as your body cannot utilize more than this quantity of protein.

Low GI and high fibre

Eat low GI foods for a sustained slow, but constant release of energy, and to maximize recovery of your muscles. Always include fibre in your diet. Five to ten servings of fruit and vegetables a day will help to keep your digestive system working efficiently, which is especially important if you are eating extra protein. Fibre will slow down the digestion of the protein giving your body more time to absorb the amino acids.

Below: Peanut butter provides essential fats and protein for building muscles and a long steady release of energy.

Above: Avoid saturated fats; choose healthy oils instead, such as olive oil or various types of nut oils.

Food supplements

Creatine supplementation will help to increase muscle mass. It is possible to gain up to 3 per cent muscle mass in one week, if you consume 7g/0.25oz of creatine a day. Creatine works by dragging water into the cells, which then stimulate protein synthesis.

There are some side effects – water retention, cramping, kidney and muscle damage and dehydration. The best form of creatine is creatine monohydrate, which is readily available and easy for the body to utilize.

People with fewer fast-twitch muscle fibres may struggle to get the maximum benefit from taking creatine. If you are a long-distance athlete looking to put on weight, use creatine after meals containing carbohydrates, as the increase in the insulin level after the meal can help with the uptake of creatine into the muscle cells. Drink plenty of water after taking creatine to compensate for its dehydrating effect.

Meal-replacement drinks If you lead a busy lifestyle, it can be hard to prepare meals with enough calories and nutritional value. A meal-replacement drink (MRP) will take care of that. Most MRP drinks contain essential amino acids and creatine

Calorie count

If you are attempting to put on muscle, try increasing your carbohydrate consumption to 50 per cent and your fat consumption to 25 per cent, while decreasing your protein consumption to 25 per cent. This will mean that instead of consuming 12 calories per 500g/1.1lb of body weight, which is an average amount, you will double your calories and consume 24 calories per 500g/1.1lb of body weight. Extra calories are essential if you want to put on more muscle, especially if you are burning off more energy because you have recently stepped up your physical training.

and glutamine to aid recovery and promote muscle growth. They typically contain 40g/1.4oz of protein and 60g/2oz of carbohydrates.

Exercise and rest

To prevent calories from being burnt, avoid cardiovascular exercise and ensure you do appropriate weight-training. Use free weights to work throughout the entire movement and provide good stability. Rest is very important. If your body has maximum recovery after a workout, it will also have maximum potential for growth.

Below: Adding protein and fruit shakes to your diet will ensure that you get a supply of high quality protein.

Eating for Endurance

For an endurance event, such as a marathon, you need to maximize the amount of fuel your body can store, take on more during the event and quickly replenish yourself after the race for a speedy recovery.

In the two or more days before an endurance event or long training session, start to prepare your body. You should top up your muscle glycogen levels by regularly eating plenty of low GI foods.

To make sure your muscles are fully hydrated, make sure that you consume 30 per cent more fluids than normal in the three to four days prior to the event. Avoid drinking any alcohol and do not eat foods that are high in fat. If you get nervous before a big event, avoid eating too much fibre, as this can upset your stomach. Also, avoid any foods with which you are not familiar. Eat five to six smaller meals throughout the day, with no more than four hours between each meal.

Below: Before the big event, when you are training, eat what you will have on race day so that you know your body is comfortable with it.

Carb loading

Although it does not work for everyone, carbohydrate loading is popular among endurance athletes. It involves lowering your carbohydrate intake to 5–7g/ 0.2–0.3oz per 1kg/2.2lb of body weight, or approximately 113–170g/4–6oz per 18kg/40lb for three days; then raising it to 8–10g/0.3–0.4oz per 1kg/2.2lb of body weight, or about 170–227g/6–8oz per 18kg/40lb, for the final three days before the event.

Try this technique in preparation for a long training session to see if it works for you before adopting it for an event.

One day before the event

At this stage you need to continue topping up your muscle glycogen levels (stored glucose, mainly in the liver and the muscles) by eating low GI foods, avoiding fatty foods, alcohol and too much fibre. Eat simple, familiar foods that you find easy to digest. If you are

Endurance length

Endurance events refer to those events lasting for more than 90 minutes, including marathons, half-marathons, cycle races and triathlons.

staying away from home and having food prepared for you, check the ingredients for anything that could upset your digestion and hydration levels. Take particular note of the salt and spice content.

The day of the event

Eat your main meal two to four hours before the start. You may need to experiment with this in training. Some people need at least three hours after eating before exercise, while others need only two hours. Consume foods that are low in fat, protein and fibre. The meal should consist of 2.5g/0.08oz of carbohydrate

Above: Plan your food intake during an event such as a marathon so that you do not run out of energy too early in the race.

per 1kg/2.2lb of body weight, or approximately 42.5g/1.5oz per 18kg/40lb.

Sometimes, having food in the form of a carbohydrate drink is a better way to aid digestion, especially if you suffer from a nervous digestion system. The carbohydrates can be a mixture of low and high GI. The high GI foods will give you the initial boost that you need, while the low GI foods will release energy steadily over the course of the event.

During the event
You could be using more than 1,000 calories per hour during an endurance event. As you can only store 2,000 calories before you start exercise, and only then if you have maximized your nutrition, it is essential to eat as you compete. Aim to take on 400–600 calories per hour, eating every 15–20 minutes. The foods should consist of 70 per cent carbohydrate, 20 per cent fat

and 10 per cent protein. Consume foods such as energy bars, gels, bananas, dried fruit, cereal bars and low GI energy drinks that contain little fibre and are easy to digest. If the event lasts for more than four hours, you will need to

Below: Take on fluid containing essential minerals, which will help you to sustain energy in your muscles.

use fat as an energy source. Therefore, you will need to have consumed adequate amounts of carbohydrate, because your body cannot utilize fat without it.

Drink 200ml/6.7fl oz of water for every 100 calories consumed to prevent water being taken from the muscles and transferred to the gut to digest the food, which will have a detrimental effect on your performance. Drinks containing electrolytes will help to replace essential minerals such as sodium, chloride, calcium, potassium and magnesium.

After the event
After exercise, your body is ready to take in and store carbohydrates better than at any other time. In the 30–45 minutes after exercise, you will be able to process carbohydrates up to three times faster than at any other time of the day, so take advantage of this fact. Consume a mixture of low and high GI foods to replenish glycogen stores quickly and prepare for the next workout. Try taking food in the form of liquid to make it easier to digest. The ratio of carbohydrate to protein after exercise should be in the region of 4:1.

Below: As soon as possible after the event, make sure you replace all the fluid that you have lost.

TRAINING PLANS

Having established your goals, you need a training plan to achieve them, safely and effectively. Use the cardiovascular, strength, flexibility and core-stability tests described earlier in the book to assess your fitness levels. Then, decide what you want to concentrate on and devise an appropriate strategy. The following plans will help you to achieve goals such as gaining strength and losing weight, becoming a better runner and de-stressing. Remember, training with a partner will improve your technique and motivation. Before you begin, start your training diary.

Above: Your exercise plan should contain different types of training to make it more challenging and fun.
Left: Once you have worked out what training to do, you will feel more motivated.

Weight-loss Plan

Losing weight is one of the most common goals of people who take up fitness training. Follow this plan for six weeks and you should see great results. Keep an accurate training diary, including a record of your body measurements, to monitor your progress.

In order to burn off fat, you need to make all your big muscles work hard to promote stronger muscles. They will then act as living tissue to burn off calories. Throughout your weight-loss workouts, try to keep your heart rate at Level 2–3, i.e. you should always be slightly out of breath. Resistance training will help to give you a faster-acting metabolism, so it should become a major part of your training. Always do resistance training to prevent further weight gain.

The importance of diet

In order to lose weight, exercise should go hand in hand with a low GI diet. Once you have established a good training pattern, focus on your nutrition, as this is the most important factor in a weight-loss programme.

Resistance is useful

You may burn more calories during a cardiovascular workout than a resistance training session, but the afterburn following a resistance training session is far greater. When your muscles are recovering, they will burn off additional

Below: The right diet, preferably a low GI diet, with exercise, are essential elements in a weight-loss programme.

Training strategies
• Resistance exercises should alternate between upper- and lower-body exercises, to allow your upper body to rest while at the same time your lower body is working, and vice versa.
• Remember to include some stretches in your warm-up routine, and also at the end of every session, to help you to stay flexible and avoid injury.
• Core-stability training is vital to help you to carry out the cardiovascular and resistance training correctly without injury, so include core-stability exercises at least once a week. Start with basic core exercises and, as you master the exercises, progress to the more advanced exercises.

calories. If you are very unfit, the chances are that you won't be able to manage more than 5 minutes of cardiovascular exercise because you will soon be uncomfortably out of breath. However, resistance training will not leave you as breathless, so it is an easier, as well as a more effective, method of

Below: You don't have to go to the gym to lose weight, you can do certain exercises at home.

Above: Resistance exercises will help muscles burn up calories, resulting in weight loss.

weight loss for the unfit person. Also, by beginning your weight-loss programme with basic resistance training, you soon gain greater strength in your muscles, which will help you to cope with longer cardiovascular sessions. Never underestimate the power of resistance training for weight loss.

Six-week weight-loss plan

As you get fitter, increase the intensity and duration of your cardiovascular exercises. You need continually to challenge your body to make it burn more calories so try doing intervals going from Level 2 (medium-intensity training) to Level 3 (high-intensity training) for up to 1 minute at a time. Take steps to stay motivated throughout your training. Consistency and regular training is the key to losing weight so pick a time to follow the plan when you will not be distracted by other events in your life. Follow this plan for six weeks to put you well on your way to significant weight loss. Be flexible – if you cannot cycle or run because of poor weather conditions, simply choose one of the other day's activities until you are able to get outside again. This weight-loss plan is suitable for men and women.

Day	Exercise	Time/Sets/Reps/Level	Comments
Monday	Rowing	5 minutes L1–L2	Warm up your muscles to reduce the risk of injury
	Leg press	3 x 20	Firms and strengthens calf muscles
	Olympic bar chest press	3 x 20	Tones and shapes the chest
	Cycling	5 minutes steady L2	Low-impact aerobic exercise that burns up calories
	Leg extension	3 x 20	Strengthens and works upper legs
	Dumbbell chest press	3 x 20	Intense workout of the upper arm, chest and shoulder
	Treadmill walk	5 minutes L2–L3	Use + 5 per cent incline
	Lunge	3 x 20	Works the upper leg and buttocks
	Lat pull-down	3 x 20	Trains the neglected back muscles
	Rowing machine	5 minutes L2	Cool down gives time to return the blood flow to normal
Tuesday	Basic core stability	Hold each exercise 20 seconds	Builds up the muscles of the trunk that control the spine
	Walking	20–40 minutes	Burn 300–400 calories per hour when walking briskly
Wednesday	Cycling	5 minutes L1–L2	Warm up and do stretches
	Step-up	3 x 20	Start with 3 x 10
	Bench press-up	3 x 10–20	Progress to full press-ups
	Treadmill walk/run	5 minutes L2–L3	Use +5 per cent incline
	Machine leg curls	3 x 20	Exercises the hamstrings
	Dumbbell flies	3 x 20	Works the middle of the chest
	Rowing	5 minutes L2–L3	Cardiovascular exercise works the upper body
	Side lunges	3 x 20	Work hips, buttocks and thighs
	Dumbbell shoulder press	3 x 15	For shoulder and upper-arm strength
	Cycling	5 minutes L2	Cool-down
Thursday	Basic core stability	2–3 seconds for each direction of the movement	Work all the major muscles in the trunk, try raises, planks, fit ball, BOSU and medicine ball exercises
	Walking	20–40 minutes	Option to run or bike
Friday	Treadmill walk/run	5 minutes L1–2	Warm up and do stretches
	Lunge	3 x 20	Works most of the muscles in the upper leg and calf
	Arnie shoulder press	3 x 15	Strengthens shoulders, upper arms and chest
	Rowing	5 minutes L2–L3	Try intervals of 1 minute easy and 30 seconds hard
	Squat	3 x 20	Works the quadriceps muscles in the upper leg
	Upright cable row	3 x 15	Strengthen neck and shoulders
	Cycling	5 minutes L2–L3	Medium- to high-intensity training
	Calf raise	3 x 20	Stretches out the calf muscles
	Triceps dip	3 x 10–20	Works the upper arm and chest muscles
	Treadmill walk/run	5 minutes L1–L2	Cool down
Saturday	Walking	1–2 hours L2	Low-impact exercise
	Or Running	1–2 hours L2	One of the best forms of cardiovascular exercise
	Or Cycling	1–2 hours L2	Aerobic exercise
Sunday	Rest day	24 hours	Eases and repairs sore muscles

Weight-gain Plan: Muscle

Gaining weight in the form of muscle is another popular fitness-training goal. It calls for a strict regime of heavy resistance training and good nutrition. It also means avoiding all cardiovascular training for at least the first six weeks.

The correct resistance training, with more sets but fewer repetitions of heavy weights, along with regular training will help break down muscles for the whole body. These muscles then grow back stronger and bigger.

If possible, always have a training partner with you to watch your technique. Good technique will help you to isolate the muscles that you want to work effectively. A training partner is also invaluable support when your muscles fatigue when training to failure.

You must train all of the major muscles in your body to get bigger. There is no point in training your upper-body muscles and not your legs, if you want your legs to be strong enough to support you and not be vulnerable to injury. Focus on the bigger muscles – chest, back and tops of the legs – rather than the small muscles – the biceps and triceps – which will not add much to your overall size.

The biggest first

Always plan your training session so that you exercise your biggest muscles first. Otherwise, the supporting smaller muscles will be too weak to help train your bigger muscles. For example, do dumbbell chest presses before triceps dips so that your triceps muscles are fresh enough to help in the dumbbell chest press. Once you have followed the plan for about six weeks, make adjustments to focus on the areas of your body in which you want to see more growth. For example, if you want bigger shoulders, do two shoulder sessions in the week instead of one.

More food, more muscle

In order to increase muscle mass, you will simply have to consume more calories. Include a selection of mainly low to medium GI foods in your diet

Above: Having a training partner to help you lift heavy weights can motivate you and make training safer.

and increase the protein content of your food to 40 per cent. If you find it hard to eat larger portions of food, particularly foods in the protein group, then supplement your meals with protein shakes and bars, and make sure that you eat something every three hours.

> **Measure up**
> Before you begin training to increase your weight by increasing muscle tissue, take measurements of your neck, shoulders, biceps, chest, waist, thighs and calves. This will enable you to monitor your progress and see changes in your body shape that will help to motivate you.

Left: While you are doing resistance training, increase the protein in your diet with eggs, fish, meat and nuts.

Six-week weight-gain plan

Day	Exercise	Time/Sets/Reps/Level	Comments
Monday	Rowing	5 minutes L1	Warm up to reduce risk of injury
	Olympic bar chest press incline	5 x 6–8	Do incline first to isolate the chest more
	Dumbbell chest press incline	5 x 6–8	Gives a workout of the chest and upper arms
	Olympic bar chest press	5 x 6–8	Tones and shapes the chest
	Dumbbell chest press	5 x 6–8	Intense workout of upper arm, chest and shoulder
	Cable flies flat bench	5 x 6–8	Workout for chest, back, shoulders and arms
	Press-up	5 x 6–8	Good for strengthening back, chest and arms
	Triceps cable push-down	5 x 6–8	Strengthens upper arms, shoulders, chest and back
	Triceps bench dips	5 x max reps	Works upper arm and chest muscles
Tuesday	Hack squat	5 x 8–10	Good for upper legs and buttocks
	Leg press	5 x 8–10	Strengthens and firms leg muscles
	Lunge	5 x 8–10	Hold dumbbells to make it harder
	Step-up	5 x 8–10	Go as slow as possible on the drop back down
	Leg extension	5 x 8–10	Strengthens and works upper legs
	Ab crunch	5 x 10	Hold weight above head
	Hanging leg raise with twist	5 x 8–10	Builds up the abdominal muscles
Wednesday	Overhand chin-up, wide grip	3 x max reps	When you can do 10 reps, add a weights belt
	Lat pull-down, overhand grip	5 x 6–8	Be careful not to use your lower back
	Lat pull-down, underarm grip	5 x 6–8	Helps to train the back muscles
	Seated cable row	5 x 6–8	Especially strengthens the middle back and forearms
	Bent-over barbell row	5 x 6–8	Generally strengthens the back
	Barbell bicep curl, narrow grip	5 x 6–8	Workout for the biceps
	Concentration curl	5 x 6–8	Exercises the biceps
Thursday	Row	5 minutes L1	Warm up
	Hanging leg raise	5 x 10	Start with 3 sets and build up to to 5 sets
	Sit-up, with Russian twist	5 x 20	10 each side
	Crunch	5 x 20	Tones and strengthens the abdominal muscles
	Reverse crunch	5 x 20	Gives stronger and sleeker abdominal muscles
	Dumbbell side bend	5 x 20	10 each side
	High cable side bend	5 x 20	10 each side
Friday	Olympic bar shoulder press	5 x 6–8	Improves shoulder strength and muscle mass
	Dumbbell shoulder press	5 x 6–8	For shoulder and upper arm strength
	Cable shoulder press	5 x 6–8	Strengthens upper arms, improves general fitness
	Shrug	5 x 6–8	Helps the trapezius muscle to become stronger
	Bent-over cable lateral raise	5 x 6–8	On each arm
	Dumbbell frontal raise	5 x 6–8	On each arm
	Overhead triceps extension	5 x 6–8	Increases strength and flexibility of the triceps
	Triceps press-up	5 x 6–8	Use decline to make it harder as you get stronger
Saturday	Dead lift	5 x 8–10	Tones the lower body and legs
	Dumbbell squat	5 x 8–10	Tones buttocks, hips and thighs
	Cable bicep curl	5 x 6–8	Works the biceps
	Barbell curl, wide grip	5 x 6–8	Builds up the outer biceps
	Concentration curl	5 x 6–8	Exercises the biceps
	Hammer curl	5 x 6–8	Works biceps, good for wrist, hand or elbow injuries
	Oblique crunch	5 x 10	10 each side
	High cable side bend	5 x 10	Works the oblique muscles at the sides of the abdomen
Sunday	Rest day	24 hours	Eases and repairs sore muscles

Six-pack Plan

Many men look in the mirror and dream of having a taut, well-defined six-pack. The truth is, though, that achieving the desired effect takes a combination of dedicated training and consistently good nutrition.

Your training plan should consist of a combination of cardiovascular and resistance training. The cardiovascular training will burn off calories and increase your aerobic fitness, making your body work more efficiently. At first, stick to Level 2 for cardiovascular exercise such as running. As you get fitter, include intervals that will have a similar effect on your muscles as weight-training, i.e. exercises that will result in significant afterburn. For example, run at Level 2 for 4 minutes, then run fast at Level 3–4 for 1 minute, repeating this pattern throughout the session.

Diet and resistance training

Resistance training will help to build and strengthen muscles, and increase your metabolism. There is a direct link between the benefits of resistance training and your diet, so you will need to adjust the combination of the two to suit your personal requirements. There is a very fine balance between eating enough to retain muscle – and in the

Below: Eat well and stick to the plan for six weeks to achieve your six-pack.

process maintaining a high metabolism – and cutting back on food in order to reduce your body fat. Don't make the mistake – as many people do – of eating significantly less, as this will only result in your muscles not having enough energy and your metabolism declining to the point where you start to deposit fat. It is important that you eat every three to four hours. Also, you should eat mainly low GI foods

Above: Don't always stick to a rigid routine; try to vary it, otherwise you will become bored with training.

and it is crucial that your diet consists of 40 per cent protein. If you find it hard to include larger portions of protein in your daily diet, then try supplementing your meals with protein shakes and bars, and make sure that you eat every three hours.

Major muscle workout

You need to work all the major muscles in your body, not just your abdominals, in order to achieve a six-pack. Your abdominal muscles are small, so exercising them in isolation will not increase your metabolism sufficiently to get rid of the layer of fat that lies on top of them. During every exercise, concentrate on tensing your abdominal muscles to make them work harder. For example, during a leg press, tense your abdominals until you can feel them working as hard as your legs. Don't neglect your diet, you need good nutrition as well as exercise.

Six-pack training plan

Day	Exercise	Time/Sets/Reps/	Comments
Monday	Rowing	5 minutes L1	Warm up
	Dumbbell squat	3 x 20	Tones buttocks, hips and thighs
	Lunge	3 x 20	Works upper legs and buttocks
	Overhand chin-up, wide grip	5 x max reps	When you can do 10 reps, add a weights belt
	Overhand lat pull-down, wide grip	5 x 12	Exercises the muscles of the back
	Olympic bar chest press incline	5 x 12	Develops the mass and strength of the pectorals
	Olympic bar chest press	5 x 12	Heavy resistance to train chest muscles
	Dumbbell bicep curl	5 x 12	Develops and tones the biceps
	Bicep hammer curl	5 x 12a	Builds up biceps and forearm muscles
Tuesday	Running	45–60 minutes L2–L3	Option to use cross-trainer
	Rowing	10 minutes L2–L3	
	Crunch	3 x 20	Build up to 5 sets, hold weights plates
	Hanging leg raise	3 x 10	Build up to 20 reps as you get stronger
	High rope crunch	3 x 20	Build up to 5 sets
Wednesday	Rowing	5 minutes L1	Warm up
	Leg press	3 x 20	Tones and strengthens calf muscles
	Leg extension	3 x 20	Works on the muscles of the upper legs
	Overhand chin-up, wide grip	3 x max reps	When you can do 10 reps, add a weights belt
	Seated cable row	5 x 12	Works on forearms and middle back
	Dumbbell chest press	5 x 12	Exercises upper arms, chest and shoulders
	Lying cable flies	5 x 12	Good workout for chest muscles
	Cable lat raise	5 x 12	Works out shoulder muscles
	Cable frontal raise	5 x 12	Works anterior deltoids (front of chest)
Thursday	Running	45–60 minutes L2–L3	Option to use cross-trainer or rowing machine
	Hanging leg raise with twist	3 x 10	Build up to 5 sets
	Sit-up with Russian twist	3 x 20	Build up to 5 sets, use weights to make it harder
	Oblique crunch	3 x 20	Build up to 5 sets
	High rope crunch with twist	3 x 20	Build up to 5 sets
	Dumbbell side bend	3 x 20	Build up to 5 sets
	Side crunches	3 x 20	Build up to 5 sets
Friday	Rowing	5 minutes L1	Warm up
	Lunge	3 x 20	Works the upper leg and buttocks
	Machine leg curl	3 x 20	Develops hamstrings
	Dumbbell shoulder press	5 x 12	Strengthens shoulders and upper arms
	Upright row	5 x 12	Targets shoulders, upper back and biceps
	Dumbbell lat raises	5 x 12	Works upper chest
	Dumbbell frontal raises	5 x 10	10 each arm
	Triceps cable push-down	5 x 12	Develops triceps
	Bench triceps dip	3 x max reps	Strengthens triceps
Saturday	Running	45–60 minutes L2–L3	Option to use cross-trainer or rowing machine
	Crunch	3 x 20	Build up to 5 sets, hold weights above head to make it harder
	V-crunch	3 x 20	Build up to 5 set
	Broomstick twist	3 x 20	Build up to 5 sets
	Kneeling cable rotation	3 x 20	Build up to 5 sets
	Dumbbell side bend	3 x 20	Build up to 5 sets
Sunday	Rest day	24 hours	Eases and repairs sore muscles

Wedding Dress Plan

On a day as important as your wedding, you will want to do yourself justice and look at your best. This workout will improve your shape and leave you feeling fit and toned for one of the most important days of your life.

This training plan will improve the parts of your body that will be most on show, or accentuated, when you are wearing your wedding dress: the buttocks, hips, underarms, abdominals, top of the chest and back of the arms.

If your wedding preparations run true to the norm, you can expect to lose some weight with the stress of it all in the last few weeks before the big day. This, combined with your workout sessions – which will also result in changes to your body shape – means that you need to be careful that your wedding dress is not suddenly a size too large. Aim to have achieved your desired shape before your last wedding-dress fitting.

Combination training

This workout plan combines a mixture of cardiovascular and resistance training. The cardiovascular training will increase your aerobic fitness, burn off calories,

make your body work more efficiently and increase your energy levels. The resistance-training exercises will work big muscle groups to burn maximum calories and tone smaller muscles, such as your arms, to give you the look you want on the day. If you feel there are some parts of your body that need improving, focus your workouts on those areas and adjust the planned sessions to allow you to work on those areas two or three times a week for

Above: You will have your wedding photographs forever, so make sure that you look as good as you can.

Below: The fitter you are, the better you will be able to cope with the pressure on your big day.

Below: If you have stuck to the training plan, you should be happy with your appearance on your wedding day.

Exercise tips

To get the best results from these exercises, make sure to eat healthily every three to four hours, consuming low GI foods, which will help your muscles to recover from exercise and maintain your energy levels.

Warm up for 5 to 10 minutes at Level 1 to Level 2 at the start of every training session, and complete stretches on the parts of your body that you will be using. Do a series of stretches again at the end of the workout.

faster results. Include core-stability training at least one day a week to help avoid injury and give you great posture. Start with the basic core exercises and progress onto the more advanced core exercises as you master them. Follow the plan for six weeks for great results.

Right: Basic core exercises will help to improve your posture and figure and get you into good shape.

Six-week wedding-dress plan

Follow this six-week plan and you will be feeling and looking great for your big day – and in the photographs afterward.

Day	Exercise	Time/Sets/Reps/	Comments
Monday	Cycling/running/cross-trainer	20–40 minutes L2	Use one or a combination
	Lunge	3 x 20	10 each leg; use dumbbells to make it harder
	Cable lat pull-down	3 x 20	Works back muscles and biceps
	Leg extension	3 x 20	Tones and works upper legs
	Dumbbell chest press	3 x 20	Isolates and works upper chest
	Incline bench	3 x 15	Strengthens and tones abdominal muscles
	Crunch	3 x 10	Start with 10 reps and build up to 20
	Bench triceps dip	3 x 10–20	Use straight legs to make it harder
Tuesday	Cycling/running/cross trainer	10–20 minutes L2	Use one or a combination
	Leg press	3 x 20	Tones and strengthens leg muscles
	Single-arm dumbbell row	3 x 15	Workout for the middle back muscles
	Leg curl	3 x 20	Exercises the hamstrings
	Dumbbell flies	3 x 15	Workout for the middle of the chest
	Oblique crunch	3 x 20	Works upper abdominals and obliques
	Dumbbell lat raise	3 x 15	Exercises the shoulders
Wednesday	Cycling/running/cross trainer	40–60 minutes L2–L3	2 minutes L3–4, alternating with 3 minutes L2
Thursday	Cycling	10 minutes L2	Warm up
	Bench drop lunge	3 x 20	10 each leg; use dumbbells to make it harder
	Single-leg hip raise	3 x 10	Workout for the buttocks
	Single-arm cable pull down	3 x 15	Mainly works lats, also biceps, middle back
	Bench press up	3 x 10–20	Works large muscles in the chest, also triceps
	Broomstick twist	3 x 20	Works obliques: the muscles at the side of abdomen
	Triceps cable push-down	3 x 15	Strengthens upper arms, shoulders, chest and back
Friday	Cycling/running/cross-trainer	10–20 minutes L2	Use one or a combination
	Side lunges	3 x 20	10 to each side to strengthen leg muscles
	Bent-over barbell row	3 x 15	Workout for the back
	Dumbbell flies	3 x 15	Exercise muscles at front of chest
	Cable adductors	3 x 20	10 each leg
	Plank	30–60-second hold	Builds endurance in abdominals and back
	Dumbbell bicep curl	3 x 15	Tones and strengthens biceps
Saturday	Cycling/running/cross trainer	40–60 minutes L2–L3	2 minutes L3–4, alternating with 3 minutes L2
Sunday	Rest day	24 hours	Eases and repairs sore muscles

Pregnancy Training Plan

Pregnancy is a very demanding time physically and mentally. However, by following the right exercise plan until late pregnancy, when you may find exercise uncomfortable, you can maintain your weight, reduce labour time, and make delivery easier.

Many women are understandably anxious about exercising when pregnant, but you can safely do a number of different types of exercise. Resistance exercises will make you stronger and less prone to injuries through overuse injuries as your baby gets bigger.

Basic core exercises will keep your spine and pelvis in line and prevent backache, while pelvic floor exercises will prevent incontinence. Regular exercise will increase your energy levels, improve self-esteem, help you to sleep better and enable you to get fitter after childbirth.

Pilates is a good way to increase the strength of your pelvic floor, support your back and position the baby for birth. Yoga will maintain muscle tone without impact. Swimming is one of the safest and most effective forms of exercise, as it works all the major muscles without any impact.

Below: Learn which exercises are appropriate so that you protect your unborn baby at all times.

Pregnancy training plan

Combine three daily sessions of pelvic floor exercises with weekly cardiovascular exercise – consisting of three 15–30-minute sessions – and two weekly resistance-training sessions.

Resistance training

Exercise	Sets/Reps/Time	Comments
Walking/running or cross-trainer	5–10 minutes L1–L2	Warm up or cycle
Seated cable row	3 x 10–12	Works back and forearms
Leg extension	3 x 10–12	Tones upper legs
Dumbbell chest press incline	3 x 10–12	Works chest and arms
Lat pull-down	3 x 10–12	Works back muscles
Seated leg curl	3 x 10–12	Exercises hamstrings
Dumbbell fly	3 x 10–12	Works middle of the chest
Dumbbell lat raise	3 x 10–12	Exercises the shoulders
Dumbbell bicep curl	3 x 10–12	Strengthens biceps
Bench triceps dip	3 x 10–12	Strengthens triceps

Cardiovascular training

Exercise	Sets/Reps/Time	Comments
Option 1: Stationary bike	10–20 minutes L1–L2	If you cannot hold a conversation, then you are going too fast
Option2: Treadmill walk/run	10–20 minutes L1–L2	Use without incline
Option 3: Cross-trainer	10–20 minutes L1–L2	Use for warm-up
Pelvic floor exercises	5–10 seconds	Stand, lie down or sit

Watchpoints

Seek advice from a midwife or doctor before you start any exercise plan, particularly if your pre-pregnancy body mass index (BMI) was over 35. While you should be keeping fit during pregnancy, this is not the time to make dramatic improvements in your fitness. Instead, aim to maintain the fitness you had before you became pregnant. Your exercise should not be above Level 2 if you are of average fitness, and no higher than Level 3 if you are above average fitness. If you cannot hold a conversation while exercising, you are training too hard.

Because of the extra weight you are carrying, you should avoid exercises with lots of impact in the third trimester.

As it is vital to minimize the risk of loss of balance and foetal trauma throughout pregnancy, you should definitely not undertake sports such as horse-riding, skiing, cycling, ice-skating and scuba diving.

Looser joints Be aware that during pregnancy a hormone called relaxin is released into the body. This hormone helps your joints to loosen in preparation

Warning

Stop exercising immediately if you feel any chest pain, headaches, dizziness, swelling, overtiredness, abdominal pain, nausea, dizziness, pelvic pain, contractions or lack of foetal movement.

Above: If you feel tired, stop training and take a rest. Don't push yourself if you don't feel like exercising.

for childbirth, but it also means that some exercises should be avoided: lunges, deep squats, step-ups and full sit-ups may damage the pelvic floor.

Relaxin, which is a hormone that relaxes the pelvic ligaments, may also affect other joints, particularly the wrists, elbows and knees, so use only light weights and do no more than 12 repetitions. Listen to your body and make sure you are comfortable during training.

Heat, hydration and hypoglycaemia

Avoid getting too hot by not exercising in hot or humid conditions and wearing the correct clothing. Stay well hydrated to keep your body temperature normal. Eat plenty before and after exercise to prevent hypoglycaemia (low blood-sugar levels) and do not exercise for more than 40 minutes.

The importance of position In the second and third trimester, the pressure of the baby on your blood vessels may cause blood to pool in your legs, so sit

down for resistance exercises and do not do any exercises involving movements above your head. Similarly, do not exercise lying on your back, as the pressure of the baby can cause low blood pressure.

Pelvic floor exercises

The easiest way to locate your pelvic floor muscles is by closing and pulling in both the front and back passages as if you were stopping yourself from urinating and defecating. Then, contract the muscles for 5 seconds to begin with, building up at your own pace to more than 10 seconds. If you struggle to achieve this when standing, try contracting your muscles when lying down, then progress to sitting up and, finally, standing.

Pelvic lift

1 *Lie on your back, bend your knees and plant your feet on the floor more than hip-width apart. Turn your toes slightly inward to engage the muscles of the inner thighs and groin area. Put palms down on the floor and breathe in.*

2 *Tense your buttocks and lift your hips off the floor. Hold for 5 seconds. Repeat ten times.*

Side stretch to alleviate heartburn

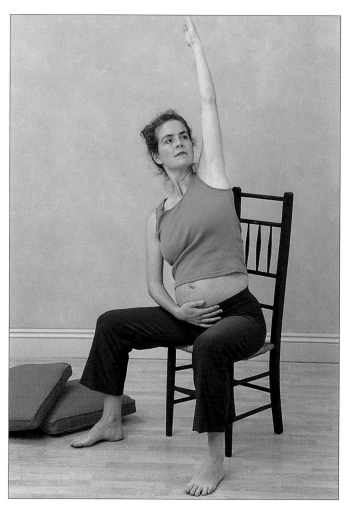

Sit on a firm chair with knees wide and feet flat on the floor. Bring your left arm out to the side and up overhead, stretching your left side. Look up at your hand, breathe deeply and hold the position. Repeat on the other side.

Postnatal Training Plan

Postnatal exercise is the best way to get back in shape and improve your self-esteem. A combination of cardiovascular and resistance training will help you to lose weight, increase your energy levels and help you cope with the emotional ups and downs.

If you feel comfortable and have had a normal birth, you can start to do some light exercise as soon as possible afterward. However, it is normal to wait for six to eight weeks before making dramatic improvements to your fitness level. During this time, you should avoid any high-impact training. Always seek advice from your doctor about the best time to start exercising.

If you have had a caesarean, you must get your doctor's approval before you begin any training. As it normally takes six to eight weeks before you are ready to begin any form of exercise, there is no point rushing to regain your pre-pregnancy fitness level. Your body has undergone major physical changes, so take your time, be patient and concentrate on your core muscles and pelvic floor strength.

What to avoid

It is important to check that your abdominal muscles have returned to normal, as they can get overstretched during pregnancy (diastasis rectus abdominis). To check the state of your abdominal muscles, lie down, then place your hand, palm down, just above your belly button, with your fingers pointing down toward your pubic bone. Try to lift your head and shoulders off the floor by tensing your abdominal muscles. You should feel them coming together. If you don't feel the abdominals

working, you should begin with pelvic floor exercises described in the pregnancy training plan and avoid doing sit-ups until you can feel your abdominals working correctly.

Your joints and ligaments will still be loose after the birth, so avoid any exercises involving significant impact or exercises such as lunges, squats, step-ups and hip adduction/abduction until you feel you have full control. Use light weights only and do no more than 12 repetitions during any session.

Above: Increase your fitness and strength, and get back into shape, while your baby is growing.

Building fitness

Start your cardiovascular fitness by walking at least three times a week for 15 minutes, building up to 30 minutes. If walking feels uncomfortable, then use the bike or do cross-trainer exercises instead. Include the pelvic floor in your training every day. You can start doing some pelvic floor squeezes the day after childbirth, if it was an easy delivery.

Postnatal exercise plan

If you apply yourself to this daily routine following childbirth, you will soon be able to resume your normal fitness training.

Exercise	Time/Sets/Reps	Comments
Pelvic tilt	10 x 10 seconds	Begin with 5 seconds and build up to 10 seconds
Pelvic floor squeeze	10 x 10 seconds	At least 4 x daily
Transverse abdominal	10 x 10 seconds	Begin with 5 seconds and build up to 10 seconds
Half crunch	3 x 10–20	Avoid tensing your neck
Reverse crunch	3 x 10–20	Keep your lower back pushed into the floor

Calories for energy

If you are breastfeeding your baby, make sure that you eat sufficient calories to enable you to have enough energy to exercise and recover. Eat low-to-medium GI foods to give you long-lasting energy.

Begin by contracting the pelvic floor for 5 seconds, and building up to 10 seconds after a few days. Once you feel ready, you can attempt faster contractions, with up to 10 every 30 seconds.

Introduce abdominal exercises as soon as you feel comfortable enough to do so, and you have had the go-ahead from your doctor. Start resistance training once your pelvic floor and abdominals are strong enough to support you in the exercises you want to do. Use the same resistance exercises that you did while pregnant before moving on to a more advanced training plan of your choice.

Below: Make sure you are fit enough to cope with the physical demands of a lively, active child.

Exercises to relieve tension in the back: floor twist

1 *Lie on your back, contract your pelvic floor, tense your abdominals and draw your knees toward your chest. Repeat a few times to loosen up the lower and middle back.*

2 *Extend left arm along floor, breathe in and drop your bent legs to the right with your right hand supporting them. To make the twist stronger, turn head to the left.*

3 *Breathe in to bring the legs back to the start position over your chest, using your right hand to help lift their weight. Repeat the movement to the left and continue several times on each side. Relax with your knees bent to finish.*

Older Person's Plan

Your metabolism declines with age, so it is vital to eat healthily and take regular exercise to maintain your muscles. If you are exercising for the first time since your youth, take any exercise slowly and seek advice from your doctor before you start.

Because your metabolic rate declines after the age of 30, you need to boost it by doing resistance exercises, that is, you apply resistance to a particular movement. This type of exercise will give you greater strength and energy and the afterburn continues to use up calories long after your training session is over.

When you are doing resistance exercises, avoid overhead exercises and those that involve keeping your balance. Listen to your body and stop well before training to failure, which could cause injury, and is unnecessary. Don't exercise beyond Level 3 (*see* page 46) during the cardiovascular exercises; you should still be able to easily hold a full conversation.

Have a training partner with you to help you to set up the weights and be on hand to assist, should you need it. If you are unsure about any exercises in the gym, ask an instructor to help you.

Below: Maintaining your fitness levels as you get older will help to improve the quality of your life.

Above: If you are unsure about what type of exercise you should do, seek help from an expert.

Breathing exercises

To avoid a rise in blood pressure, use the breathing exercises, especially when doing resistance exercises. Working with the wrong weights can lead to a rise in blood pressure, so make sure that you use weights that are light enough for you to do at least 15 repetitions.

Exercises for strong bones

To avoid osteoporosis, include impact exercises, such as step-ups and walking. Do not move too quickly after leg exercises, as it will take some time for the blood to be redistributed through the body.

Exercise sessions to maintain strength and flexibility

Attempt to do each session once a week. Use the first 5 minutes of each session to get warmed up. As well as these sessions, continue to exercise out of the gym with walks of varying pace and terrain.

Session	Exercise	Time/Level/Sets/Reps	Comments
One	Cycling	5–10 minutes L1–L2	Use as warm-up
	Leg extension	3 x 15–20	Strengthens and tones upper legs
	Standing squat	3 x 15–20	Don't let your knees go forward of your feet; use dumbbells to make it harder
	Overhand cable lat pull-down, wide grip	3 x 15–20	Works back muscles and biceps
	Dumbbell chest press	3 x 15–20	Works upper arms, chest and shoulders
	Incline bench	3 x 15	Strengthens and tones abdominal muscles
	Cable triceps push-down	3 x 15–20	Exercises triceps
	Treadmill walk	5–10 minutes L2–3	Use incline to make it harder
Two	Treadmill	5–10 minutes L1–L2	Builds general fitness and stamina.
	Seated leg curl	3 x 15–20	Tones up back of upper thighs
	Hip raises	3 x 15–20	Progress to single-leg hip raises
	Single-arm cable pull-down	3 x 15–20	Works lats, also biceps and middle back
	Dumbbell fly	3 x 15–20	Works the middle of the chest
	Dumbbell bicep curl	3 x 15–20	Optimum workout for the biceps
	Cycling	5–10 minutes L1–L2	Warm down
Three	Rowing	5–10 minutes L1–L2	Use correct technique to avoid injury
	Step-up small step aerobics step	3 x 15–20	Exercises and tones leg muscles
	Dumbbell side bends	3 x 15–20	Works obliques and abdominal muscles
	Straight arm cable pull-down	3 x 15–20	Exercises the back muscles and the triceps
	Knee press-up	3 x 5–10	Progress to bench press-ups, then full press-ups when you feel ready
	Dumbbell lat raise	3 x 10–15	Works the deltoid muscles
	Cycling	5–10 minutes L1–L2	Use to warm down

Above: Resistance training is the key to maintaining your muscles as you age.

Core-stability exercises

Include some basic core-stability exercises once a week for good posture and to hold your spine and pelvis in place. Start with basic core exercises, such as a plank, side plank raise, plank to single-leg raise and single-leg stand, and gradually progress to the more advanced levels.

Nutrition

It is very important that you plan a healthy diet and eat low GI foods in order to maintain your energy levels, and eat every three to four hours to keep your metabolism high and prevent weight gain.

If you feel very tired or faint during training, eat high GI foods, which will result in a rapid increase in your blood sugar level.

Make sure also that you have a diet that is high in protein to maintain muscle strength and to help them recover from your workouts. Remember – the more muscle you have, the more active your metabolism will become.

Right: Your exercise will be more enjoyable if you share the activity with someone else.

De-stress Plan

You may think that you are simply too busy to exercise or too exhausted to find the motivation. But the less exercise you do, the less energy you have, so take what little time you have, get to the gym and use this plan to improve your overall fitness.

A regular exercise plan will give you the energy you need to take on everyday challenges. While you are exercising, you should concentrate on the task in hand, which should prevent you from dwelling on other stresses in your life.

Try the two sessions of the de-stress plan and in between the sessions, do some cardiovascular training for 20–40 minutes, such as running, rowing, cycling and cross-trainer exercises. These sessions should be at a level where you start to feel out of breath. Spend most of your cardiovascular session in Level 2 and include up to 10 x 1-minute efforts at Level 3 to further increase your heart rate and improve your recovery rate. Having these 1-minute efforts to concentrate on will focus your mind fully on the exercise. You could make these 1-minute efforts shorter but increase the intensity to work at Level 4.

Rest between your efforts needs to last long enough for you to recover enough to tackle the next effort. Start with 3 minutes between each effort and

Above: Try interval training to make best use of your exercise session. This is riding fast for 1–10 minutes, resting to recover, then repeating a few times.

Left: Stress at work can be managed by exercising to increase energy levels.

Increasing weights

For the resistance exercises, pick a weight that you can comfortably use for the time allocated for each exercise. If you are using dumbbells, have a range of weights close by so that you can quickly switch weights to make the exercise easier or more difficult. As you increase in strength, you will be able to gradually increase the weight that you can lift.

drop it to 90 seconds when you feel fit enough. It is hard to motivate yourself to exercise when you are stressed from a day's work so set yourself targets in your workouts. Aim to lift a bigger weight or run farther in a certain time. You must also keep your exercise as regular as possible so you keep up a level of fitness that enables you to feel good when you exercise rather than wishing you hadn't let your fitness slip away from you.

Nutrition

It is important to eat healthily if you have a busy life. If you spend 10 minutes a day making healthy food, you will find everyday tasks easier, and your energy levels will remain constant, so you can fit more into your day. Stick to eating low to medium GI foods and stay hydrated. Alcohol will not help you to de-stress – it will only make you more tired and even less inclined to exercise.

Releasing tension

Boxercise is one of the best ways to de-stress, so if you have a training partner who will hold the pads for you, go for it. Begin with 5 minutes at a time, building up to around 15 minutes. Try doing a boxercise session in place of some of the cardiovascular exercises in your training week.

Below: A boxing session is a great way to unwind and get rid of stress.

De-stress exercise plan

Take 10 to 20 seconds' rest between each exercise to allow your body to recover just enough to complete the next set without your heart rate going down. To make your de-stress plan complete, include at least one session of core-stability exercises, starting at the basic level and working up through the levels, to improve your posture and prevent injuries such as back pain in everyday movements or through too much time spent being sedentary.

Make sure you warm up for 5 to 10 minutes at Level 1 to Level 2, then spend 5 minutes stretching to prepare your muscles for the workout. Try to do at least two workouts a week.

Session	Exercise	Time/Level	Comments
One	Cycling	5 minutes L1–L2	Warm up
	Treadmill	5–10 minutes L2–L3	Builds fitness
	Overhand lat pull-down, wide grip	30 seconds	Works back
	Step-up	60 seconds	30 seconds on each leg
	Press-up	30 seconds	Build up to 60 seconds
	Single-arm dumbbell row	60 seconds	30 seconds on each arm
	Lunge	60 seconds	30 seconds on each leg
	Dumbbell chest press incline	30 seconds	Increase weight as strength increases
	Rowing	5 minutes L3–L4	Go as far as possible
	Dumbbell shoulder press	30 seconds	Works shoulders
	Dumbbell squat	60 seconds	Works buttocks
	Bench triceps dip	30 seconds	Build up to 60 seconds
	Crunch	60 seconds	Tones abdominals
	Treadmill walk/run	5 minutes L2–L3	For stamina
	Warm down	5 minutes	Stretches
Two	Cycling	5 minutes L1–L2	Warm up
	Rowing	5–10 minutes L2–L3	Works upper body
	Bent-over barbell row	30 seconds	Works back muscles
	Side lunge	60 seconds	Strengthens legs
	Dumbbell chest press	30 seconds	Works chest, arms
	Single-arm cable pull-down	60 seconds	30 seconds on each arm
	Side step up	60 seconds	30 seconds on each leg
	Press-up	30 seconds	Works upper body
	Treadmill walk/run	5–10 minutes L2–L3	Builds stamina
	Arnie shoulder press	30 seconds	Works deltoids
	Calf raise	60 seconds	Works calf muscles
	Dumbbell bicep curl	30 seconds	Works the biceps
	Sit-up with Russian twist	30 seconds	Build up to 60 seconds
	Rowing	5 minutes L2–L3	Works upper body
	Warm down	5 minutes	Stretches

Outdoor Training Plan

For people who find gyms intimidating or just plain inconvenient, the following outdoor programmes are ideal, especially in a park where you can use benches and trees in place of gym equipment.

If you like to walk or jog with a partner, it is not always possible to match your running pace, which can leave both of you frustrated. The faster person wants to go faster, and the slower person feels they are letting their training partner down by slowing them up. By introducing the approach to training outlined here, the fitter person can follow these exercise plans while waiting for their partner to catch up.

Build up strength

For the first two weeks, do 20 seconds of each exercise, building up to 40 seconds and then 60 seconds once you are confident of your strength. Jog or walk between the exercises to keep your heart rate at Level 2 to Level 3. If you would prefer to walk rather than run, use fast walking to keep your heart rate high, and include some hills to make the session more beneficial.

Below: Running outside in the fresh air is exhilarating, and gives you the chance to explore new places.

Outdoor exercise plan

Each session is only about 30 minutes long; do session one and two each week, on different days, and after just three to four weeks of training you will notice how much easier they are. Your recovery rate between exercises will also have improved dramatically.

Session	Exercise	Time/Sets/Reps/Level	Comments
One	Walking/jogging	5 minutes L1–L2	Warm up
	Running	5 minutes L2–L3	Cardiovascular exercise
	Lunge	60 seconds	30 seconds on each leg
	Running	2 minutes L2–L3	Good for general fitness
	Bench step-up	60 seconds	30 seconds on each leg; use a park bench
	Running	2 minutes L2–L3	
	Bench press-up	60 seconds	Begin with 30 seconds; build up to 60 seconds
	Running	2 minutes L3–L4	
	Side lunge	60 seconds	30 seconds on each side
	Running	2 minutes L3–L4	
	Bench triceps dip	60 seconds	Works upper arms and chest
	Running	5–10 minutes L2–L4	Include 5 x 30-second hill runs at L4
Two	Walking/jogging	5 minutes L1–L2	Warm up
	Running	5 minutes L2–L3	
	Standing squat	60 seconds	Strengthens lower body
	Running	2 minutes L2–L3	
	Side step-up	60 seconds	Use park bench
	Running	2 minutes L2–L3	
	Bench drop lunge	60 seconds	Use park bench
	Running	2 minutes L3–L4	
	Triceps press-up	60 seconds	Use park bench; begin with 30 seconds; build up to 60 seconds
	Running	2 minutes L3–L4	
	Calf raise	60 seconds	Lean against back of park bench or tree
	Running	5–10 minutes L2–L4	Include 5 x 30-second sprints at L4

At the start of your workout, do your normal stretches using a park bench, which you can hold on to, lean against or place your leg on. Remember that core-stability training still needs to be part of your routine. If the ground is dry, do core exercises outside; if it is wet, do them in the comfort of your home. Try to include some core exercises at least once a week, beginning with the basic exercises and gradually progressing to the intermediate and more advanced exercises when you feel able to.

Bench step-ups

These can be done as part of a circuit or added to a running or walking session.

1 *Place one foot on the bench. Push up using the muscles in your front leg to lift you up so that both legs are standing on the bench.*

2 *Once you are standing upright on the bench, slowly lower yourself back to the ground using one leg at a time. Repeat using the other leg to start.*

Bench press-ups

Outdoor benches in parks or urban streets are ideal for doing press-ups since they are at a perfect height for these types of exercises.

1 *Start the press-ups by lowering yourself to the plank position with hands on the bench and elbows bent at 90 degrees.*

2 *Press up carefully until your arms are straight, then pause for a second before slowly lowering yourself back down to the start position.*

Bench triceps dips

Outdoor benches are normally the perfect height for triceps dips.

1 *Start by getting to the plank position with hands on the bench, fingers facing outward and your elbows bent at 90 degrees. Lower yourself so that your knees are bent and your feet are flat on the ground in front of you.*

2 *Once you have lowered yourself down, hold the position for a short time, then carefully begin to press back up to the straight arm starting position. Have a rest, then repeat the exercise. If your arms feel stiff, rub or shake them.*

Clothing
Wear several layers of clothing so that you can easily take them off if you get hot and maintain your body temperature at a comfortable level.

Precaution
Always carry a water bottle so that you can stay hydrated, and a mobile phone in case you have an injury or other emergency.

Travel Plan

When you are away from home, it is not always easy to get to the gym – which can be the perfect excuse to stop your fitness training. However, with the following plan, you have no reason to stop exercising.

This plan is designed for the traveller who has a limited amount of space in which to exercise, such as a hotel room, and no equipment to hand. For weights, you can improvise by using bottles of water. To support your back while doing floor exercises, use a blanket or folded towel. Remember – being on holiday is no excuse not to keep up with your exercise programme.

If you are staying at a hotel that offers the use of a gym to its guests, you just need the motivation to go every morning before you get involved in other activities. Having a gym so close at hand may even improve your fitness levels. And if the hotel does not have a gym, follow the traveller's fitness plan whenever you have a spare 20 mintues and you will feel the benefits.

The training sessions will keep your heart rate up and give your muscles a good workout. For maximum benefit, allow only 10–20 seconds between each exercise. If you want to keep your heart rate up during the session, you can also include marching or jogging on the spot between each exercise.

Improvised exercises

Above: Even if you have only a limited space, there is usually enough room to stretch so you can stay flexible.

Above: If you don't have suitable weights, simply use water bottles to do some lat raises.

Travel tips

Include some basic core exercises every other day to keep your trunk muscles working well, especially if you are spending a significant amount of time sitting down.

Stretch after your warm-up, and also at the end of each session, to prevent your muscles from shortening during periods of travel.

Left: Even though you are immobile when you are travelling, it can still be a tiring process. It is therefore important to keep up your exercise wherever and whenever you can, so that you can maintain your energy levels.

Traveller's exercise plan

Each session should only take about 15 minutes, and you should always start with a good 5 minutes' warm-up at Level 1 to Level 2, followed by some stretches for the muscles you are going to use. Do just one or all the sessions when they fit into your schedule.

Session	Exercise	Time/Sets/Reps/Level	Comments
One	Walking/marching on spot	5 minutes L1–L2	Warm up
	Standing squat	60 seconds	Use water bottles as weights
	Press-up	30 seconds	Build up to 60 seconds
	Crunch	60 seconds	Exercises abdominal muscles
	Calf raises	60 seconds	Lean against the wall or door
	Body weight shoulder press	30 seconds	Strengthens shoulder muscles
	Oblique crunch	60 seconds	Works oblique abdominal muscles
	Frontal raises	60 seconds	30 seconds each arm, use water bottles as weights
	Hip raise	60 seconds	Strengthens buttock muscles
	Triceps dip	30 seconds	Build up to 60 seconds
Two	Walking, marching on spot	5 minutes L1–L2	Warm up
	Lunge	60 seconds	30 seconds on each leg
	V-crunch	30 seconds	Build up to 60 seconds
	Single-leg squat	60 seconds	30 seconds on each leg
	Plank	30–60 seconds	Builds endurance in abdominal muscles and back
	Double-leg jump	60 seconds	Land as softly as possible
	Side plank	60 seconds	Strengthens oblique abdominal muscles
	Upright row	30 seconds	Use water bottles as weights
	Side crunch	60 seconds	30 seconds on each side
	Bicep curl	30 seconds	Use water bottles as weights
Three	Walking, marching on spot	5 minutes L1–L2	Warm up
	Wide-leg power squat	60 seconds	Exercises quadriceps
	Decline press-up	30 seconds	Build up to 60 seconds; put feet on chair or bed
	Leg criss-cross	30 seconds	Build up to 60 seconds
	Superman	60 seconds	Works buttocks and abdominal muscles
	Lateral jump	60 seconds	Strengthens and tones the thighs, hamstrings and buttocks
	Lateral raise	30 seconds	Use water bottles as weights
	Reverse crunch	60 seconds	Works lower abdominal muscles
	Triceps press-up	30 seconds	Build up to 60 seconds
	Single-leg hip raise	60 seconds	30 seconds on each leg

Above and left: You don't have to give up exercising if you are travelling; you can manage without any equipment.

Speed and Power Plan

Training for speed and power calls for a very fine balancing act. You need to get faster and stronger, but without adding too much muscle bulk, which will only slow you down. This plan will help you to fine-tune your training strategy.

Plyometrics and sprint training will help train your fast-twitch muscle fibres to give you the increased speed and power you want. However, without initial resistance training to develop strong muscles, you may find it difficult to increase your speed and power.

Follow this plan for six weeks, using the One Repetition Maximum (ORM) test for strength and timed sprints to see if you are getting faster. The speed and power training plan gives you the structure of the programme for a week.

Exercise exchange

After three weeks, you can try exchanging some of the exercises with other, similar, exercises. For example introduce some other resistance training exercises for legs to challenge your muscles in different ways. You could change hack squats for leg presses, and the single-leg hip raise with cable

> **Layered clothing**
> It is important to keep your muscles warm throughout your training session, especially when you want them to perform powerfully with fast contractions. The solution is to wear a number of layers of clothing, so that you can easily adjust them to suit your level of intensity and the conditions in which you are training.

kick backs. Do the same for your upper-body exercises. Adjusting the exercises and changing the order will challenge your body further, making it faster and stronger. Include some core-stability training every week. Your core muscles will play a vital role in helping you to avoid injury and enable you to create forward speed, with all your muscles recruiting in the correct order.

Above: To gain speed and power, you may consider taking extra protein in the form of drinks, which you can make from a protein powder formula.

Speed and power training plan

Always do 5 to 10 minutes' cardiovascular warm-up, which should be at a higher intensity than a warm-up for normal gym training. You need to get as much blood as possible circulating to the big muscles that you want to use. Follow the warm-up with stretches, to prepare your body for the hard training session. Stretch your muscles at the end of the workout to help them recover and avoid injury. Your speed and power should be much improved if you stick to this plan for about six weeks.

Day	Exercise	Time/Sets/Reps/Level	Comments
Monday	Running	10 minutes L1–L2	Warm up
	8 x 100m/109-yd sprints	L4	Stretch to prevent injury
	300m/328-yd jog recovery	L1	Stretch to help recovery
	8 x 50m sprints	L4	Don't overstride, keep to 90 strides per minute
	350m/383-yd jog recovery	L1	Try to maintain good technique
	Running	5 minutes L1	Cool down
Tuesday	Cycling	5 minutes L1–L2	Warm up
	Hack squat	5 x 8–10	Exercises quadriceps muscles
	Dead lift	5 x 8–10	Works thighs and buttocks
	Wide-leg power squat	5 x 8–10	Works the quadriceps muscles
	Dumbbell squat	5 x 8–10	Tones buttocks, hips and thighs
	Lunge	5 x 8–10	Try bench drop lunges to make it harder
	Calf raise	5 x 8–10	Use weights to make it harder
	Single-leg hip raise	3 x 20	Tones and strengthens the buttocks

Day	Exercise	Time/Sets/Reps/Level	Comments
Wednesday	Cycling	5 minutes L1–L2	Warm up
	Double-leg squat jump	5 x 20	To prevent injury, make sure your plyometrics technique is correct
	Side lateral jumps	5 x 20	Works quadriceps and buttocks
	Single-leg squat jump	5 x 20	10 each leg
	Step-up	5 x 20	10 each leg
	Crunch	3 x 20	Workout for the abdominals
	Hanging leg raises	3 x 20	Begin with 10, build up to 20
	Knee cable rotations	3 x 20	Exercises abdominal muscles
Thursday	Running	10 minutes L1–L2	Warm up
	4 x 200m/219-yd sprint	L4	Develops fast-twitch muscle fibres
	200m/219-yd jog recovery	L1	Use good technique for stretching, don't bounce
	6 x 100m/109-yd sprint	L4	Helps increase speed and power
	200m/219-yd jog recovery	L1	Aids easy recovery between sprint efforts
	8 x 50m/55-yd sprint	L4	Increases leg turnover
	150m/164-yd jog recovery	L1	Stretching actually encourages relaxation
	Running	5 minutes L1	Cool down
Friday	Running	40 minutes L2–L4	Use the first 5–10 minutes to warm up to L1, then 10–20-second sprints at L4 every 3 minutes
Saturday	Rowing	5 minutes L1–L2	Warm up
	Overhand chin-up, wide grip	5 x max reps	Develops back muscles
	Olympic bar chest press	5 x 8–10	Tones and shapes the chest
	Bent-over barbell row	5 x 8–10	Strengthens the back muscles
	Dumbbell chest press, incline bench	5 x 8–10	Builds up the chest, shoulder and arms
	Arnie shoulder press	5 x 8–10	Srengthens shoulders and upper arms
	Cable frontal raise	5 x 8–10	Works front of shoulders
	Dumbbell bicep curls	5 x 8-10	Optimum workout for the biceps
	Triceps cable push-down	5 x 8-10	Works the triceps
	Bench triceps dip	3 x max reps	Strengthens triceps
Sunday	Rest day	24 hours	Eases and repairs sore muscles

Nutrition

You can increase the density of your muscles by stepping up the calorie content of your diet. Study the information on how you should eat to gain muscle. Always have a recovery drink, consisting of a mixture of carbohydrate and protein, to aid a speedy recovery and prepare your muscles for their next training session, or recovery between sessions could be twice as long.

Right: Gaining speed and power won't just happen overnight; it will take time, hard work and dedication to your training plan.

Racket Sports Plan

Playing racket sports – particularly tennis, squash and badminton – is a good and highly enjoyable way of keeping fit and competing with a partner. It can also be one of the best ways to de-stress after a hard day's work.

Racket sports demand a great deal of your time if you are to play them properly and enjoy them to the full, with a competitive edge: you need power, speed, stamina and good stability.

Boost your fitness

With such intense physical demands, you need to do more for your fitness than just play the game – no matter how regularly you practice. Take time to complete these two sessions in every ten-day period to give you the best chance of improving your game and preventing injury. You will soon find that you can get to the ball quicker and make it harder for your opponent to get a winning shot past you.

It is vital that you do regular core-stability training at least once a week to prepare your body for the constant pounding and change of direction. Begin with basic core exercises and work your way up to the advanced exercises and the fit ball, BOSU and medicine ball exercises.

On the days between racket and gym sessions, you should focus on building up your cardiovascular fitness with a

Above: Reaching a good standard in racket sports takes a lot of effort. It also requires strength and stamina so that you can last out in a long game.

Below: Core-stability exercises are essential to avoid injuries and they will help to make you a better player.

Above: Fluid intake will have a beneficial effect on your performance. If you are dehyrated, you lack concentration and feel under par.

Below: Rotational exercises will help your reflexes become sharper and will make you a good competitor.

Racket sports exercise plan

Before you play any competitive racket sport or start a training session, always try to fit in at least 5 to 10 minutes' warm-up, consisting of activities such as walking and jogging, cycling or rowing, followed by a warm-down of some stretches. Also, it is a good idea to stretch after your tennis game or training session to help your muscles to recover faster and avoid injury.

Session	Exercise	Time/Sets/Reps/Level	Comments
One	Cycling	5–20 minutes L1–L2	Warm up; option to row or run
	Leg press	3 x 20	Firms and tones leg muscles
	Side lunge	3 x 20	Strengthens hips, buttocks and thighs
	Step-up	3 x 20	Tones and firms leg muscles
	Rowing	10–20 minutes	2 minutes at L2 and 1 minute at L4
	Lateral pull-down, overarm grip	3 x 12–15	Works the lats (muscles in the back)
	Dumbbell chest press, incline bench	3 x 12–15	Builds up the chest, shoulders, arms
	Arnie shoulder press	3 x 12–15	Strengthens shoulders and upper arms
	Crunch	3 x 20	Abdominal workout
	Reverse crunch	3 x 20	Tones and strengthens rectus abdominis
	Oblique crunch	3 x 20	Works upper abdominals and obliques
	Dumbbell bicep curl	3 x 12	Optimum workout for the biceps
	Bench triceps dip	3 x 20	Exercises triceps
Two	Rowing	5 minutes L1–L2	Warm up; option to use bike
	Plank	30–60 seconds	Builds up abdominals and back
	Superman	3 x10	Works buttocks and abdominal muscles
	Hip raise	3 x 20	Tones and strengthens the buttocks
	Press-up to dumbbell row	3 x 20	Good for core stability
	Double-leg jump	3 x 20	Builds power and speed
	Lateral jump	3 x 20	Strengthens the thighs, hamstrings and buttocks
	Overhead slam	3 x 10	Engages buttocks, chest and abdominals
	Single-leg squat with cable row to frontal raise, start position	3 x 10	Reinforces a strong core
	Cable wood chop, high to low	3 x 10	10 each side
	Dumbbell side bend	3 x 20	Works obliques and abdominal muscles

20- to 40-minute run. Also, make sure to vary the pace of the run to simulate the varying pace in the rackets game. Include five to ten 20-second sprints and some 30–60-second hill intervals.

Nutrition

Racket sports combine many attributes of fitness, making them a great way to lose weight. However, it is always important to eat healthily and include a mixture of low and medium GI foods that contain adequate protein to help your muscles recover and strengthen.

As with all intense physical activity, you need to be careful not to become dehydrated during the game. Always have a water bottle nearby and use energy drinks to keep hydrated if you know you will be playing or training for more than an hour.

Below: In racket sports, there is demand on the muscles to contract fast so that you can leap into the air.

Below: Fitness will enable you to get into position faster to return the opposition's shot.

Golf Plan

It may look like an amiable, leisurely pastime, but golf is a very complex sport that involves high-speed muscular movements with rotation and which, at the same time, demands a solid base as well as great focus and control.

To become a better golfer, you have to practise as much as possible – there are no short cuts. As with many other sports, however, it is not just a matter of practising the game itself. In fact, in order to be able to practise for long periods of time using such a complex muscular movement, you will have to be fit. Otherwise, your body will simply

Below: One of the main goals when training for golf is to remain free from any injury by building up fitness.

break down through overuse injuries, which will prevent you from improving, or even enjoying, your game.

The two sessions outlined here will help you work the muscles you need for the golf swing, which will, in turn, help to improve your game and avoid injury. Session one aims to build basic strength to enable your muscles to train harder for longer. Session two is more advanced: it uses rotational exercises with balance and core stability to simulate the stresses on the body during

Above: A long round of golf will make you dehydrated, especially in hot weather, so always carry a drink with you when you are on the course.

your golf swing. It is important to use one side of the body at a time for some of your resistance exercises, as golf will affect your muscular symmetry. To prevent injury, the muscles on both sides of your body need to be well balanced.

The key to great golf
Flexibility and core stability are essential attributes for a successful golfer. Core stability, in fact, is perhaps more important for golf than for any other sport. One slight wrong movement in your trunk could have a detrimental effect on your golf swing. Make sure you progress through the core-stability exercises, beginning at the basic level.

Flexibility is also a major factor in golf; you need to be able to rotate at the trunk with great flexibility, so take time to

Switch on core muscles
Try to fit in some basic core exercises just before you tee off. They will help you to switch on the core muscles so that they support your game from the first stroke onward.

Golf exercise plan

On days between your twice-weekly gym sessions, you should try to improve your cardiovascular fitness to improve your aerobic efficiency and stamina on the golf course. Do 20–40 minutes of some form of cardiovascular exercise, such as running, rowing, cycling or cross-training twice a week. The fitter you are, the more energy you will have to focus on your game.

Session	Exercise	Time/Sets/Reps/level	Comments
One	Rowing	5–10 minutes L1–L2	Warm up; option of cycling or cross-trainer
	Dumbbell squat	3 x 20	Progress to single-leg squats
	Side lunge	3 x 20	10 to each side
	Single-leg squat	3 x 20	10 on each leg. Focus on keeping your hips level
	Single-arm cable lat pull-down	3 x 12–15	On each arm
	Bent-over barbell row	3 x 12–15	Strengthens the back
	Cable fly, standing	3 x 12–15	Develops pectorals
	Arnie shoulder press	3 x 12–15	Strengthens shoulders and upper arms
	Bent-over lateral raise	3 x 12–15	Exercises shoulders and back
	Single-arm triceps cable push-down	3 x 12–15	Mainly works the triceps
	Wrist curl	3 x 12–15	Change the angle of the wrist curl every session
	Oblique crunches	3 x 20	10 each side
Two	Rowing	5–10 minutes L1–L2	Warm up; option of cycling or cross-trainer
	BOSU squat	3 x 20	Progress to single-leg BOSU squat
	Plank knee tuck	3 x 20	10 each side
	Cable wood chop on BOSU	3 x 20	Begin without BOSU, progressing to standing BOSU
	Single-hand medicine ball press-up	3 x 20	10 each arm
	Medicine ball lunge and lean	3 x 20	10 each leg
	Medicine ball lunge and rotate	3 x 20	10 each leg
	Squat to cable shoulder press	3 x 20	Begin with 10 reps and build up to 20
	Press-up to dumbbell row	3 x 20	10 rows each arm
	Squat to cable side twist	3 x 20	20 each side
	High cable side bend	3 x 20	Movement works the abdominals

do regular stretching before and after every practice session and game. If your muscles are not flexible, you will become increasingly prone to injury, and you will not be able to get your body into the positions necessary for a great golf swing.

Nutrition

The longer your golf game, the more important your nutrition. If you play 18 holes, you will typically walk 8–10km/ 5–6 miles, perhaps also carrying your clubs. Eat the correct foods before, during and after the game, and stay well hydrated. Eat low GI foods for a slow, steady release of energy. Always have a drink with you to prevent dehydration, especially during the hot summer months.

Right: Squats are a great way to build up strength in the leg muscles, and increase your fitness for golf.

Above: Side stretches will help you to stay flexible, which is essential for golf.

Contact Sports Plan

Contact sports rely on many different fitness attributes. Which one you choose, and how you tailor your fitness plan, depends on whether you want to focus on your speed, power, strength, endurance, stability or flexibility.

Contact sports range from team sports, such as rugby and football, to individual sports, such as boxing and martial arts like tae kwon do. For a team contact sport, such as rugby, you should train according to the position you play in. For example, if you are a forward, you will want to be strong and powerful, so you should concentrate on heavy resistance training with low repetitions and increased emphasis on your upper body. If you play in the back rows, you will need speed and stability to be able to run fast and

Below: In contact sports, stability is vital if you are to avoid being injured. You also need flexibility and speed.

change direction. You will also need some muscular strength to take the tackles and take on the opposition, so your training plan should include a mixture of resistance-training and core-stability exercises, with particular emphasis on plyometrics.

Train and adapt

The three sessions outlined here will give you a basic fitness level that you can then progress from and adapt. Between your three weekly gym sessions, do regular cardiovascular training. Most of this can be undertaken during actual practice in your sport, but extra cardiovascular training will give you an added advantage.

Above: If you have access to a gym before your sport, you can warm up using the cross-trainer.

Try to do two 40-minute runs, mixed with ten hill sprints of 10–20 seconds and ten flat sprints lasting 10–20 seconds, to get your body used to high-intensity workouts and faster recovery. A weekly boxercise session will prepare you for hand–eye co-ordination and improve cardiovascular fitness and upper-body strength.

Core stability and flexibility

To help prevent injury and enable you to use all your strength, speed and power effectively, core stability is vital. Work your way through basic, intermediate and advanced core-stability training sessions for the best results. Flexibility in contact sports is often neglected, so make time to stretch once you are warmed up, and exercise to let your muscles prepare for training and fast recovery.

Contact sports exercise plan

Session one works your legs, session two works your upper body and session three is partly for speed and partly for trunk stability. If your sport requires more endurance and less muscle bulk, increase to 12–15 repetitions for each set during the resistance exercises.

Session	Exercise	Time/Sets/Reps	Comments
One	Rowing	5–10 minutes L1–L2	Warm up; option to cycle, run or use cross-trainer
	Hack squat	5 x 8–10	Good for upper legs and buttocks
	Dead lift	5 x 8–10	Works thighs and buttocks
	Single-leg squat	5 x 8–10	With dumbbells
	Step-up	5 x 8–10	With dumbbells
	Lunge	5 x 8–10	On each leg, holding dumbbells
	Cable adductor/abductor	5 x 8–10	Works strong muscles in upper legs
	Calf raise	5 x 8–10	Use weights to make it harder
	Crunch	3 x 20	Hold weights in hands above head to make it harder
	Reverse crunch	3 x 20	Abdominal workout
	Hanging leg raise with twist	3 x 10	Build up to 20 reps
Two	Rowing	5–10 minutes L1–L2	Warm up; option to cycle, run or use cross-trainer
	Over-arm chin-up, wide grip	5 x max reps	Exercises the lats, biceps and mid back
	Dumbbell chest press, flat bench	5 x 8–10	Develops and tones the chest
	Single-arm dumbbell row	5 x 8–10	Workout for the middle back muscles
	Press-up	5 x 8–10	Strengthens back, chest and arms
	Cable shoulder press	5 x 8–10	Strengthens upper arms, improves general fitness
	Arnie shoulder press	5 x 8–10	Strengthens shoulders and upper arms
	Bent-over cable lateral raise	5 x 8–10	Develops rear deltoid (shoulder) muscles
	Sit-up with Russian twist	3 x 20	Works abdominals and obliques
	Oblique crunch	3 x 20	Works upper abdominals and obliques
	Dumbbell side bends	3 x 20	Works obliques and abdominal muscles
Three	Row	5–10 minutes L1–L2	Warm up; option to cycle, run or use cross-trainer
	Double-leg jump	3 x 20	Good core stability needed for this jump
	Lateral jump	3 x 20	Strengthens and tones the thighs, hamstrings and buttocks
	Lunge jump	3 x 20	Good for buttocks, quadriceps and calf muscles
	Squat throw	3 x 20	Strengthens core muscles of abdomen, hip and buttocks
	Over head slam	3 x 20	Engages hamstrings, hips and buttocks
	Press-up to dumbbell row	3 x 20	Good exercise for core stability
	Dumbbell bicep curl	3 x 8–10	Optimum workout for the biceps
	Bench triceps dip	3 x max reps	Keep legs straight to make it harder
	Broomstick twist	3 x 20	Works obliques: the muscles at the side of abdomen
	Kneeling cable rotation	3 x 20	Exercises the abdominals
	Side crunches	3 x 20	Strengthens and tones obliques
	Warm down	5–10 minutes	Stretches

Nutrition

You will need to adjust your nutrition depending on what it is you want to achieve. In order to lose weight, to gain muscle, or to increase your endurance choose a diet that is appropriate for your requirements.

Right: Resistance training will help your body take the physical knocks from the opposition without injury.

Swimming Plan

There is more to becoming a good swimmer than just being able to dive in and swim a few lengths in the pool. The training plan outlined here will improve your fitness level in the water and give you greater strength.

Choose two of the three training sessions outlined here to do on the days you are not swimming at high intensity. If you are going to do resistance training on the same day as swim training, then decide which session you want to get the most out of and do that first. Be aware that the resistance training may leave you feeling sluggish in the water later in the day. However, if you swim first, you may struggle to make the improvements you want in your resistance training.

Core stability and flexibility

To form a strong connection between your upper and lower body, you need to have strong core stability. There is no point in having strong shoulders and legs if the centre of your body is weak, as this will only result in energy loss when training or competing. So, begin with the basic core-stability exercises,

Below: Regular stretching of the arms will keep your muscles long and powerful for swimming.

Above: Stretch your body after swimming, paying particular attention to the arms and shoulders.

twice a week, gradually building up at your own pace to the intermediate and advanced exercises.

In order to get a full range of movement for all swim strokes, it is important to stay flexible, so regularly stretch all areas of your body after every session in the pool or the gym.

Above: Stretch your neck to avoid it getting stiff from trying to lift your head, or turn the neck to the side to breathe.

In particular you should pay careful attention to your back, chest, shoulders and arms.

Nutrition

Consume low to medium GI foods every three to four hours and eat high GI foods during training sessions.

Stay well hydrated when you are swimming. It's easy to think you don't need anything to drink because you are exercising in water – however, some pools can be hot, which can dehydrate you. Always have a water bottle at the side of the pool.

Right: Always have the right equipment, such as goggles, so that you can relax and enjoy your swim.

Swimming exercise plan

All three of these sessions include a combination of upper- and lower-body exercises as well as exercises to build abdominal strength. If you have weak areas, you can spend more time on them. For example, if you have weak shoulders, you may want to include more shoulder exercises.

Session	Exercise	Time/Sets/Reps/Level	Comments
One	Row	5–10 minutes L1–L2	Warm up; option to use cross-trainer
	Overhand chin-up, wide grip	3 x max reps	Develops shoulders and upper back
	Olympic bar chest press	3 x 10–12	Tones and shapes the chest
	Overhand lateral pull-down, wide grip	3 x 10–12	Targets the lats
	Cable fly	3 x 10–12	Develops pectorals
	Leg press	3 x 20	Strengthens and firms leg muscles
	Leg extension	3 x 20	Strengthens and works upper legs
	Arnie shoulder press	3 x 10–12	Strengthens shoulders and upper arms
	Cable triceps push-down	3 x 10–12	Exercises triceps
	Reverse crunch	3 x 20	Tones and strengthens rectus abdominis
	Hanging leg raise	3 x 20	Builds up the abdominal muscles
Two	Cross-trainer	5–10 minutes L1–L2	Warm up; option to use rowing machine
	Seated cable row	3 x 10–12	Strengthens the middle back and forearms
	Dumbbell chest press, incline bench	3 x 10–12	Builds up the chest, shoulder and arms
	Single-arm cable lateral pull-down	3 x 10–12	Each arm
	Medicine ball one-hand press-up	3 x 10–12	Each arm
	Hack squat	3 x 20	Good for upper legs and buttocks
	Machine leg curl	3 x 20	Exercises the hamstrings
	Dumbbell frontal raise	3 x 10–12	Each arm
	Overhead triceps extension	3 x 10–12	Increases strength and flexibility of the triceps
	Oblique crunch	3 x 20	Works upper abdominals and obliques
	Broomstick twist	3 x 20	Works obliques: the muscles at side of abdomen
Three	Rowing	5–10 minutes L1–L2	Warm-up; option to use cross-trainer
	Single-arm dumbbell row	3 x 10–12	Workout for the middle back muscles
	Dumbbell chest press, decline bench	3 x 10–12	Targets the pectoral muscles
	Single-arm straight arm pull-down	3 x 10–12	Exercise aimed at outer back
	Dumbbell fly, flat bench	3 x 10–12	Strengthens chest
	Lunge	3 x 20	10 on each leg
	Calf raise	3 x 20	Strengthens the calf muscles
	Cable lateral raise	3 x 10–12	Each arm
	Single-leg squat to cable row to frontal raise	3 x 10–12	Each arm
	Dumbbell biceps curl	3 x 10–12	Develops biceps
	Kneeling cable rotation	3 x 20	10 each side
	Cable side bend	3 x 20	Works the oblique muscles of the abdomen

Running Plan

Being a successful runner involves more than simply running. You need to do the correct core-stability and resistance-exercise training for support and to help you to avoid injuries. You also need gradually to increase the distances that you run.

The distance of your running event, for example, a marathon or a 5km/3-mile race, will dictate the amount of running that you have to do. You should aim to run three to four times a week, varying the distances, speeds, inclines and length of intervals to challenge your body and improve your fitness. Do not run more than two days in a row unless you are an elite runner, as this will make you prone to injury. If you want to do cardiovascular training on other days, choose low-impact exercises, such as cycling, rowing or swimming.

The cross-trainer is an excellent tool for keeping fit if you are recovering from a running injury, because it works the running muscles using similar movement patterns to running.

Below: To improve running times, use exercises that are directly related to the same movements.

Core-stability and resistance training

Your fitness training programme should involve resistance training twice weekly and regular core-stability training. Begin with basic level core-stability training, then gradually work your way up to the intermediate and advanced exercises. Core stability is essential for running because of the constant impact on one leg and the resulting lateral movement, which can cause injury. Do some core-stability exercises immediately before your fastest runs so that your core muscles are already switched on before you start running.

Resistance training will give you the strength to resist the constant impact of running and provide the power to drive you forward, thus making you faster. Do the resistance-training exercises on the days that you are not running. Do not, however, do a resistance session before going for a run, as your muscles will be tired and therefore unable to support you adequately while you run. This is only likely to make you more prone to injury.

Above: Run with people of your own ability to avoid injury, and push yourself to make improvements.

Stretching

It is important to stretch before and after every session. The main muscles that you need to pay attention to are the lower back, hamstrings, quadriceps, hip flexors and calf muscles. Take 5 minutes to complete your stretches – they are just as important as running or resistance training.

Nutrition

Being lightweight is an advantage for runners, so eat healthily to keep your weight low, choosing foods that are low to medium GI, and eat regularly to keep your metabolism high and help your body to recover between training sessions. In the 2 hours before, as well as during and immediately after a long running session, eat a mixture of low and high GI foods to enable faster recovery and to replace muscle glycogen (stored glucose).

Exercise plan for runners

Session one and two will strengthen your running muscles. Session three works some of the smaller muscles and helps combine the core and major muscles used in running. Session four is for the upper body. You should do all of these exercises at least once every two weeks to maintain upper-body strength and muscle tone.

Session	Exercise	Time/Sets/Reps/Level	Comments
One	Running	5–10 minutes L1–L2	Warm up
	Leg press	3 x 20	Strengthens and firms leg muscles
	Dumbbell squat	3 x 20	Tones buttocks, hips and thighs
	Crunch	3 x 20	Abominal workout
	Step-up	3 x 20	Exercises and tones leg muscles
	Lunge	3 x 20	Works the upper leg and buttocks
	Reverse crunch	3 x 20	Tones and strengthens rectus abdominis
	Leg extension	3 x 20	Strengthens and works upper legs
	Calf raise	3 x 20+	Strengthens the calf muscles
	Oblique crunch	3 x 20	Works upper abdominals and obliques
	Dumbbell side bend	3 x 20	Works obliques and abdominal muscles
Two	Running	5–10 minutes L1–L2	Warm up
	Hack squat	3 x 20	Good for upper legs and buttocks
	Dead lift	3 x 20	Works thighs and buttocks
	Leg criss-cross	3 x 20	Tones the abdominal muscles
	Side step-up	3 x 20	Works leg muscles
	Side lunge	3 x 20	Strengthens hips, buttocks and thighs
	Broomstick twist	3 x 20	Works the muscles at the side of the abdomen
	Leg curl	3 x 20	Exercises the hamstrings
	Calf raise	3 x 20+	Strengthens the calf muscles
	Kneeling cable rotation	3 x 20	Exercises the abdominals
	High cable side bend	3 x 20	Movement works the abdominals
	Dumbbell bicep curl	3 x 20	Optimum workout for the biceps
Three	Run	5–10 minutes L1–L2	Warm up
	Cable hip adduction	3 x 20	Improves stability
	Cable hip abduction	3 x 20	Targets hip abductor muscles and buttocks
	Cable kick back	3 x 20	Strengthens buttocks and hamstrings
	V-crunch	3 x 20	Works 'six-pack' abdominal muscles
	BOSU squat	3 x 20	Progress to single-leg squats
	Gluteal bridge	3 x 20	Progress to feet on fit ball
	Medicine ball, lunge and lean	3 x 20	Builds strength and power
	Medicine ball, lunge and rotate	3 x 20	Improves link between upper, lower and core muscles
	Press-up to dumbbell rows	3 x 20	Good exercise for core stability
	Sit-up with Russian twist	3 x 20	Works abdominals and obliques
Four	Run	5–10 minutes L1–L2	Warm up
	Lateral pull-down	3 x 12–15	Works the lats (muscles in the back)
	Dumbbell chest press	3 x 12–15	Workout of the upper arm, chest and shoulder
	Seated cable row	3 x 12–15	Strengthens the middle back and forearms
	Cable fly	3 x 12–15	Develops pectorals
	Arnie shoulder press	3 x 12–15	Strengthens shoulders and upper arms
	Bent-over dumbbell lateral raise	3 x 12–15	Strengthens upper back and shoulders
	Dumbbell frontal raise	3 x 12–15	Exercises shoulders
	Bench triceps dip	3 x 12–15	Exercises triceps
	Cable bicep curls	3 x 12–15	Develops and strengthens biceps
	Warm down	5–10 minutes	Leg stretches

Cycling Plan

Cycling may appear to be an easy way to get fit and, up to a point, it is. Taking it one step farther, however, by increasing your strength and power to enable you to cycle faster, for longer, calls for a detailed plan.

There are many different types of cycling disciplines, including track racing, long-distance stage races, cross-country, mountain biking, downhill mountain biking and cyclo-cross, to name but a few. They all require slightly different types of training intensity and duration.

The information on page 56 tells you how to set up your bike correctly and the type of session that you can include in your training to make you go faster. However, as with many of the sports covered in this book, if you want to become really good at cycling, you need to get off your bike and into the gym.

Core-stability and resistance training

You will need to undertake core-stability training twice a week to strengthen your trunk muscles and help support your back, especially the lower

Below: Cycling off-road requires considerable effort and hence demands a lot of your core stability muscles.

back, if you are to become a more proficient cyclist. The bent-forward position of the cyclist requires you to have a strong core, as a weak core will soon result in an aching back. Core-stability training will also make your muscles recruit in the correct order and help you to avoid lateral movement, thus ensuring that all your power is going into driving the bike forward, rather than being lost sideways, especially when you are climbing hills out of the saddle. So, begin with the basic core exercises and gradually build up to the intermediate and advanced exercises.

Resistance training will help you to become more powerful. Remember that the stronger the engine, the greater the potential for speed. You should do two resistance-training sessions per week, focusing on your legs, along with a small number of upper-body exercises. It is also vital that you stay flexible, so always remember to do some stretching after every cycle ride or fitness training session in the gym.

Above: Track cycling requires huge amounts of training and power to win races.

Below: Having the fitness and strong legs able to shift your body weight is essential for cycling. This lunge will help to build up the leg muscles.

Nutrition

For obvious reasons, lightweight cyclists are better cyclists. The heavier you are, the more weight you have to move, especially when it comes to going uphill. You should, therefore, eat a diet consisting mainly of low to medium GI foods to keep your weight down and maintain your energy levels. Eating every three to four hours will help to maintain a high metabolism and allow your muscles to recover faster between training sessions. In the two hours before, as well as during and after long rides, eat a mixture of low and high GI foods to aid faster recovery and to replace muscle glycogen (glucose stored in the muscles).

Right: When you are cycling in remote areas, eat low and high GI foods regularly to maintain the metabolism.

Exercise plan for cyclists

Session one and two will provide basic muscular strength. Session three is more advanced and involves working your core muscles and limbs at the same time. Try to do each of these three sessions within a period of ten days.

Session	Exercise	Time/Sets/Reps/Level	Comments
One	Cycling	5–10 minutes L1–L2	Warm up
	Hack squat	3 x 20	Good for upper legs and buttocks
	Dead lift	3 x 20	Works thighs and buttocks
	Leg extension	3 x 20	Try doing this with just one leg
	Lunge	3 x 20	10 each leg; hold dumbbells to make it harder
	Side lunge	3 x 20	10 to each side
	Cable adductor	3 x 20	10 each leg
	Cable kickback	3 x 20	10 each leg
	Crunch	3 x 20	Workout for the abdominals
	Oblique crunch	3 x 20	Works upper abdominals and obliques
	Arnie shoulder press	3 x 12–15	Strengthens shoulders and upper arms
	Dumbbell biceps curl	3 x 12–15	Develops biceps
Two	Cycling	5–10 minutes L1–L2	Warm up
	Leg press	3 x 20	Try using single legs
	Dumbbell squats	3 x 20	Progress to one-leg squats
	Leg curl	3 x 20	Try using single legs
	Step-up	3 x 20	10 each leg; hold dumbbells to make it harder
	Side step-up	3 x 20	10 each leg
	Cable abductor	3 x 20	10 each leg
	Calf raise	3 x 20+	Strengthens the calf muscles
	Reverse crunch	3 x 20	Tones and strengthens rectus abdominis
	Side crunch	3 x 2	Strengthens and tones obliques
	Cable lateral raise	3 x 12–15	Develops shoulder muscles
	Triceps cable push-down	3 x 12–15	Strengthens triceps muscles
Three	Cycling	5–10 minutes L1–L2	Warm-up
	Medicine ball lunges with leans	3 x 20	10 each side
	Medicine ball, lunges with rotations	3 x 20	10 each side
	Squat to cable shoulder press	3 x 20	Exercises the legs and shoulders
	Press-up to dumbbell row	3 x 10	Good exercise for core stability
	Squat throw	3 x 10	Strengthens core muscles of abdomen, hip and buttocks
	Single-leg squat with cable row to frontal raise	3 x 20	10 each side – good for developing balance and stability
	Lunge with medicine ball to wood chop	3 x 20	10 each side
	Kneeling cable rotations	3 x 20	10 each side

Triathlon Training Plan

With their intense determination and high pain threshold, triathletes are prone to overuse injuries. A sensible training plan, including strength and core-stability training, can reduce these risks and help them achieve their full potential.

Triathlon is one of the fastest growing sports in the world. Triathlon is usually taken seriously and training is to prepare for the competition. Perhaps one of the reasons it is so popular is because many competitors are good or were good at one or two of the disciplines, and having reached the peak in one of those, they want a new challenge. Competition is more attractive than in other endurance sports since you can race against people of similar age and ability as well as being on the course with the world's best.

Base training

Aim to do three key training sessions – one swim, one cycle, one run – each week to see a progressive improvement.

These sessions require your full focus and energy to get the most out of them. The other three sessions in the week are base sessions that provide increased aerobic and strength maintenance, which will enable your three key sessions to be more beneficial. Without these base sessions you will be prone to over-training and injuries. The key sessions should be two days apart and adapted to the distances you do in competition. For example, if you are training for an Ironman competition, you will need to do one swim of between 65 and 90 minutes, one cycle ride lasting up to 6 hours, and one run lasting between 80 and 120 minutes. If you want to compete in Olympic distance triathlons

you will need to do one swim lasting between 20 and 40 minutes, one cycle ride lasting over 90 minutes and one run lasting between 40 and 60 minutes.

Transition

The transition (movement from one form of exercise to another) in triathlon from swim to bike and bike to run is one of the most difficult parts of this sport. When you leave the water after the swimming it is hard to get your legs working as efficiently as you would want them to because all the oxygenated blood has been sent to your upper body to help in the swim. It can take a few minutes before you really feel your legs working. To help make this transition

---

Strength and core-training exercises

These exercise sessions should form part of your training plan, twice a week, right up to the week of the actual race itself.

Session	Exercise	Sets/Reps/TimeLevel	Comments
One	Rowing	5–10 minutes L1–L2	Warm up
	Lat pull-down, wide grip	3 x 12	Exercises the muscles of the back
	Single-arm cable pull-down	3 x 12	Works lats, also biceps and middle back
	Press-up to single-arm dumbbell row	3 x 12	Begin with 5 on each arm and build up to 12
	Plank	3 x 60 seconds	Begin with 10 seconds and build up to 60
	Medicine ball press-up	3 x 12	Begin with 5 on each arm and build up to 12
	Medicine ball throw-down	3 x 20	Builds strength and stability
	Dumbbell lat raise	3 x 12	Exercises the shoulders
	Dumbbell frontal raise	3 x 12	Exercises shoulders
	Bench triceps dip	3 x 20	Exercises triceps
	Hanging leg raise	3 x 10	Builds up the abdominal muscles
	Crunch with Russian twist	3 x 20	Strengthens the abdominals and lower back
Two	Cycling	5–10 minutes L1–L2	Warm up
	Lunges with twists	3 x 20	10 each side
	Lunges with medicine ball wood chops	3 x 20	10 each side
	Fit ball sit-up	3 x 20	Exercises the abdominal muscles
	Machine leg curl	3 x 20	Try using single legs
	Single-leg squat	3 x 10	Works gluteus, hamstrings, quadriceps and core muscles
	Side plank	3 x 60-second holds	Begin with 10 seconds and build up to 60
	Single-leg hip raise	3 x 10	Workout for the buttocks
	Calf raises	3 x 20	Strengthens the calf muscles
	Side crunch	3 x 20	Strengthens and tones obliques

Above: During the swim part of the triathlon, keep focused and try to ignore the other competitors.

smoother in competition try and practise the transition from swim to bike as frequently as you can so that you can quickly adapt from one sport to another. As you leave the swim try and kick more with your legs to distribute more blood to your legs and prepare them for running out of the water and on to the bike section. For the transition of bike to run you have to tackle the problem of trying to stride out. Your stride length on the bike is very short as it is just the length of the cranks, which can lead to tightening of the muscles in the hips and back of legs, mainly the hamstrings and calf muscles.

This is a common time for injuries to occur. To prevent this from happening use a short stride pattern for the first few minutes of the run and then gently lengthen your stride allowing your muscles to stretch out and give you an effective stride length. Practise your transition from bike to run in training but be careful about when you do your bike-to-run transitions. In training, avoid

bike-to-run sessions after long hard bike sessions. The long bike ride will make the muscles in your legs tired. Not only do your leg muscles need to be fresh to power you forward on the run, they also need to act as shock absorbers to absorb the impact as your feet strike the ground. Tired legs going into the run may make you more prone to injuries, so make sure you engage your core muscles when your legs feel tired to support your body properly. Speed of transition is important as your time in

Above: Lat pull-downs work the muscles in the back. A strong back is essential when competing in a triathlon.

transition is included in your overall time. You need the appropriate equipment to make transitions faster and to practise changing out of swim gear into bike gear and going from bike

Below: Transition from swim to run can make your legs feel weak, so practise it many times beforehand.

Above: The longer the distance of the triathlon, the more influential the bike leg will be on the overall result.

gear to running gear. Saving a few minutes in transition is easier than trying to make up 2 minutes on the bike or run.

Equipment

Choosing the correct equipment is vital if you are to feel at ease during every stage of the triathlon. The swimming part is simple, unless you are going to wear a wetsuit, in which case get your wetsuit fitted by a specialist swim or triathlon store. If you are swimming in open water you may need outdoor tinted goggles. Swim in your wetsuit to get used to how it affects your stroke and take your wetsuit off during training to make the transitions faster. Your bike needs to be set up correctly to enable you to be in a comfortable aerodynamic position and get the best power output. In training practice, get in and out of your cycling shoes quickly and try

Left: When others are suffering in the later stages of the triathlon, a strong run will take you up the leader board rapidly.

Triathlon training plan

The following training plan assumes that you are training for an Olympic distance triathlon in about six weeks' time, that you have a good level of fitness and that you are able to train for six sessions per week, in addition to doing two strength/core sessions each week. Everyone responds differently to training sessions, so adjust your training to what suits you best. Practise your transition by doing a 'swim to bike' or 'bike to run', with no rest period. These are marked on the plan with a *.

	Monday	Tuesday	Wednesday	Thursday	Friday	Saturday	Sunday
Week 1	Swim 1	Cycle 1	Run 1	Swim 2	Rest	Cycle 4	Run 4
Week 2	Swim 4	Cycle 2	Run 2	Swim 3	Rest	Cycle 4	Run 4
Week 3	Swim 1	Cycle 1	Run 3	Swim 4	Rest	Cycle 3	Run 4
Week 4	Swim 3	Cycle 4	Run 3	*Swim 3 + Cycle 3	Cycle 1	Rest	*Cycle 1 + Run 1
Week 5	Swim 1	Cycle 1	Run 2	*Swim 4 + Cycle 2	Cycle 1	Rest	*Cycle 3 + Run 1
Week 6	Swim 4	Cycle 3	Run 30 mins L2	Swim 2	Rest	Cycle 40 mins L2	Race

Swim sessions
Warm up and cool down 100–200m/109–218yd, L1–L2
1 – timed 1,500m/1,640-yd swim, L3
2 – 10 x 100m/109-yd sprint at L3–L4 with 30 seconds' rest between each one

3 – 3 x 400m/437-yd at L3–L4 with 2 minutes' rest between each one
4 – 2 x 800m/875-yd at L3 with 4 minutes' rest between each one

Cycling sessions
Warm up and cool down for 5–10 minutes at L1–L2
1 – timed 20km/12.4-mile time trial on a flat route, L3–L4
2 – 6 x 4-minute hills at L4 with at least 5 minutes' rest between hills, L2

3 – 1½ hours with 20-second sprints every 5 minutes on flat route, L2–L3
4 – 2 hours using two gears too hard for the middle 10 minutes of every 30 minutes, L2–L3

Running sessions
Warm up and cool down with a 5-minute jog at L1–L2
1 – timed 10km/6-mile run on flat L3
2 – 8 x 2-minute runs on hills at L3–L4 with at least 4 minutes' easy jog between hills, L2

3 – 6 x 1,000m/1,094-yd fast L3–L4 on the flat with 500m/547-yd easy jog between them, L2
4 – 1 hour steady run, L2–L3

attaching them to the pedals before the start. Choose cycling shoes that are easy to get in and out of with minimum straps. For running, select shoes that are light and easy to get in and out of. Consider using elastic laces to save time.

Your weakest discipline
Every triathlete has a discipline that is not as strong as the other two. Spend time on your weakest discipline to bring it up to the standard of the others. Use the off-season to take advantage and double up on training sessions involving your weakest discipline. However, consider where you need to make the real improvements. If you are doing an Ironman and swimming

is your weakest sport, you need a plan. Most of the time is spent on the bike and run so if you do shave off 5 minutes in the swim it will not make much difference to the outcome.

More time spent on the bike and running might mean that you can take a bigger chunk of time off the end result. In shorter sprint events it is more important to get each discipline to equal strength, and as fast as possible.

Training for triathlon is hard; listen to what your body tells you to avoid over-training and injuries. Rest is as important as your training. Practise swimming with others who are in training, especially in open water, to get used to having people surrounding you and get to know the

conditions of open water. You may need to adjust your swimming stroke to have a higher arm action on recovery if the water conditions are rough.

Nutrition
Training for a triathlon will burn a massive number of calories, so you need to eat lots of low to medium GI foods every three to four hours to maintain energy levels, followed by medium to high GI foods in the two hours before, during and after training sessions so that you can replace muscle glycogen (stored glucose). Your body will be at risk of dehydration, so keep your fluid intake high and weigh yourself to test hydration levels after training sessions and competition.

Resources

Further reading

Anderson, Bob, *Stretching*, (Shelter Publications Inc, US, Sept 2000)

Andrews, Greg, and Doughty, Simon, *The Cyclist's Training Manual*, (A & C Black Publishers Ltd, 2007)

Baker, Cherry, *Pregnancy and Fitness*, (A & C Black Publishers Ltd, 2006)

Bean, Anita, *The Complete Guide to Sports Nutrition*, (A & C Black Publishers Ltd, 2006)

Bean, Anita, *The Complete Guide to Strength Training*, (A & C Black Publishers Ltd, 2008)

Brooks, Douglas, *The Complete Book of Personal Training*, (Human Kinetics Europe Ltd, 2004)

Brzychi, Matt, and Fornicola, Fred, *Dumbbell Training for Strength and Fitness*, (Blue River Press, 2006)

Burough Nina, *Walking for Fitness*, (Dorling Kindersley, 2004)

Cash, Mel, *The Pocket Atlas of the Moving Body*, (Ebury Press, 1999)

Clark, Charles and Maureen, *The Healthy Low GI Low Carb Diet*, (Vermilion, 2005)

Cordain, Loren, *The Paleo Diet*, (John Wiley and Sons, 2003)

Delavier, Frederic, *Strength Training Anatomy*, (Human Kinetics, 2005)

Delavier, Frederic, *Women's Strength Training Anatomy*, (Human Kinetics Europe Ltd, 2002)

Detz, Jeanine, *Ultimate Core Workout*, (Ulyssess Press, 2005)

Difiore, Judy, *The Complete Guide to Postnatal Fitness*, (A & C Black Publishers Ltd, 2003)

Fishman, L., *Sciatica Solutions*, (W.W. Norton and Co, 2007)

Friel, Joe, *Total Heart Rate Training*, (Ulysses Press, 2006)

Friel, Joe, *The Triathlete's Training Bible*, (Velo Press, 2009)

Garcia, Lizbeth, *101 Ways to Burn Fat on the Ball*, (Fairwinds Press, 2006)

Graimes, Nicola, *The Big Book of Low-Carb Recipes*, (Duncan Baird Publishers, 2005)

Griffin, Sue, *Training the Over 50's*, (A & C Black Publishers Ltd, 2006)

Hildritch, Graeme, *The Marathon and Half Marathon*, (The Crowood Press Ltd, 2007)

Hope, Richard, and Lawrence, Debbie, *Advanced Circuit Training*, (A & C Black Publishers Ltd, 2008)

Hope, Richard, and Lawrence, Debbie, *Fitness Professionals Circuit Training*, (A & C Black Publishers Ltd, 2007)

Jackowski, Edward, *Fit to Tee*, (Sterling, 2007)

Jarmey, Chris, *The Concise Book of Muscles*, (Lotus Publishing, 2008)

Key, Sarah, *Sarah Key's Back Sufferers*, (Vermilion, 2000)

Krupnik, Mikhail, *Prepare for Combat: Strength Training for Martial Arts*, (Basic Health Publications, 2006)

Laughlin, Terry, *Total Immersion*, (Simon and Schuster Ltd, 2004)

Lawrence, Matt, *The Complete Guide to Core Stability*, (A & C Black Publishers Ltd, 2007)

Massey, Paul, *The Anatomy of Pilates*, (Lotus Publishing, 2009)

McNeeley, Edward, and Sandler, David, *The Resistance Band Workout Book*, (Burford Books, US, 2006)

Milligan, James, *Swiss Ball for Total Fitness*, (Union Square Press, 2001)

National Academy of Sports Medicine, NASM, *Essentials of Personal Fitness Training*, (Lippincott Williams and Wilkins, US, 2007)

Nelson, Arnold, *Stretching Anatomy*, (Human Kinetics Europe Ltd, 2006)

Norris, Christopher, *The Complete Guide to Stretching*, (A & C Black Publishers Ltd, 2007)

Oliver, Ian, *Boxing Fitness*, (Snow Books, 2005)

Peterson, Lars, *Sports Injuries: Their Prevention and Treatment*, (Informa Healthcare, 2000)

Rolf, Christer G., *The Sports Injuries Handbook: Diagnosis and Management*, (A & C Black Publishers Ltd, 2007)

Schoenfeld, Brad, *Sculpting Her Perfect Body*, (Human Kinetics Europe Ltd, 2007)

Walker, Brad, *The Anatomy of Sports Injuries*, (Lotus Publishing, 2007)

Walker, Brad, *The Anatomy of Stretching*, (Lotus Publishing, 2007)

Weiss, Adam, *The Abs Smart Fitness Plan*, (McGraw-Hill Contemporary, 2009)

Whitmarsh, Cindy, *Ultrafit: Challenging Workouts – Amazing Results*, (Fairwinds Press, 2006)

Wolcott, William, *Metabolic Typing Diet*, (Broadway Books, 2002)

Zinczenko, David, *The Abs Diet*, (Rodale International Ltd, 2006)

Websites

www.mylifept.com (author's website)
www.brianmac.co.uk
www.bristishcycling.org.uk
www.britishtriathlon.org
www.endurancelife.com
www.marathonguide.com
www.mens.fitness.magazine.co.uk
www.muscle-fitness.co.uk
www.physioroom.com
www.theglycemicindex.com

Magazines

220 Triathlon
Ace Tennis
Brides
Cycling Weekly
Fairway to Green
Men's Fitness
Men's Health
Muscle Fitness
Runner's World
Triathlete
Triathlete's World
Ultrafit
What Mountain Bike

Index

PICTURE ACKNOWLEDGEMENTS

The publisher would like to thank the following picture libraries for the use of their pictures in the book. Every effort has been made to acknowledge the pictures properly. We apologize if there are any unintentional omissions, which will be corrected in future editions.

l=left, r=right, t=top, b=bottom, c=centre

Alamy: 11bl, 14bl, 14br, 17bl, 49tr, 50b, 226, 227.

Corbis: 12 (both), 14t, 15bl, 18tr, 18bl, 20tr, 21tl, 21tc, 21bl, 48, 49b, 50t, 63bl, 72bl, 132bl, 133tr, 133bc, 195br, 198tr, 204tr, 206t, 207tc, 218br, 219, 230tl, 239, 242tr.

Getty: 9, 10tr, 10bl, 11, 13tl, 13b, 15cl, 15r, 16, 19bl, 19bc, 19br, 23br, 24 (both), 27cr, 27bl, 28 (all), 36, 37, 39tc, 39tr, 39b, 40t, 41b, 43tr, 44t, 46 (both), 47 (both), 62tl, 62tr, 62br, 63br, 67, 68t, 70l, 71tr, 73 (both), 130, 164, 165tl, 165tc, 165tr, 168br, 170bl, 190, 191, 192tc, 192bl, 192bc, 193br, 196br, 197tl, 198bl, 199bc, 199br, 202bl, 204bl, 204br, 205tr, 205br, 206bl, 207br, 208, 208bc, 208br, 212bl, 216 (both), 218bl, 221tr, 223tl, 224 (both), 225l, 228, 230bl, 232, 234tc, 234tr, 235bc, 235br, 236tr, 238bl, 240b, 241, 244tr, 244bl, 245tr, 247tl, 247br, 248 (both).

iStockphoto: 20bl, 49tl, 233.

Philip O'Connor: 1, 2, 3, 4.1, 4.2, 4.3, 4.4, 4.5, 4.6, 4.7, 6–7, 8, 10tl, 17t, 19t, 22 9both), 23tl, 23tr, 23bl, 25 (all), 26, 27tl, 27tr, 29 (both), 30 (all), 31 (all), 32 (both), 33 (all), 34 (both), 35 (both), 38, 40b, 41t, 42 (all), 43tl, 43b, 45 (all), 51, 52, 53 (all), 54, 55t, 56 (both), 57, 58, 59 (all), 60, 61 (all), 62bl, 64 (all), 65 (all), 66, 68b, 69 (both), 74, 75bl, 75bc, 75br, 76–129, 132cl, 134, 135 (all), 137 (all), 138–140, 141tl, 141tc, 141tr, 142tl, 142tr, 143 (all), 144tr, 144br, 145 (all), 146tr, 146br, 147 (all), 148cr, 149 (all), 150tr, 151 (all), 153 (all), 155 (all), 156br, 157 (all), 159 (all), 161 (all), 162bl, 163 (all), 166, 167, 170cr, 171 (all), 172–189, 212tr, 212br, 214tr, 229 (all), 230tr, 231 (both), 234bl, 234br, 237 (both), 238tr, 240tc, 240tr, 242bl, 244br, 247tr.

Photoshot: 18tl, 21tr, 205tl.
Science Photo Library: 152cr.
Superstock: 75tl, 209t.